Other Books by Author:

Digby: The Gunpowder Plotter's Legacy

George Digby: Hero and Villain

Outram in India

The Rise and Fall of Bartle Frere

Two Generals
Buller and Botha in the Boer War

Roy Digby Thomas

authorHOUSE®

AuthorHouse™
1663 Liberty Drive
Bloomington, IN 47403
www.authorhouse.com
Phone: 1-800-839-8640

© 2012. Roy Digby Thomas. All rights reserved.

No part of this book may be reproduced, stored in a retrieval system, or transmitted by any means without the written permission of the author.

Published by AuthorHouse 10/11/12

ISBN: 978-1-4772-3009-1 (sc)
ISBN: 978-1-4772-3010-7 (hc)
ISBN: 978-1-4772-3011-4 (e)

Any people depicted in stock imagery provided by Thinkstock are models, and such images are being used for illustrative purposes only.
Certain stock imagery © Thinkstock.

This book is printed on acid-free paper.

Because of the dynamic nature of the Internet, any web addresses or links contained in this book may have changed since publication and may no longer be valid. The views expressed in this work are solely those of the author and do not necessarily reflect the views of the publisher, and the publisher hereby disclaims any responsibility for them.

Contents

Other Books by Author: i

ACKNOWLEDGEMENTS. ix

INTRODUCTION. xiii

MAPS. xv

HISTORICAL CONTEXT. xvii

chapter 1.
ORIGINS. 1

chapter 2.
LEADERS IN WAITING. 11

chapter 3.
CONFLICT IN AFRICA. 19

chapter 4.
EGYPT AND IRELAND. 37

chapter 5.
PREPARING FOR WAR. 47

chapter 6.
LET BATTLE COMMENCE. 61

chapter 7.
BULLER TAKES OVER. 71

chapter 8.
COLENSO. 85

chapter 9.
WHAT NEXT? -- 99

chapter 10.
SPION KOP. --- 107

chapter 11.
LADYSMITH IS RELIEVED. --------------------------------- 121

chapter 12.
AFTER LADYSMITH. -- 131

chapter 13.
DEFENCE OF THE TRANSVAAL. ------------------------- 137

chapter 14.
THE LAST PITCHED BATTLE. ------------------------------ 149

chapter 15.
GUERRILLA WARFARE. ------------------------------------- 153

chapter 16.
PEACE. -- 163

chapter 17.
AFTER THE WAR. -- 171

chapter 18.
FALL FROM GRACE. --- 193

chapter 19.
SOUTH-WEST AFRICA. -------------------------------------- 209

chapter 20.
END GAME. --- 213

EPILOGUE.	221
APPENDIX.	227
BIBLIOGRAPHY.	229
JOURNALS AND PERIODICALS.	233
ORIGINAL SOURCES.	235
ENDNOTES.	237
INDEX.	243

ACKNOWLEDGEMENTS.

Without great assistance from a number of people, this book would not have been published.

As with previous books I have written, Joe Roberts spent many arduous hours ironing out my grammar and eliminating mistakes. He also provided valuable advice on the structure of the book that, with its two opposing personae, was technically difficult to get right. I am much indebted to him.

Heartfelt thanks also to Bob Markham, who produced the maps that are indispensable to a book that moves the action around the country.

The front cover is a reproduction of a painting of Sir George White greeting Lord Douglas Hamilton when Ladysmith was relieved, by John Henry Frederick Bacon. I am grateful to the National Army Museum, London for permitting me to use it. The portrait of Buller is from the National Portrait Gallery, London. My thanks to both institutions.

Anthony Coleman, a good friend, voted last year the best professional guide of the Natal battlefields, ran his beady eye over my narrative on the relief of Ladysmith and offered valuable advice, from which the book has benefitted enormously. I am in his debt.

A series of periodicals written at the time of the Boer War, "To Pretoria with the Flag," was unearthed at an obscure auction by a good friend, Joan Scoones, and proved very valuable.

Last but not least, thanks to my family: Eileen, my wife, and sons Glyn and Warren who helped with the drafts and encouraged me to keep going when I started to sink in the quicksands.

R.D.T.

Redvers Buller.

Louis Botha.

INTRODUCTION.

On December 15, 1899, two generals looked at each other's army across the Tugela River and prepared for battle. Redvers Buller, Commander-in-Chief of the British Army in South Africa, was attempting to break through the Boer lines and relieve the town of Ladysmith, which was under siege. Louis Botha, commanding the Boers, was there to stop him. The tussle between these two was vital to success in the Boer War. If Buller won, reinforcements pouring into South Africa from Britain, Australia, Canada and India could sweep forward and capture the Boer headquarters at Pretoria. If Ladysmith fell to the Boers, some of Britain's finest fighting men would be captured, and the Boers would feel capable of winning the war. They would see the way open to the port of Durban, a vital point of entry into South Africa. If they could capture Durban they would deny the British a landing place for their reinforcements and open a supply route to the landlocked Transvaal.

What occurred at Ladysmith significantly affected the lives, and the futures, of both generals. The siege became a focal point of the war. The prestige, credibility and future prospects of both sides rode on the outcome. Buller was a professional soldier, well educated, vastly experienced. Botha was a farm boy with little formal education and no formal military training. Although the two men could not have been more different, their careers were to follow similar parabolas. Both rose rapidly to lead their country's fighting force. Both achieved huge prominence at Ladysmith and were feted by their countries for the part they played there. Soon, though, they were to face criticism and rejection by their own people.

What were the circumstances that led to this curious similarity in career paths? Why did men who achieved so much, who were idolised by their nations, end their lives in ignominy? This book attempts to provide new insights into what motivated them, their strengths and weaknesses. At the centre is the ebb and flow of the Boer War. For both men it was their first military engagement in outright command. As with so many such wars, the political environment in which they operated played heavily upon their lives, and was to bear down on their achievements and final fates.

Many books have been written about the Boer War. It was covered intensively by the press at the time. Newspaper reports, photographs and criticism appeared in Britain on a daily basis, and the public followed progress avidly. Since the two World Wars the Boer War has faded into the background, and virtually nothing more has been written about it. This is a pity, for new information has come to light in the last fifty years. We can look on the conflict, the actions of both sides, the significance for the British Empire and the future of South Africa with fresh eyes and the knowledge of what happened thereafter. Most books have been written from one viewpoint or the other: either British or Boer. There are very few that have attempted to be even-handed. By tracing the lives of two of the main protagonists, I have attempted to show the war from both sides.

MAPS.

South Africa -- xvi
Northern Natal -- 60
Battle of Colenso --- 84
Spion Kop --- 106
The Breakthrough -- 120

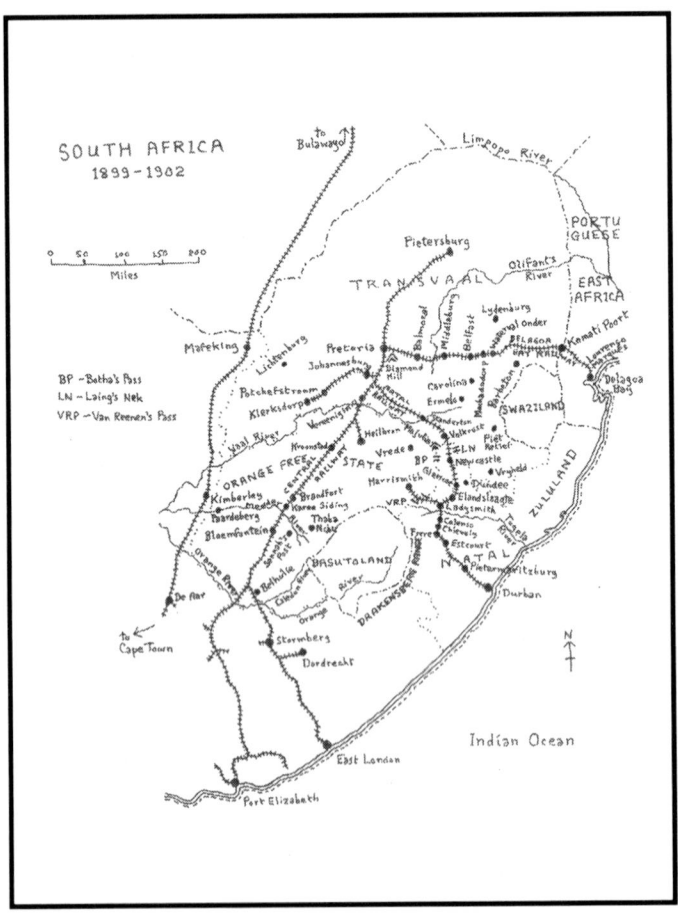

HISTORICAL CONTEXT.

Some aspects of the Boer War are familiar to many people. The place names – Ladysmith, Mafeking, Kimberly, Spion Kop, Majuba – are remembered, and can still be seen as street names in English cities. The circumstances leading up to the Boer War are less well known. For those readers who are not familiar with South African history, these notes may provide a useful lead-in to the book.

The Dutch were the first Europeans to found a colony in South Africa. Jan van Riebeeck, who landed at Cape Town on April 6, 1652, established a viable outpost farming cattle, sheep and vegetables. Although the colony shipped some of this output back to Holland, the Cape's essential importance was as a staging post for the Dutch East India Company ships en route to and from India. Labour was scarce: the local tribe, the Khoikhoi, nomadic by nature, were disinclined to work on the land. The Dutch overcame the problem by importing slaves from the west coast of Africa, and later from India and Malaya. The settlement expanded rapidly, augmented in 1688 by the arrival of French Huguenots, fugitives from religious prejudice in their own country.

Life was not easy in this remote outpost. By 1657 the settlers had started to move out from Cape Town in search of fresh land and independence from the Dutch East India Company. As the settlement expanded from its Cape Town base it came increasingly into contact – and conflict – with the indigenous people. Land hungry, the new settlers used their modern weapons to subjugate first the Khoikhoi (known as Hottentots by the Dutch), the bushmen (nomadic hunters), and then the Bantu tribes moving down from the north to inhabit the eastern coast of South Africa.

For nearly 150 years the Dutch colony was left in peace by the other European powers, whose ships were able to use Cape Town as a supply stop but had no interest in colonising a settlement so far from home and civilisation.

In 1795 the Dutch monarchy was overthrown and replaced by a French satellite administration calling itself the Batavian Republic. Britain, already concerned about the rise of Napoleon in France, became alarmed at the threat to its lucrative trade routes to the east. On July 9 four British sloops-of-war sailed into Simons Bay near Cape Town and landed a military force which swiftly succeeded in capturing Cape Town.

Peace in Europe formalised by the Treaty of Amiens in 1802, saw the Cape returned to the Batavian Republic, but the truce between Britain and France was a fragile one. When in 1805 the first shots in the Napoleonic Wars were fired, Britain moved quickly to reoccupy the Cape on a more permanent basis, and take control of the territory.

From the start the British were in conflict with the Dutch settlers. The employment of slaves was a thorny question for Europeans, and the anti-slavery movement in Britain succeeded in persuading its government to outlaw the practice. In 1828 an Ordinance was passed by the Cape authorities declaring "Hottentots and other free people of colour" equal before the law, and removing legal restrictions on their movements.[1] The Slavery Abolition Act of 1833 outlawed slavery throughout most of the British Empire. Enforced in the Cape in 1834, this Act and the preceding Ordinance had the result of setting free 38,000 slaves and depriving the settlers of their labour pool.

The immigrants who settled in South Africa were a hardy and independent breed. Mainly of Dutch origin, followed by French Huguenots, they had left their homelands in order to escape persecution and restrictions, and to forge a fresh and free life for themselves and their families.

Increasingly, under the British, their new overlords, they found themselves subject to new laws. The removal of their slave labour force was the last straw. This forced the 5,000 or so largely Dutch farmers (the Boers, as they were called), with about 5,000 coloured servants, to move away from the Cape in search of new pastures and freedom from interference. They spread out across the high plateau of grasslands to the north and crossed the Drakensberg into fertile north Natal. As they moved north across the Orange and Vaal Rivers they clashed with the indigenous Bantu tribes living there but managed through the use of the gun to overcome resistance and establish widespread farms for their cattle and sheep, tended by the Africans.

The British Government's attitude towards this exodus was ambivalent. On the one hand it sought to maintain control over its expanding colony, on the other it was reluctant to commit additional finances to this new territory which yielded little in return.

In 1843 Britain created a new colony by annexing Natal, where some of the Boers had settled. This was mainly to control and protect its valuable port, Port Natal, later to be named Durban. By doing so they effectively land-locked the settlers in the hinterland: their only realistic outlet to the sea was through Durban or Cape Town. The Boers, whilst accepting with reluctance the annexation, would have nothing to do with the British in the other interior territories.

Although the Cape Province and Natal were crown colonies, Britain's fundamental interest in South Africa was as a staging post to its most important colony, India. Strategically it was vital that the sea passage be secured, and a naval base was developed at Simonstown, close to Cape Town, for this purpose. Britain's international interests were so far flung and onerous that South Africa was seen as little more than a nuisance, with little value to the Empire. It was considered to be a constant drain on overseas funding at a time when Britain had a number of demands on its finances.

Nevertheless, imperial attitudes insisted that Britain keep control of its colonies, and laws were drawn up aimed at maintaining influence over the interior territories in which the Boers settled. These independent trekkers found this unacceptable: after all, that was why they had left the Cape. They campaigned to establish independent republics, and Britain reluctantly acceded to their request. The high plains of inland South Africa held little of value for the British, and simply added another responsibility. In 1852 the Sand River Convention and in 1854 the Bloemfontein Convention granted the Transvaal and Orange Free State respectively their wishes.

The discovery of diamonds at Kimberley in 1866, and gold in the Transvaal in 1871 (although it was only in the 1880's that the rich seams of the Witwatersrand were unearthed) transformed Britain's interest in South Africa. Suddenly this far-away place promised vast wealth for the British Empire, and foreigners (called 'Uitlanders' or Outlanders by the white inhabitants) poured into Pretoria and Johannesburg, the two major cities in the Transvaal, in search of riches. Many of these were from the British Isles.

Like settlers in any foreign country, from the time that the Boers settled in the Transvaal they experienced an uncertain existence. They were constantly seeking fresh pastures and larger farms for their herds of cattle and sheep. In the process of expansion they upset the neighbouring Zulu and Swazi tribes and were subject to sudden raids on their isolated communities. They were resistant to interference from a central, ruling body, and spread sparsely across a huge territory. They were reluctant to pay any taxes, and with export of produce controlled by the British colony ports, the fledgling republic found it difficult to survive financially.

In Britain, the parliamentary election of 1874 returned the Conservative Party to power. Benjamin Disraeli became Prime Minister. A noted imperialist, he caught the public mood, conscious of British Imperial glory. He argued that the previous government with their parsimonious approach and their indifference to the Empire had neglected the colonies, and considered them a burden. Necessary reforms and advances in self-government had not taken place.

The financial plight of the Transvaal offered the British an opportunity to impose their will and introduce the necessary reforms. In 1877 the British annexed the Transvaal. They claimed that this was necessary in order to rescue the Republic from financial ruin. They also argued that their soldiers could more effectively protect it against marauding indigenous tribes. Initially there was only minor resistance to the British move. Many settlers were relieved to have the financial burden and pressure of defending their lands against the Africans lifted from their shoulders to some extent. For many Boers, however, annexation soon became a cause for friction.

The question now arose: how was Britain to control its diffuse and widespread South African interests? Canada had been in a similar situation, with English and French inhabitants. There the problem was solved by the creation of a (rather loose) federation.

In 1877 Bartle Frere was appointed Governor-General of the Cape Colony with a brief from the Colonial Office to confederate the various parts of South Africa in a similar fashion to that successfully achieved in Canada. The annexation of the Transvaal was the first building block in that process. However Frere realised that without the inclusion of Zululand, on the border of Natal, a confederation would be neither secure nor complete. In 1879 he thus engineered a war against the Zulus, confident that the British army, hitherto invincible elsewhere in the world, would quickly subdue them.

The first engagement in that war at Isandhlwana on January 22, 1879, was a disaster for the British and ultimately cost Frere, and his military commander Lord Chelmsford, their posts. Of 800 white soldiers who took part, British and colonial, 779 were killed and the British force routed.[2] It took three months for Chelmsford to prepare for a fresh onslaught. The overwhelming firepower of the British finally told and Zululand was subdued before the end of the year.

With the military threat of the Zulus removed, Boer resentment to annexation of the Transvaal mounted. The Boer leader at the time was Stephanus Johannes Paulus (Paul) Kruger, a craggy, ultra-conservative Calvinist farmer. He was to dominate the Transvaal Boers and champion their cause. Dogmatic in his opinions, he would not tolerate opposition to his views. His strong leadership and readiness to listen to their grievances made him revered by his followers. He campaigned long and hard for the Republic to be reinstated. Initial negotiations with Bartle Frere made some progress. Frere was prepared to allow the Transvaal self-government within limits, whilst retaining external relations under British rule. He could envisage this arrangement as feasible within a federal South Africa. This might have led somewhere if Frere had not been recalled in disgrace for going to war with the Zulus against the express instructions of the British Government.

This was a major disappointment to the Transvaal Boers. They trusted Frere, and believed they could have reached an amicable agreement with him. With his departure went the Boers' dreams, and General Garnett Wolseley, sent to South Africa by the British Government to determine the future of the country after the Anglo-Zulu war, would not honour any of the undertakings Frere had made. He was contemptuous of the Boers: "Ignorant men, led by a few designing fellows.... talking nonsense on the High Veld."[3] He told them to forget about independence: "So long as the sun shines, the Transvaal will remain British territory."[4]

The disastrous defeat at Isandhlwana gave Disraeli's opponent, William Gladstone, the opportunity to air his criticisms to telling effect. In what was known as the Midlothian Campaign he castigated British policy in South Africa, arguing that Britain should pursue the path of morality and justice, free from the taint of self-interest. He believed in self-government for colonial subjects. He was swept back into power in a decisive election in 1880.

It was therefore understandable that the Boers now turned to Gladstone in the belief that he would champion their cause. With self-government denied them, the independence they had sought on leaving the Cape was lost. However Gladstone had been persuaded that the future for South Africa lay in federalisation, which would involve the Boers in a unified structure. His party was not sympathetic to Boer aspirations, which it saw as divisive. Moreover, there did not seem to be a place in the structure for the indigenous African tribes. The finances of the Transvaal remained in a parlous state. Thus he informed the Boers "… our judgement is that the Queen cannot be advised to relinquish the Transvaal."[5]

In November 1880 Boer anger boiled over. The flash point was the non-payment of taxes by a farmer, Piet Bezuidenhout. This was a common occurrence among the Boers. The authorities seized his ox wagon and put it up for sale in the public square in Potchefstroom on November 11. An ox wagon was a Boer's prize possession, his mobile home, allowing him to roam the veld in self-sufficiency. Some one hundred protesters assembled. When an official mounted the platform to read the conditions of sale one of the protesters, Piet Cronje, dragged him off and kicked him. The ox wagon was restored to Bezuidenhout and hauled back to his farm.

Armed Boers, who occupied some of the principal buildings in Potchefstroom drove off the soldiers from the Scots Fusiliers sent to arrest Cronje. Attempts by the soldiers to regain control of the town resulted in shots being fired.

The first Boer War had begun.

On December 13, 1880, the Boers formally rebelled against British rule. A rally of 5,000 men, women and children at Paardekraal, a farm near present-day Krugersdorp, proclaimed the Transvaal to be free of British rule. A triumvirate of their leaders, Kruger, M.W. Pretorius and General Petrus Jacobus Joubert, was elected to govern the Republic. The Boers' flag, the Vierkleur (four colour) was hoisted and rifles were handed out to anyone who could shoot. Louis Botha's father supported the rebellion by gathering together as much ammunition as he could and taking it personally by wagon to the Transvaal Boer headquarters at Heidelberg.

Wealth provided by the goldfields enabled the Boer administration to arm itself with the most modern weapons from Europe. Denied access to the two South African ports of Durban and Cape Town, they imported the arms through Delagoa Bay, a port in the Portuguese-controlled territory of Mocambique, which adjoined the Transvaal.

A series of skirmishes in isolated towns ensued. The British forces in the Transvaal were well scattered in small garrisons, not expecting a general rising. They were ill equipped to handle local insurgency from mobile groups of sharp-shooting horsemen. On December 16 the Volksraad (people's council) in Pretoria unilaterally declared the Transvaal an independent Republic. On December 20 two companies of the British Army from the 94th Foot, marching from Lydenberg to Pretoria, were ambushed at Bronkhorst Spruit. They lost 56 men before surrendering to the Boers.

Britain was not prepared to allow the Transvaal its independence, or have its authority challenged. Since the Zulu War a substantial body of British troops had been stationed in Natal. Under the command of Sir George Colley they prepared to move on Pretoria to reassert control. They set out from Natal with 500 infantry and 70 mounted infantry to relieve the beleaguered garrisons. The Boers did not wait for them to enter the Transvaal. With 2,000 armed men they crossed the frontier into Natal and took up a strong position at Laing's Nek, near Volksrust, guarding the main road to the Transvaal.

On January 23, 1881, Colley approached the pass and ordered the Boers to disperse. The Boers demanded that the annexation of the Transvaal be rescinded. They insisted that the Republic be reinstated as a protectorate of the British monarch. This was substantially what the Boers had agreed with Frere. It would afford them protection from external powers while providing self-rule over domestic affairs. Colley's response was to charge their position, but the Boers under General Joubert were well prepared for them. 195 British casualties were incurred before they were forced to retire.

When the Boers did not follow up their victory Colley tried again. On February 8, 1881, reinforced by artillery, he marched up the main road. Near the Ingogo River the entrenched Boers opened fire on the column. Colley was forced to retreat, having suffered heavy casualties. He now studied the Boer positions, and realised that they were concentrated at the foot of a high hill, Majuba, which dominated the main road, and appeared not to be occupied. Whoever held the hill would control the surrounding territory. Moreover, if the British were to enter the Transvaal they needed to control Majuba.

On February 26, at ten o'clock on a moonless night Colley moved forward again with 494 soldiers and 64 sailors, and climbed Majuba Hill. The summit was reached at three in the morning with the soldiers exhausted and disorganised. Carrying 58 pounds of equipment each, they experienced difficulty keeping together, and once they reached the top, a plateau 400 yards long by 300 yards wide, and found it unoccupied, they made no attempt to entrench or establish defences. Dawn showed the Boers spread out below them on the plain: "...we seemed to hold them in palm of our hands," wrote one British correspondent.[6]

The Boers were very alarmed to find the British above them. Volunteers were called for to climb the hill. Although movement towards the hill was reported back to Colley, he appeared unconcerned. "We will wait until the Boers advance on us, then give them a volley and charge."[7] By now the Boers were within rifle range and beginning to pour fire into the undefended British position from several points. One bullet killed Colley on the spot, and his deputy, Lieutenant Ian Hamilton, had his left wrist shattered. Within minutes the British troops had turned and fled. 280 British soldiers were killed in the rout. Rider Haggard, in his book, *Cetywayo and his White Neighbours* wrote that the Boer force numbered between two and three hundred men. Sir Ian Hamilton, who was present at Majuba, told him later that the Boers numbered no more than one hundred.

The result of this encounter was that the Boers were encouraged to assert their demands. They observed that the British were poorly led, and could be defeated. Moreover, the favourable peace terms now offered encouraged them to believe the British wished to avoid war at almost any price, and were reluctant to commit military resources to the territory. The British were stunned. They had regarded the Boers as an undisciplined rabble of farmers who would pose no military threat; now these back-woods men had soundly beaten seasoned, professional soldiers who were accustomed to British dominance on the battlefield.

Prime Minister Gladstone immediately entered into discussions with the Boer leaders, and yielded on every point demanded by the Boers. On August 3, 1881, the Pretoria Convention made the Transvaal a self-governing state subject to British control of foreign policy. The old South African Republic was alive again.

In 1887 a rich seam of gold was discovered on the Witwatersrand

(Ridge of White Water). The trickle of prospectors from overseas, already attracted by the diamond fields and gold discoveries elsewhere, became a flood. These Uitlanders were mainly single men in search of a quick fortune. They cared little for the country. In camps around Johannesburg they scandalised the locals. "A loafing, drinking, scheming lot," a politician called them, who would "corrupt an archangel, or at any rate knock a good deal of bloom off its wings."[8] The Transvalers – conservative, god-fearing farmers and small tradesmen - were a different breed.

Paul Kruger had been appointed President of the new Republic in 1883, and dominated proceedings. He granted a number of concessions that could be seen as monopolies on the railways, dynamite, and other commodities. An English paper at the time described him as:

> "Personally corrupt, since he was not above charging very heavy travelling expenses for a certain trip in which he was the guest of the Cape Colony; winking at or openly justifying corruption in others; laying up a colossal fortune out of the stealings of himself and his friends from the State.....[He wore] a shabby frock coat deluged with coffee stains, a seedy silk hat without gloss, an immense scarf of office which sorts grotesquely with this apparel, and ill-fitting trousers barely long enough to meet the boots, are his familiar habiliments. He smokes and drinks coffee incessantly. He has the fervent piety of a Torquemada; believes himself under the peculiar protection of God; and interlards his discourse with religious ejaculations, as if God could smile upon tyranny and corruption."[9]

To stop Cape railway traffic that was bringing new goods to the Transvaal, Kruger imposed prohibitive "import" taxes at the Transvaal border. When traders attempted to circumvent these taxes by offloading their goods at the border and sending them on by ox-wagon he blocked drifts along the Vaal River.

It was not long before the Uitlanders came into conflict with the Boers. They were fast outnumbering the local population. The Uitlanders contributed eighty per cent of the Transvaal's taxes. They paid 33 pence in the pound Income Tax compared with the burghers' 3 pence. Without political representation, the Uitlanders were at the mercy of the dictates of Kruger and his Volksraad. In August a petition signed by 35,000 Uitlanders seeking an extension of the franchise was presented to the Volksraad. Attempts to gain a voice in local affairs were refused out of hand. Kruger feared that if he granted the Uitlanders the franchise they would come to dominate the administration of the Transvaal and introduce far-reaching changes. Almost certainly the burghers way of life would not survive, and Kruger himself would be ousted. The newcomers saw the Volksraad as corrupt and inefficient, unwilling to recognise the changes taking place as Johannesburg rose from the veld into a thriving, teeming city.

Enter Cecil Rhodes, a dominant figure in the diamond industry from which he had become extremely rich, and Prime Minister of the Cape Colony. He saw advantages in championing the Uitlanders. Rhodes had a dream of uniting South Africa under the British flag, and then expanding to encompass the territories to the north of South Africa. He even contemplated a time when Cape Town and Cairo would be directly linked by a railway running up the spine of Africa.

Kruger raised the political temperature in January, 1895 in an after-dinner speech. He referred to Germany as a "grown-up power that would stop England from kicking the child Republic."[10] Rhodes found this unacceptable; something had to be done about the troublesome president. Rhodes worked closely with the men who controlled the gold mining industry in the Transvaal. These magnates were as frustrated as the other Uitlanders by the lack of a franchise or any say in the affairs of the Republic. Rhodes conceived a plan to provoke the newcomers into an uprising against the Boers. This involved an invasion from the northwest of the Transvaal, in the belief that the new, Uitlander inhabitants of Pretoria and the new gold town of Johannesburg would spontaneously support him. There is some evidence to suggest that the British Government knew of Rhodes' plans and tacitly approved.

A close friend of Rhodes, Leander Starr Jameson, the Administrator of Rhodesia, was chosen to lead the raid, which was launched on December 29, 1895. Far from achieving its aims, the raid was a fiasco. The Boers were fully aware of what was planned, and confronted the invasion force before it could reach Johannesburg. The Uitlanders were much more interested in making money than fighting for their rights, and failed to support the invasion. Jameson and his men were captured, and the attempt fizzled out in ignominy. Jameson was led off to prison in Pretoria in tears. This raid was a turning point in South African history.

The Dutch in the Cape and the Boers in the Orange Free State lost any trust they still had in the British. They were alienated and pledged their support to Kruger. Rhodes was forced to resign as Premier of the Cape.

A telegram from Kaiser Wilhelm of Germany dated January 3, 1896 addressed to Kruger and published in the Cape Times caused a stir:

> "I tender to you my sincere congratulations that without appealing to the help of friendly Powers you and your people have been successful in opposing with your own forces the armed bands that have broken into your country to disturb the peace, in restoring order, and in maintaining the independence of your country against attacks from without."[11]

This produced a storm of protest in England and among English-speaking South Africans. Germany was accused of interfering in South Africa. The British Government, almost certainly complicit in the Raid, innocently argued that they had publicly repudiated it. On January 2 a large crowd assembled in Pretoria to see the captured leaders of the Raid paraded through the town.

Kruger recognised that the Raid represented an undertow of intent on behalf of the British that once again threatened the Republic, and would not go away. A census taken in 1896 showed that there were 50,907 white people living in the Johannesburg area, of whom 6,205 were Transvalers and the rest Uitlanders. The Boers were becoming heavily outnumbered in their own republic. They made preparations to defend themselves, taking stock of arms, ammunition and men. New, modern weapons were ordered from France and Germany, shipped to the Transvaal through the Portuguese-controlled port of Delagoa Bay, in Mocambique. On March 10 Kruger visited Bloemfontein to sign a agreement between the Orange Free State and the Transvaal Republic bringing closer union. The scene was being set for renewed conflict.

The new High Commissioner of the Cape Colony, Sir Alfred Milner, was a man on a mission. A brilliant graduate of Balliol College, Oxford University, the leading scholar of his time, he inherited from his German father a strong streak of ruthlessness, and set opinions. He considered that Kruger's treatment of the Uitlanders was outrageous. Like his predecessor, Bartle Frere, Milner could see that if the cherished dream of a united South Africa were to be realised, it would only be possible with the full and willing participation of the Transvaal and Orange Free State Republics. The Boers who presided over the republics, Kruger in the Transvaal and Marthinus Steyn in the Orange Free State, were most unlikely to surrender their independence willingly. It would only be achieved by reforms that gave the Uitlanders full involvement in their administration and legislation, or war.

The British government had another agenda as well. If Britain were to control the gold and diamond fields, it needed to control the South African ports. The Boers, landlocked in the Transvaal and Orange Free State Republics, were desperate to secure a secure and permanent outlet through Delagoa Bay, in Portuguese territory. This was something Britain strongly opposed. Not only would this port allow the Transvaal to export its produce, but also it would give other European powers, notably the Germans, an independent entry point. In the scramble for Africa taking place, after 1880 the Germans were the greatest threat. Moreover, they were the European power most in sympathy with the Boers.

By 1900 Transvaal was producing a quarter of the world's gold supply and had absorbed more than £114 million of mainly British capital in the development of the industry.[12] South Africa was fast becoming a valuable prize worth fighting for. Milner commenced lobbying the British Colonial Secretary, Joseph Chamberlain, for intervention in the Transvaal. Chamberlain was one of the foremost politicians in England. A Liberal Unionist, he had taken the lead in electioneering and campaigning for his party. When Lord Salisbury, a Conservative, formed a government in 1895 in coalition with the Liberals, he offered Chamberlain any Cabinet position he wished with the exception of Foreign Secretary or Leader of the House. To everyone's surprise, rather than choose the Treasury or Home Secretary, Chamberlain opted for Colonial Secretary. A post seen traditionally as of little interest, Chamberlain saw the post as an opportunity to expand the British Empire and use Britain's resources, both commercial and military, better. He was a passionate imperialist, and believed in spreading British influence overseas. He said:

> "I believe that the British race is the greatest of the governing races that the world has ever seen....It is not enough to occupy great spaces of the world's surface

unless you can make the best of them. It is the duty of a landlord to develop his estate."[13]

Milner's ambitions for South Africa therefore received a sympathetic ear from Chamberlain, who nevertheless advocated caution. Chamberlain's policy was to accept a settlement over the Uitlanders if it were sincere, and agree to a new convention guaranteeing the Transvaal internal independence. Ironically, this was precisely what Bartle Frere had offered in 1879 before his removal as Governor-General. Aware of the pressure building for recognition of the newcomers, many of the Boer leaders felt concessions to the Uitlanders should be made, but Kruger adamantly opposed them.

Finally, on May 31, 1899, Milner and Kruger met in Bloemfontein to discuss the issue. Jan Smuts, in his role as State Attorney, accompanied Kruger. Smuts was to play an increasingly important part in the negotiations and the war that followed. When it became apparent that a crisis faced the Transvaal, Smuts drew up a final offer to Britain, giving in on the extended franchise but adding conditions that made it unacceptable. Kruger conceded that Uitlanders could have the vote after seven years of residence. This proposal stipulated that before burgher rights were acquired prospective citizens would have to take the oath of allegiance to the Transvaal Republic. Moreover, they would not be able to replace the President by voting in someone else. These terms were certain to be unacceptable to the Uitlanders. Milner demanded that the term of residence before gaining the franchise be reduced to five years. This came as a surprise to the Boers, as they had previously believed Milner himself to be content with seven years.

Kruger, while appearing to bend, seemed intent on making sure that the newcomers could not influence the Volksraad. Earlier legislation had confined Uitlanders' vote (after qualifying for citizenship) to the "Second Raad," a second house with virtually no say in the running of the Republic. However it was apparent to everyone that Milner was bent on war. The High Commissioner was gambling that there would be lukewarm support in the republics for armed conflict, that the British South Africans would side with the mother country, and that if it came to war it would be one-sided, and soon over. He was attempting to manoeuvre the Boers into declaring war, so Britain would not be seen as the aggressors.

It was evident that the Transvaal was not yet prepared to declare war.

In order to temporise, amended reforms, meeting many of Milner's demands, were made. Milner had a different agenda. He wanted the republics to be destroyed, and set about persuading the British Government to back him. Only surrender of the republic's legislative sovereignty would be acceptable. Fred Graham, Under-Secretary at the Colonial Office disagreed strongly:

> "To speak frankly I think there is some danger of our being rushed by the party in So. Africa which, while its sympathy with the Uitlanders is genuine, has for its chief aim the wiping out of Majuba and the speedy annexation of the Transvaal."[14]

Chamberlain was under no illusions as to the dangers of going to war. Unlike Milner, he did not think it would be over quickly, or that it would be one-sided. Most important of all, he was concerned about the legacy of ill feeling that would result. He warned:

> "A war in South Africa would be one of the most serious wars that could possibly be waged. It would be in the nature of a civil war. It would be a long war, a bitter war, and a costly war… It would leave behind it the embers of a strife which I believe generations would hardly be long enough to extinguish."[15]

The Uitlanders in the Transvaal had no doubt that war was coming. Since August British refugees had been fleeing from the Transvaal. The gold mines were deserted, the shops abandoned. Iron workers and boilermen, with all their possessions, followed. The trains south to Cape Town were packed to capacity. Those that could not join this exodus south somehow made their way to Lorenco Marques in Mocambique. They jammed the wharfside, looking for a ship home to England. The economy of the Transvaal, already in poor shape, was left in tatters. More importantly, by taking up every available means of transport, they denied the Boer militia means of moving their men to Natal.

Chamberlain rebuked Milner for not trusting Kruger. He told him: "If these [concessions] appear to be substantial it is our policy to accept them as such and not to minimise them."[16] He had the support of a massive majority through the coalition Conservative/Liberal Unionist government. To keep the pressure on Kruger, however, he made

Two Generals

belligerent speeches, whilst at the same time keeping the centre Liberals, led by Sir Henry Campbell-Bannerman, onside. He proposed a seven-year franchise and a joint enquiry to establish whether the new franchise would meet the need of "immediate and substantial representation."[17] Parliament gave its assent.

Kruger trusted Chamberlain and Milner even less than they trusted him. Negotiations dragged on without making progress until the Boers realised that Milner's attitude could not be modified. On September 5 and 8 a debate in the Volksraad addressed the relationship with Britain. On September 8 a decision was taken by London to increase the number of British and colonial troops in South Africa to 27,000. In response the Boers drew up an ultimatum demanding that all outstanding points in the dispute be referred to arbitration, that British troops on the borders of the republic be withdrawn and that other troops already on the way to South Africa be turned back. When the British received the ultimatum, Milner dismissed it out of hand. It was in effect a declaration of independence, and an abrogation of the agreement that had followed Majuba. There was now no turning back.

Both sides played for time. The Transvalers wanted to marshal their resources, while the British did not wish to be seen as the aggressors. On October 11 the British Agent in Pretoria, Sir W. Conyngham Greene, delivered the reply to Kruger: Milner deemed the ultimatum "impossible to discuss."[18] He was told that this answer was regarded as a declaration of war. Milner had what he wanted.

xxxi

chapter 1.
ORIGINS.

BOTHA.

In 1880, in northern Natal, an eighteen year-old boy was taking sheep to winter grazing when he met a band of Zulus. After the Anglo-Zulu War, Zululand was broken up into thirteen principalities, and petty chiefs were vying for power. Bands of Zulus were roaming the land. The most aggressive of these was led by a Zulu captain, Mapelo. He and his warriors approached the boy and commenced driving off his cattle. Unsurprisingly the boy's African helpers fled, leaving him alone. He could do nothing to resist Mapelo, so sat on his wagon, rifle in hand, with a reserve of only six cartridges.

Mapelo knew him, greeted him and took a seat next to him. The boy had received word that a few hours before Mapelo had cut the throat of a missionary. He was aware of the peril facing him. As they talked (the boy spoke Zulu fluently) Mapelo became provocative. The boy, despite his young years, remained unruffled, reasoning calmly why he and his sheep should not be molested.

Suddenly Mapelo rose and instructed everything to be returned to the young farmer. The boy gave him some sheep for a feast and moved on, unharmed. Thus was spared the life of the man destined to lead his nation to independence and unity. The boy was Louis Botha.

BULLER.

A young captain of the British Army's 60th Rifle battalion was struggling up the Winnipeg River in Canada when it happened. He was standing in a strong current, attempting to push a boat off a rock. His men on shore were pulling the boat with a rope. Suddenly they let the rope go slack. The boat swung round and hit the captain, forcing him under water. The weight of the boat was on top of him, preventing him from surfacing.

His aide reacted quickly by leaping on the rope and jamming it against a tree. This stabilised the boat for long enough for the captain to extricate himself from a very dangerous situation. The twenty-eight years old Captain, Redvers Buller, like Botha, had survived an early threat to his life.

BOTHA.

Louis Botha was born on September 27, 1862, the seventh child of Louis and Salomina Botha (nee van Rooyen) of Greytown in Natal. His father cut a striking figure: tall, dark-featured with blue eyes, athletic, a crack shot. Although a farmer born and bred, he was interested in politics, shrewd and progressive in his outlook for the nascent Boer nation. His mother was described as the "beauty of Greytown," a town in northern Natal. [19]

The Botha family had been cattle farmers for over a hundred years, initially in Swellendam in the Cape. They joined the exodus of Dutch families from the Cape when the British, who had ultimately taken control of the territory from the Dutch in 1806, enforced the Slavery Abolition Act of 1833. They settled in the grasslands of northern Natal, and became successful cattle farmers there.

Life was tough. Their home was burnt down several times, either by marauding African tribes or by sparks from the kitchen fire. They had few comforts, and lived by the gun, which protected the family from wild beasts as well as the indigenous Africans who saw the white settlements as an infringement on their lands.

Like their fellow Boers, the Bothas rarely spent much time in one place. Having established a farm, they liked to go on hunting and trading expeditions, and frequently moved to fresh pastures. Often they would take a covered wagon and horses into the veld (the high grasslands of the interior), stalking and shooting the abundant game. They lived off the countryside, drying and salting meat from the animals they shot into "biltong" – a delicacy still enjoyed by South Africans. The wagons carried casks of butter and lard, bags of meal and potatoes. The family would be away from home for weeks, visiting friends on their farms along the Helpmekaar Ridge.

Botha Senior was a prosperous stockholder, independently minded, "who seldom interfered with others."[20] He spoke High Dutch and Afrikaans, a simplified version of Dutch, but no English. He read hardly at all, and displayed virtually no cultural awareness. He was a proficient hunter, an outstanding horseman and a shrewd and intelligent farmer. Engelenburg, a close friend of his son, wrote:

> "Someone who knew him well tells me that he was gifted above average, a lover of his country and a fluent speaker…one would always notice people standing round him in order to hear what he had to say."[21]

His thirteen children all worked on the farm. The only formal education available was a small local school and the occasional wandering Dutch tutor. Wild animals on the veld were still numerous: jackals, wolves, and occasionally lions. The children learnt self-reliance at an early age, riding horses and ponies almost from infancy and learning to shoot as soon as they reached their teens. They worked hard, living largely in the open air.

Life was simple and narrow, alleviated by regular social gatherings in the farming community. Deneys Reitz, a contemporary of Botha and later to be a stalwart of the Boer resistance, described what it was like to be a boy growing up on a South African farm in those days:

> "We learned to ride, shoot, and swim almost as soon as we could walk, and there was a string of hardy Basuto ponies in the stables, on which we were often away for weeks at a time, riding over the game-covered plains by day, and sleeping under the stars at night, hunting, fishing and camping to our heart's content."[22]

In 1867, when Louis Botha was five, the family moved. His father had lent money to impecunious friends and neighbours. He had stood surety for a neighbour's bill that could not be honoured, and the creditor called on its backer. Botha was forced to sell his farm to meet the debt. The Bothas settled on a less prosperous farm of some 5,000 acres, Vroodepoort, in Vrede, a rather barren and isolated small town in the northeastern Orange Free State. They stocked it with sheep, cattle and horses. In addition they grew corn, oats and vegetables for the family's needs. Six years later, having recovered from the financial setback, they moved to a farm of much better quality. Louis' father bought Leeuwkop from an Englishman, and commenced ostrich farming there.

BULLER.

Redvers Henry Buller, like Louis Botha, came from a large family, but there the similarity ended. He was born on December 7, 1839, the second son of James Wentworth Buller and Charlotte Juliana Jane Howard, daughter of Lord Henry Molyneux Howard and niece of Bernard Edward Howard, twelfth Duke of Norfolk. The family was prominent in both Devon and Cornwall from the seventeenth century onwards.

The name Redvers can be traced back to Richard de Redvers (also called de Ripariis or Rivers) who lived in Devon in the eleventh century. Through the ages the family had been politically prominent in the Whig Party as well as local affairs, and could boast of a prominent judge among their number. Although several Bullers had been military men, it could not be said that the family had a tradition of military service. However, a distant cousin, General Sir George Buller, fought in South Africa some thirty years before Redvers. Sir George's last service was in the Crimea, where he distinguished himself by displaying "cool-headed common sense" when there was not much of that evident among British officers.[23]

Redvers spent his early childhood at the family seat of Downes, in Devon. Life was very quiet and secluded for the children, and they made their own entertainment. The grounds and garden offered ample opportunities for outside pursuits, and also perils for young children. Redvers developed a reputation for being accident-prone. He sliced off the top of a finger with a turnip cutter, had to be rescued with difficulty by his governess when he fell into a garden pond, and was shot by a cousin with an arrow that entered the corner of his eye and left a permanent mark.

At the age of seven Buller was sent to boarding school. A severe disciplinarian who flogged his pupils regularly and often indiscriminately ran it. Although considered to be very clever, Buller was criticised for not working, and was chastised accordingly. This harsh treatment left a lasting impression on the young boy. In later years Buller showed his sister an old bible stained with his tears. He would read it while his schoolmaster stalked about the classroom flicking the boys with a driving whip. He never forgave his first schoolmaster for this treatment.

BOTHA.

An attractive-looking boy, with violet-blue eyes, Louis Botha enjoyed company. He was by nature warm, friendly and courteous, secure in his solid family environment. He was a good listener, ready to respond to the needs of others, and was described as having a natural tact.[24] At the frequent party gatherings he played the concertina, and was fond of pranks. His easy charm made him very popular, but from his early youth he showed a steely purpose and drive, disciplined and unwavering when defending his principles. His father recognised this, saying to his wife: "Mark my words, Mother, mark my words: that son of yours is going to make a name for himself."[25] Others also recognised his leadership qualities. His daughter recalled Botha meeting an old man at the agriculture show in Bloemfontein after he had been made Commander in Chief of the Boer Army. He greeted the man, who was surprised to be recognised. Botha said: "The last time I met you I was 12 years old and you said I was going to be the leader of my people."[26]

In early 1877 Theophilus Shepstone, on his way from Pietermaritzburg to Pretoria spent a night on the Bothas' farm. Shepstone, head of Native Affairs in Natal, had been given the task by the British Government of annexing the Transvaal. The independent republic had managed its finances badly, being unable to collect sufficient taxes from the farmers spread across the countryside. On meeting Shepstone, Botha Senior expressed strong objections to the annexation that was to precipitate the conflict that followed. This meeting left a lasting impression on young Louis, then a boy of fifteen, who respected his father's opinions and patriotism.

BULLER.

Like Botha, inclined to be independently minded, Buller developed a stubborn streak that resulted in a refusal to be cowed or diverted from his purpose. Nothing stimulated him more than a difference of opinion, and the force of his personality was such that few dared to stand up to him in argument. He grew up a shy, reserved young man, not quick to make friends.

From his boarding school he went on, true to family tradition, to Harrow, but his stay there was short. Some unexplained difference of opinion with the authorities caused him to move on to Eton, where he developed a reputation for having a will of his own which did not always coincide with his seniors.[27] His academic record there was not distinguished, possibly because his health was not good. The enduring legacy left him by Eton was a love for the classics. He spent his final school year at a "crammer," Flemings in Tunbridge Wells, presumably to help him pass his exams. Flemings had a name for preparing ill-taught boys for the Sandhurst entrance examination.

Buller seems to have been happier at home, at Downes. There he picked up from workmen and employees the practical skills of animal husbandry, woodcrafts and the work of the smithy. His bent for suffering accidents persisted. Struggling to lop branches in the woods his axe slipped and cut his leg so severely that the local doctor advised amputation. Buller announced that he would rather die than live with one leg. He recovered, though the injured leg was to trouble him for the rest of his life.

BOTHA.

The high veld around Vrede dry, treeless and bleak experienced very cold winters, and the farmers would move their stock to lower altitudes. Zululand, with its lush vegetation, was an attractive wintering location, although attempts to stay for any length of time provoked clashes with the Zulus living there. During his visits to Zululand Louis, who found learning foreign languages easy, became fluent in the local African dialects. This frequently was an advantage, and as we saw was to come to his rescue when he encountered Mapelo.

Botha's father died on July 13, 1883. His children, thirteen brothers and sisters, with their husbands and wives, gathered at the Vrede farm, Klipplaat, to discuss how the estate should be divided. Louis argued strongly that it would benefit them all if the estate remained intact. In the last days of his father's long illness he had managed the farm, and now offered to continue doing so for the family. This was not as presumptuous as it sounds, for Louis' elder brothers often sought his advice, unusual in a culture where deference was normally given to seniority. "It is hard to disobey Louis," his brothers and sisters would say: his common sense approach always made them listen.[28]

On this occasion they considered him too young at the age of twenty to assume responsibility, and it was decided to divide up the farm. Disappointed, Louis moved out, taking with him a younger brother and his share of the farm, a herd of carefully selected cattle.

He headed back to northern Natal, his childhood home. He re-established contact with an old friend of his father, Lukas Meyer, who was a leader of the Boers in Vryheid, a town close to the Transvaal border. Meyer was a huge man, six feet four inches tall and broad with it. He had fought against the British after the annexation of the Transvaal in 1877 and was known as the Lion of Vryheid. He was a leader of men, and immensely popular with the local Boers. Botha had first met him as a boy at his parents' home. Meyer was more than just a farmer. He had received a good education, and his tastes were cultured and refined as a consequence. The young Louis had formed an instant attachment to him, and now sought his company and leadership.

The king of the Zulus during the Anglo-Zulu war, Cetshwayo, had been captured and imprisoned by the British, finally dying in 1884. When Botha returned to Natal, Meyer was supporting the newly crowned Zulu king, Dinizulu, a youth of sixteen and son of Cetshwayo. He was faced with a challenge from Usibebu, the strongest of the Zulu generals, who was contesting the young man's right to the throne. It looked as though Usibebu's seasoned warriors would win the day against a cowed and demoralised royal force.

Dinizulu had appealed to the British for protection without success. He therefore turned to his traditional enemies, the Boers. Meyer agreed to help in return for grants of land in Zululand. Early in May 1884 he took a select group of a hundred Boers to Dinizulu's aid. Botha, with his friend Cheere Emett, was part of this group. Dinizulu was able to summon up 7,000 loyal warriors in support.

At the decisive battle of Magut on the Pondola River in 1884 the

Boers showed their courage by standing their ground and shooting with deadly accuracy. Usibebu's army wavered and fled. On May 21, 1884 Dinizulu was crowned king of the Zulus in the presence of his Boer allies, including Botha. The Boers' reward was three million acres in Zululand itself which was promptly named "De Nieuwe Republiek" (The New Republic) with Vryheid as the capital and Meyer as its president. Botha, who had accompanied Meyer on the expedition against Usibebu, was made a member of the Executive Council. At the age of twenty-two he had established himself in the Boer community.

BULLER.

When Buller was sixteen his mother died. She met him at Exeter railway station on his return from school to Devon for the Christmas holidays. Suffering from tuberculosis, there she collapsed, and could not be moved. Redvers, tended her for two days on a screened off bench in the busy terminal before she died. A woman of strong character, Buller's mother was both shy and gentle, and had centred her life on her family. She spent more time with her children than was normal in those times, and they adored her. She was well read and a fine mimic. Redvers was very close to her, and the loss affected him deeply. His devotion to her was such that to the day of his death he kept many of her small personal belongings. He took it upon himself to tend to and protect his younger siblings, showing a sense of responsibility beyond his years. In this he was very akin to Louis Botha.

His father outlived his wife by ten years. Lacking his wife's warmth of character, he could not fill the void Redvers sought in a parent, although he enjoyed the company of his children. The emotional distance between Redvers and his father prompted the young man to consider a future outside the bosom of the family. His elder brother, James, would inherit the estates, and he was thus disinclined to remain at Downes. Neither religion nor the law attracted him. He preferred the outdoor, adventurous life. With the Crimean War recently over and the Indian Mutiny in its final stages, the army was in the public eye and represented an attractive option. Instead of entering Sandhurst however, a commission was bought for him by his father. On May 10, 1858, he received a letter from the Horse Guards that read:

"I am directed by His Royal Highness the general Commanding in Chief to acquaint you, that, on your lodging the Sum of £450 in the hands of Messrs McGrigor, His Royal Highness will submit your Name to Her Majesty for the purchase of an Ensigncy in the 60th Foot."[29]

Thirteen days later Redvers received his commission, and on July 14, at the age of eighteen, he reported for duty at the Rifle Depot, Winchester.

chapter 2.
LEADERS IN WAITING.

BULLER.

BULLER DID not have to wait long after receiving his commission to see active service. Within six months he was in India. In 1859 he sailed on the ship *Ceylon* to Alexandria, then crossed the Egyptian desert to Suez and sailed on to India in the *Alma*. He was stationed at Benares (now Varanasi) for a year before moving on to China and the Opium Wars. He was present at actions in Sinho, Taku and the capture of Peking (Bejing). He did not get on with the captain commanding his regiment, regarding him as the biggest fool in the regiment. Buller was not in the habit of keeping his opinions to himself, and thus quarrelled frequently with his superior.

In September 1861, coming out of China unscathed, he sailed with his battalion for England, rounding the Cape of Good Hope. Within a year he was promoted from Ensign to Lieutenant and posted to the fourth battalion of the King's Royal Rifle Corps, serving in Canada, where he was to be for seven years.

Buller was fortunate in his posting, for he came under the command of one of the greatest regimental commanders the British Army ever produced: Robert Beaufoy Hawley. Not only did Hawley reform drill routines by cutting out unnecessary commands and therefore simplifying movements but he also believed in the self-reliance and individuality of his officers and men. Consequently, he developed a regimental system that depended upon men taking the initiative and thinking for themselves, while at the same time adhering to collective drills that were reliable and easy to follow. Every officer had a specified responsibility: captains to command their companies, whilst unusually subalterns and sergeants commanded smaller units. Buller was to say later, on his return to England, that he owed

> "All I know of soldiering, and very largely such success as I may have achieved in the Army, to my old and revered Colonel, General Hawley."[30]

For six years Buller learnt from Hawley the duties of a company officer. This was a quiet period in Canada, with few onerous tasks, and plenty of scope to indulge in shooting, fishing and boating in the Canadian lakes and forests, recreation that Hawley encouraged. Buller's progress was noticed. A contemporary, Lieutenant William Butler, wrote in his autobiography later:

> "At this time Redvers Buller was the best type of regimental officer to be found. Young, active, daring, as keen for service as he was ready to take the fullest advantage of it, he stood even then in the front rank of those young and ardent spirits who might be described as the ruck of Army life which is waiting to get through."[31]

Hawley recognised Buller's potential by appointing him Acting-Adjutant when his adjutant went on long leave. Buller was surprised by the appointment, protesting that he knew nothing yet about soldiering. He only agreed to the post when Hawley promised to teach him…and then only after considering the appointment for twenty-four hours.

Buller set about learning with great intensity. He had not modified his manner. He was still inclined to voice his opinions strongly, heedless of the effect this had. This resulted in clashes with Hawley when the two differed, as Buller would not back down, but the older man was wise enough to tolerate the young hothead, and their friendship survived.

In the summer of 1869 the fourth battalion returned to England, its overseas tour having ended. Buller was pleased to spend time at home in Downes: eleven of his previous twelve years had been spent abroad.

By 1870 he was senior enough to buy his captaincy. No vacancy existed in his own unit, so he was posted to the regiment's First Battalion, then assembling in Thunder Bay, Canada for a punitive expedition.

BOTHA.

When Botha was appointed to the Executive Council of the newly formed Vryheid Republic, he was charged with surveying the farms to be allotted to the citizens, known as burghers, after the drawing of lots. This was not without risk, as his survey took him out into Zululand where the local tribes continued to harass the would-be settlers. The task took him over a year to complete. He not only accomplished this to the satisfaction of the Council, but impressed them so much that he was asked to participate in the laying out of the town of Vryheid.

Botha had established himself in the community.

At the age of twenty-four, on December 13, 1886, he married Annie Emett, the eldest daughter of John Cheere Emett, a Swellendam farmer who had settled in Harrismith in the Orange Free State. He met his wife through her brother, Cheere Emett, who had taken part in the Zululand expedition and had struck up a friendship with Botha. The family was of Irish descent, related to a well-known Irish patriot, Robert Emett. Annie was educated at St Michael's Home, Bloemfontein. She was an excellent musician and had a lively personality with a well-developed sense of humour. Apparently when the couple met it was love at first sight. Her family favoured an alternate suitor whom she did not like. They wondered what she could see in the "little Dutch Boy" (although Botha was a massive figure of a man).[32]

To avoid conflict with her family she accepted a teaching position in Bloemfontein at her old school, known as "The Home." She taught there for three years, returning home with her feelings towards Botha stronger than ever. She spoke little Afrikaans and he not much English, having lived most of his life in an exclusively Afrikaans community. However, as he explained: "There is a language of the eyes that transcends the barriers of speech."[33]

Annie and Louis moved into a farm of three and a half thousand acres called Waterval, near Vryheid, close to Annie's family. A comfortable homestead was built in stone. The Bothas' existence, however, was a simple and hard-working one, for the countryside was sparsely populated and farms somewhat isolated. Initially they were financially stretched, but in time Botha would come to own sixteen thousand acres in the area, as well as other farms in the Transvaal. He established a flock of 6,000 sheep, 600 cattle and a string of 400 fine horses. Annie quickly became fluent in Afrikaans, and taught Louis English, though they always conversed in Afrikaans. Louis was reluctant to speak English in public, and preferred to address his audience in Afrikaans.

BULLER.

Canada had been unified as a dominion under British rule in 1867. One of the first acts of the new dominion was to buy from the Hudson Bay Company for £300,000 all the territorial rights to the Northwestern Territories, a wild, untamed and barely civilised area. When surveyors were sent to the territory to determine what was there, the isolated communities (mainly hunters and trappers), showed alarm at their potential loss of independence.

The residents of the Red River Settlement were mixed-race French-Indians who foresaw the English-speaking colonists moving into their territory. They objected to the presence of the British, and set up a Provisional Government, declaring that this was independent of the Canadian Dominion which was a recently-formed federation of the Canadian provinces. The Ottawa Government sent out William McDougall as Lieutenant-Governor of the territory, but he was denied entry by the rebels and forcibly turned back. This was not acceptable to Ottawa, and it was decided to send a brigade to quell the uprising.

Buller was reluctant to return to Canada so soon, but duty called and he could not resist a challenge. The logistics were daunting: 1200 miles, mainly by way of the lakes Huron and Superior, then by road for 50 miles, and then a series of smaller lakes by boat for another 550 miles. This final stretch had never been navigated by anything larger than birch-bark canoes. Special boats were built, between 25 and 30 feet in length, with a beam of 6 to 7 feet to carry fourteen men. The expeditionary force was commanded by Colonel Garnett Wolseley, who had seen action in India, and was regarded very highly by the British Army. The 60th Rifles were chosen as part of an elite force to accompany him.

Buller caught up with them at Thunder Bay on June 10. He was thirty years old, and was about to be tested severely for the first time.

Adverse weather conditions and the difficult terrain made progress arduous. The route had not been previously mapped, and the soldiers did not know what to expect. The boats had to be manhandled over rough terrain between stretches of water, together with provisions and arms. Inevitably in such a specially chosen force there was close rivalry between the groups. Buller's battalion excelled in the conditions, and this was noticed by Wolseley. The 60th Rifles responded to Buller's leadership, and appreciated his concern for their well being, as well as the strong and courageous lead he provided.

Buller's expeditionary force walked into the Red River Settlement unopposed on August 22. The rebels had left the settlement hours before the force arrived, thus avoiding conflict. An amnesty was agreed, and the incipient rebellion petered out. Wolseley was so impressed by Buller that he recommended that he be promoted to Brevet Major. The War Office decreed that, as there had been no fighting, the promotion should go by dint of succession to the two most senior captains, and Buller was denied. He returned to Montreal, and the following year was transferred to the Staff College in England.

BOTHA.

Life at Waterval was indeed a pleasant one. The size of farms meant that homesteads were widespread. Farmers led a fairly lonely existence mainly of hard work, so when they gathered socially the atmosphere was convivial. Botha, with his good looks, musical talent and easy, extrovert nature, was popular. Many people sought him out for advice and consultation, despite his young years. Annie was a fine singer and accomplished hostess. Three sons and two daughters were born there in the ensuing years, and the farming business prospered. Botha was an astute businessman who knew his farming, and had a reputation for being a fine judge of cattle.

By 1894, eight years later, he was a respected senior member of the local community, a Veldcornet (General's assistant) in the local militia at a salary of £200 per annum and sufficiently wealthy to be able to turn his mind to other matters. He spent some months as Resident Justice and Native Commissioner in the Boer protectorate of Swaziland where he stopped a wholesale traffic in liquor and gained valuable administrative experience. It was an isolated and lonely post, and he returned to Vryheid with some relief.

Outside of the protection of the town, though, life was hazardous. On one occasion, travelling through the countryside, Zulus surrounded him, threatening to kill him in the belief that he had supported Usibebu. Fortunately he was recognised in time.

On another occasion he was visiting his favourite bull, and turned to stroke another animal. The favourite, ignored, charged at Botha and gored him through the ribs. For a while it was thought he might die, but his strong constitution pulled him through, although the effects of his injuries were felt for years afterwards.

The new Republic of Vryheid lasted just over four years. Victory over Usibepu had given Meyer and his followers' control over Zululand. All three surrounding states – Natal, the Transvaal and Orange Free State – objected. Vryheid was too small and confined to be able to administer its own affairs and survive. In 1886 the British proclaimed Zululand to be within their sphere of influence, refuting the grant of 3 million acres which Meyer had received. Dinizulu, inexperienced in such political matters, proved an unreliable ally to the Boers. He tried to improve his fortunes by playing opposing interests against each other. Consequently he was forced to flee into exile. The only safe guarantee for the New Republic was removed. The burghers of the Transvaal regarded it as their territory. Soon the South African Republic absorbed it.

BULLER.

Buller did not stay long at the Staff College. Within two years, in 1873 Wolseley had called upon him to join an expedition to confront the Ashanti tribe, which was threatening the chain of trading posts set up by the British on the Gold Coast in West Africa. There Buller gained valuable experience of an entirely different form of warfare, one he had not encountered before. He was assigned the onerous duty of intelligence officer, a difficult task in such wild country with virtually no local support. There was no precedent for this post, and information concerning the enemy's positions and plans was hazy to say the least.

Buller formed a corps of interpreters and deployed commissioners to the local native kings. The notebook in which he recorded the information he gleaned is still in existence. He developed a strong dislike of the press. On one occasion he threatened to horsewhip correspondents who filed copy which displeased him, and on another threw out of the mess tent a reporter who said he would read personal mail in search of a story.

Buller was kept very busy, but appears to have acquitted himself well. Within two weeks of assuming the post Wolseley was able to surprise the depots near Elmina from which the Ashanti received their supplies, acting on intelligence supplied by Buller. The British pushed inland through dense forest and a network of waterways towards the Ashanti capital, Kumasi. They were frequently ambushed but the local tribe could not match the British modern rifles, supported by seven-pounder guns. The capital was captured, ransacked and set ablaze.

Buller returned to England, physically exhausted. He felt ready for a quiet spell at home.

chapter 3.
CONFLICT IN AFRICA.

BULLER.

BACK AT Downes, life for Buller was uneventful. His father had died in 1865, and the estates had passed to his elder brother, James Wentworth Buller. When James died in 1874, Buller effectively became squire. He was 34 years old. It was convenient for him to remain in England and he joined the War Office. In three years there he learnt the ways of that body and some of the intricacies of administering the military affairs of a worldwide empire. His experience was thus so different from that of Botha in his tight-knit community. Buller gained access to exalted social circles, and dined with the Prince of Wales, later to be King Edward VII. Deskwork was not the exciting career for which he had joined the army, however. Bureaucracy frustrated him, as a contemporary put it:

> "...a corporal and a file of men could not move from Glasgow to Edinburgh without the sanction of the War Office"[3434]

When the chance for action in the field came again he jumped at it. At the beginning of 1878, aged 39, he was offered a position on special service as a staff officer to General Frederic Thesiger (later Lord Chelmsford) who was going to South Africa to replace General Sir Arthur Conynghame as Officer Commanding the British forces in that country. This coincided with uncertainty in Europe over Russia's expansionist ambitions. Constantinople was being threatened and many thought this may lead to war.

Buller did not believe that another war in Europe was imminent and felt that a spell in South Africa would provide him with valuable experience. So it proved to be. He wrote:

> "...when I went to South Africa in 1878, all I asked, Collie, Wolseley, Baker et-all said I was mad to go, but it was the making of me. I believe myself that we are all such perfect fools as far as being able to foretell what is going to happen that we are almost always in the right when we accept what does happen; merely resolving to do the best we can in whatever position Providence leads us into."[35]

He sailed from Plymouth on February 1, 1878, on the *S.S. American*. On the same ship was a friend from the Ashanti campaign, Colonel Evelyn Wood. At the age of twenty Wood had distinguished himself during the Indian mutiny of 1857. In charge of a troop of light cavalry he had routed a band of rebels, and then rescued a local merchant who was threatened with hanging by rebels. For this he was awarded the Victoria Cross. Wood and Buller were to join forces at a later date.

Buller's first post was in the eastern Cape. In 1820 the British government had sponsored immigration to a settlement there in order to secure the Empire's position and protect the coastline. The settlers had been encouraged to farm, although many were tradespeople, and struggled to make a living. There were already a number of Boer farms in the area. Inevitably, the white settlers clashed with resident indigenous tribes. As the Boers sought to expand their pastures, they encroached upon tribal lands, and the tribes resisted their advances. To make matters worse, the tribes themselves were at war with each other. The Gcalekas on the coast resented the progress made by the Fingoes, further inland, who had co-operated with the colonial authorities and prospered.

Buller reached East London on March 4 and was posted to Kingwilliamstown, close to the Transkei border and at the heart of the disputed territory. The town was full of settlers who had been displaced from their farms and had sought refuge there. Buller's role was that of a Staff Officer attached to Commandant Frost, a colonial officer responsible for operations in the area. There was friction between the British contingent and the colonial officers over who administered the eastern Cape. These latter officers reported to the Prime Minister of the Cape Colony, whilst the British officers were responsible to the Governor-General, an imperial minister. The two factions could not agree about how the African tribes should be resisted and handled, and predictably neither was prepared to yield to the other.

Within six weeks Buller was given command of the Frontier Light Horse, a disparate collection of British, Boer and foreign men described as "a terror to every one but the enemy."[36] He wrote to his sister: "They are in terribly bad order and I fear there is not much credit to be got out of being associated with them, but I will do my best; it is at any rate something to be one's own C.O."[37]

Buller soon pulled them into some sort of order by applying strict discipline and imposing his personality upon the force. He administered stern justice and was quick to dispense with men who were not prepared to toe the line. On one occasion, having given his men time off after a tough patrol, a drunken trooper threw abuse at him. Buller appeared to ignore this, and marched the unit off. A few miles into the countryside he ordered the man to dismount and clear off.[38]

In developing the unit he commanded Buller did not follow the conventional, rather formal drills of the British cavalry. Through the Boers in the unit he learnt the merits of fluid, rapid movement and the democratically based formations of commandos living off the land. In the process he gained considerable respect for the Boers' methods of fighting. Unlike the Boers, however, he applied British discipline and order.

Such was the power of his personality that very quickly his men came to respect him and avoid transgressing. Among British commanders Buller was perhaps the most assiduous at attending to his men's needs, and understanding them. He was always prepared to take the same risks that he asked his men to take. They loved and respected him, and were thus motivated to do what he asked. Perhaps more controversially, his strong opinions meant that few were prepared to oppose him or question his judgement. The writer Rider Haggard knew him well. He wrote:

> "Sir Redvers was always very kind to me, but he was not a man to cross in an argument. Once, at his own table, I heard him differ from the late Lord Justice Bowen

in a way that made me glad I was not Lord Justice Bowen."[39]

Results were quick to come. In a series of skirmishes with resistant tribes the Frontier Light Horse drove all before them, pressing the Africans back across the Kei River. Mobility, increasingly good discipline and courage stood Buller's force in good stead. Evelyn Wood later wrote that Buller's leadership had helped smooth relationships between the British Army and the colonials, who previously had been hesitant to serve as irregulars in the South African campaign.

With the eastern Cape under control, he was asked to turn to more pressing problems. Whilst the British were engaged in the eastern Cape they could not attend to the widespread unrest occurring elsewhere in South Africa. Of the tribes in South Africa confronting the settlers, the Zulus were the largest and most warlike. They challenged Boer claims to the rich pasturelands, whilst the Boers sought to expand their farms into Zululand.

Bartle Frere, Governor General of the Cape, had been given a brief by the Colonial Secretary in London to confederate the disparate states within South Africa into a unified country. He quickly realised that this would not be possible without including Zululand, located to the north of Natal and bordering both Natal and the Transvaal. It was soon obvious to him that the Zulus were unlikely to enter willingly into such a confederation on terms acceptable to the settlers or indeed the British. Frere therefore decided that the only solution was war, aimed at bringing the Zulu nation to its knees. General Thesiger, who had commanded operations in the eastern Cape with some success, was appointed Commander-in-Chief of the British army designated to invade Zululand.

Buller and his Frontier Light Horse were instructed to join this force. On June 2 he wrote:

> "There is a rumour that I am to march to the Transvaal with the 90th under E. Wood and some guns. It sounds too good to be true, but it would be great fun should it prove correct."[40]

With his unit reinforced to 203 men, Buller journeyed north through the Transkei, reaching Pietermaritzburg, the capital of Natal, on August 23, 1878. There he joined Thesiger, who had succeeded to the title of

Lord Chelmsford. The strategy for an invasion of Zululand was to involve five columns: one near the coast advancing on Eshowe, a column under Wood which would start from near Utrecht in the north, and the main force near Dundee in northern Natal. A smaller force would be held in reserve to support the main column while the fifth would execute a holding operation on one of the Zulu allies, Sekukuni, who was threatening the Transvaal. Buller was assigned to Utrecht under the command of his old friend Evelyn Wood.

On December 11, 1878, Frere issued an ultimatum to the Zulus. Either they complied with a series of demands, the most stringent of which was that the Zulus abandon some of their more objectionable (to the British) tribal customs. Additionally a British Resident was to be established in Zululand to administer the territory. There was no likelihood of the Zulu king accepting these conditions, and on January 11, 1879, the main British column crossed the Buffalo River at Rorke's Drift, and invaded Zululand. The plan was for the northern and southern columns to commence their advance at the same time, all three columns converging on the royal seat at Ulundi, in the middle of Zululand.

Unfortunately for the British, at the first set battle at Isandlwana involving the main column major blunders by the British senior command resulted in an overwhelming victory to the Zulus. Surprised by the speed at which the main Zulu army advanced from their capital, Ulundi, the British failed to entrench or secure their position in any way. With half of the invading column away looking for the Zulu army, 20,000 Zulus overwhelmed the remainder. Of 800 soldiers, British and colonial, 779 were killed. The advance was stopped in its tracks, with Chelmsford retreating hastily to Pietermaritzburg.

Wood crossed the Blood River on January 10 and established a camp inside Zululand at Bemba's Kop. Chelmsford asked him to resist the Zulus in the north while the main column advanced. Buller's Light Horse scouted through a range of forty miles of rolling plains interspersed with isolated, tabletop mountains. He brought back 600 cattle that he had rounded up, but reported only minor skirmishes with small bands of Zulus. He did however report evidence of Zulus congregating on two mountains, Zunguin and Hlobane, which stood in the way of Wood's progress and would need to be taken if northern Zululand were to be controlled.

On January 21 Buller and Wood advanced on Mount Zunguin,

capturing it with little difficulty and displacing a tribe called the abaQulusi, who retreated to Mount Hlobane. Wood was able to look across to Hlobane and see 4,000 Zulus drilling on the slopes. The mountain dominated the landscape, rising to a thousand feet above the plain. On top was a level plateau five miles long and a mile wide. Precipitous, rocky cliffs surrounded it.

After a day's rest Wood moved on Hlobane. As he did so, a note arrived from Chelmsford announcing the disaster at Isandlwana. Wood's column was now exposed; he was well in advance of the rest of the British force, with little expectation of support arriving. He abandoned his advance, retreated to his base on the White Umfolosi River, and considered his options. An experienced field officer, he was unlikely to make the mistakes that had caused the disaster at Isandlwana. He needed to find a strong defensive position, and wait. The camp was moved to Kambula, ten miles upstream. This was a commanding ridge with clear sight of the plains on all sides, a position Wood felt confident of defending. He was able to persuade a number of Boers from the Utrecht and Wakkerstroom districts to join him. They felt themselves and their families exposed and threatened by the Zulus

For nearly two months Wood stayed at Kambula, sending forth foraging parties who made a nuisance of themselves among the Zulus. He and Buller were hardly out of their saddles. Buller wrote to his sister:

> "In the saddle for eighty hours does not leave one much time for writing or sleeping… for I have nearly 160 miles of country to patrol with a very inadequate force."[41]

Buller showed a prodigious work rate, seemingly never tiring. His Frontier Light Horse ranged far and wide, riding forty to fifty miles a day, rounding up cattle and attacking Zulu settlements wherever they were found. His correspondence at this time indicates an ambition for promotion, but also a yearning to be home. Writing to his sister on March 21, he says:

> "I am gradually stepping up the ladder and am now in command of a considerable force of Cavalry, having over 560 in camp and 250 more daily expected. I am fearing that the reinforcements from England will bring out so many senior officers that there will be no room for

poor junior me, and I shall have to recede to my former position as C.O. of the F.L.H. [Frontier Light Horse]. Still, to have been a Brigadier of Cavalry for even so short a time is something for an Infantry Captain any way. My great wish is that they should finish the war and let me get home."[42]

Sooner or later the British would have to tackle the Zulus on Mount Hlobane. The sides of the mountain looked unscalable, but a reconnoitre of approaches revealed two possible routes to the top. The western slope would be accessible to infantry, while a narrow, rocky path on the eastern slope promised possible, but hazardous, access for cavalry. It was decided that Buller would lead a strong force up the eastern approach, while a force under Lieutenant Colonel Russell would create a diversion to the west. Russell was not well regarded; Wood had nearly removed him from his post previously. Russell was to be the major weakness in this campaign.

Buller had with him a number of auxiliary troops drawn from Natal's indigenous population. In fact Chelmsford persuaded the Natal government to allow him to recruit 7,600 men from this group, despite the government's misgivings that a trained, armed group of local soldiers would cause them trouble later. Most of them carried traditional assegais (spears) and hide-covered shields, but some were provided with rifles. The auxiliaries performed very well, and supported the British campaign ably and at times bravely. These auxilliaries, scouting behind the mountain, saw smoke and fires to the east. They assumed, correctly, that these were the campfires of a Zulu army. However they did not report this to the white mounted troops accompanying them, as they had learned that their words were never heeded.

On March 27 Buller, with 675 men, positioned himself at the eastern end of Hlobane. Of these 503 were mounted: 156 were from the Frontier Light Horse, 70 Transvaal Rangers (Boers) and 277 Natal Africans. At 3.30 a.m. on March 28 he started up the mountain. Soon the slope was too steep to ride up, and the men dismounted, but Buller urged them on. As they climbed, they were assailed by groups of Zulus hiding in the caves that littered the slope, but they were brushed aside, and the force reached the upper plateau at daybreak. The summit turned out to be a long ridge, and before long Buller found bands of Zulus both in front and behind him. He was surrounded.

Russell, meanwhile, with 640 men was making slow progress climbing the western slope. By 6.30 a.m. his vanguard of black auxiliaries had reached a low plateau below the summit, to be informed that Buller's force was in possession of the upper plateau. Russell judged that the final scramble up a stony, narrow slope could not be negotiated and that there was little more he could do to help Buller. Without informing his deputy, he set off with his force for a point six miles to the west, and took no further part in the battle.

At this stage everyone's attention was drawn to the southeast. There on the grassy plain, no more than three miles away, was the main body of the Zulu army, 22,000 men, heading straight for Hlobane. It was drawn up in battle formation, with the "horns" thrust out on both wings and a dense mass of warriors in the centre. Wood had received advance intelligence that the army was approaching, but thought he had at least two days of leeway before it arrived. In fact the army had started early from oNdini, well over 100 miles away and reached Hlobane in under six days. All thoughts of attack were banished.

Exposed on the plateau without support from Russell, Buller had somehow to get his force down from Hlobane and back to the safety of Kambula. Zulus now occupied the slope up which he had climbed. The only way down was the western slope up which Russell had come. What remained of Russell's force, on the lower slopes under the command of his deputy, Lieutenant Browne, did its best to hold back the pursuers. Buller sent forward the Africans, who on foot were able to get down and escape. The Boers on their nimble horses picked their way down too. Buller was left with stragglers and the remnants of his force, harried on all sides by Zulus.

By now the main Zulu army had joined those on the mountain, and Buller's force was taking heavy casualties. He retreated as best he could, but the Frontier Light Horse, who made a stand to enable the others to get down the mountain, was decimated. A number of horses fell, leaving nearly half the horsemen without mounts. Buller remained with the Frontier Light Horse, calmly marshalling his troops. Aware that any man on foot was almost certain to be chased down and killed by the Zulus, he was insistent his men descended the mountain with their horses, even sending one back to fetch his mount when he abandoned it. On three occasions as they retreated he galloped back to pick up men without mounts, the last of whom was within eighty yards of the pursuing Zulus.

One of the troopers rescued by Buller, George Ashby, facing the pursuing Zulus, had his rifle burst. Buller came galloping by and offered to take him up on his horse. Ashby refused, as he realised Buller's horse would not easily bear two heavy men. Buller stayed with him, however. Ashby was able to find another rifle and the two men retreated, firing as they went.

When he reached Kambula Buller rounded up some fresh horses and rode out again in the rain to look for survivors. He returned after midnight with seven men he had found, lost, in the hills eight miles away. He had not slept for over forty-eight hours. For his efforts he was awarded the Victoria Cross, and his reputation, already high, was further enhanced. Wood told the Queen that what Buller had done that day was wonderful, and later Chelmsford was to write to the British Commander-in-Chief in London, the Duke of Cambridge:

> "With any other leader the enormous steepness of the ascent & the other physical difficulties would have been sufficient to prevent an attack by mounted men; but Lt. Col. Buller is a man of iron nerve & extraordinary courage, and is able to lead those under him where others would fail. How he escaped being killed himself I cannot understand, as he was, I believe, the very last man in the retreat and must have had any number of Zulus all around him."[43]

Fifteen officers, seventy-nine European men and one hundred black auxiliaries were killed. Buller would never leave a wounded man on the battlefield if he could help it. Later, in England, Wood told Buller's sister that he had earned the Victoria Cross every time he went out in Zululand.[44]

A feature of Buller's record that recurs again and again, was the affection and respect accorded him by officers and men alike. A seventeen year-old said of him:

> "Tough and brusque he was, but his troopers discovered that he was both accessible and sympathetic. If we were lying in the rain, so was Buller. If we were hungry, so was he. All the hardships he shared equally with his men. Never did Buller, as commander, have a patrol tent

to sleep under whilst his men were in the open. He was the idol of us all. "[45]

The assault on Hlobane had one positive factor in its favour. By diverting the Zulu army from its original line of advance it gave Wood time to organise his defences at Kambula before the inevitable onslaught on that stronghold. In addition to the earthwork redoubt built on the top of the hill he arranged a wagon laager three hundred yards to the rear. Between the redoubt and the laager he positioned four guns in the open, while in the redoubt were a further two guns. The laager itself was secured strongly with the wagon wheels chained together and any gaps filled with mealie bags. His garrison numbered 2086 officers and men. All but 58 of the irregular auxiliaries dispersed after the battle on Hlobane.

Early on March 29 the Zulu army could be seen advancing from the southeast. Wood was concerned that it would bypass his stronghold and fall on the undefended town of Utrecht. Indeed, Cetshwayo had instructed his generals not to engage the British force in fixed positions, but to harry the garrison in every possible way so as to entice Wood to come out and fight in the open. However, success at Hlobane had led the younger Zulu warriors to believe they could achieve an easy victory at Kambula. They now resisted any attempts to stop them confronting the British.

Young Zulu warriors had much to gain from battle. In peacetime, boys between fourteen and eighteen years old gathered at amakhanda, enormous military homesteads available for the king to mobilise. They were formed into regiments called amabuthos. They were not allowed to marry until they had "washed their spears" – killed in battle. Therefore they were impatient to be tested, and looked for confrontation.

The Zulu army halted about four miles distant from Kambula to give the commanders time to draw up their final plans and the witch doctors the opportunity to apply final ministrations. Then they recommenced the advance in the familiar "horns" formation, the two wings ahead of the main body, or "chest." The left wing moved wide and headed in the direction of Utrecht, which was not garrisoned and therefore was defenceless. Suddenly this force wheeled to the right and rapidly advanced, stopping some three miles from the British lines. Meanwhile the right horn had also spread out, halting a mile and a half away, just out of range of the guns. Wood estimated the Zulu front to stretch over 10 miles.

It appears that the Commander in Chief, Mnayamana, Cetshwayo's closest associate and most influential man in Zululand after the king, intended to follow the original plan and stand off the redoubt. When Wood ordered the tents to be struck and battle positions assumed the Zulus took this as a sign that the British were preparing for immediate flight. The right horn suddenly broke from its stationary line into columns and rushed forward. It is said that the two horns consisted of the two rival amabuthos of unmarried men, desperate to be first among the British tents.

Buller rode out with the Mounted Infantry to within rifle range and fired into the right horn of the army. The young iNgobamakhosi regiment was goaded into retaliating, and attacked prematurely, leaving the rest of the army no alternative but to join in. Buller wrote:

> "They did not stand our attack as I pressed home, and the advance of their right column, about 2,000 strong, turned & charged us. I need not tell you that the 80 or 90 men I had got on their horses pretty quick, & we scampered back to camp holding a running fight with them as we went."[46]

In fact despatches reported that with great precision and coolness Buller's force fell back, dismounted again, repeating the operation until the Zulus were within range of the artillery. The Zulus clearly did not understand this manoeuvre, commenting later that the "mounted redcoats were very much afraid, and quickly cried out and ran away."[47]

The Zulu advance was halted in its tracks when the four seven-pounder guns below the redoubt opened up. Supported by accurate rifle-fire from the 60th Light Infantry in the main laager and redoubt at three hundred yards, heavy casualties were inflicted on the attackers. This charge set off the main assault, but Woods defences were well marshalled, and although many Zulus came close to the defences they could not breach them.

By mid-afternoon hundreds of Zulu bodies littered the battlefield and Wood was able to release infantrymen in a bayonet charge. By provoking the premature response from the right horn, Buller had prevented the Zulus from surrounding the British position in their usual flanking movement, and the rear of the defences was never challenged.

By sunset the battle was over, and the Zulus were seen to be retreating in some disorder. Exhausted by their efforts, they were in no condition to defend themselves. They were pursued mercilessly by the cavalry. Few prisoners were taken.

The Zulus estimated that they lost around two thousand warriors that day, but the total was probably much higher. The wounded were either carried or staggered prodigious distances from Kambula. Bodies were found a long way from the battlefield in the days that followed. Despite Mnayamana exhorting his men to stay together, most of the Zulu regiments broke up and dispersed to their homes, their morale broken. Few returned to oNdini and the king.

Kambula was to prove, in retrospect, the defining battle of the Anglo-Zulu War. Commandant Schermbrucker, who fought at Kambula, recognised it as the British victory "which really broke the neck of the Zulu power."[48] The Zulu army that attacked the British represented the flower of the army, with many of the young men from crack amabuthos killed. Many families lost sons, including several of the leading generals. Cetshwayo now recognised that overall victory was no longer possible. His army had incurred heavy losses and morale was very low. The British had learnt their lesson and would not be caught in the open without overwhelming firepower. His only hope was a negotiated peace. This the British were disinclined to do; Isandhlwana had to be avenged. Unconditional surrender was the only option.

Wood remained at Kambula until the end of May, when Chelmsford was ready to make the final push against the Zulus. Certain now of his men, Buller readily volunteered the Frontier Light Horse for the most difficult assignments. There were minor skirmishes during this period, and we gain a good description of Buller during a reconnaissance mission. The Zulus allowed the main force to pass them, intending to attack the column from the rear. Wood, seeing what was happening, ordered twenty men led by Buller to turn and charge:

> " Leading his men at a swinging canter, with his reins in his teeth, a revolver in one hand, and a knobkerrie he had snatched from a Zulu in the other, his hat blown off in the melee, and a large streak of blood across his face, caused by a splinter of rock from above, this gallant horseman seemed a devil incarnate to the flying savages, who slunk out of his path as if he had been – as indeed

they believed him – an evil spirit, whose very look was death." [49]

On June 1 Wood moved forward, joining up with Chelmsford's main force on the march towards the Zulu capital, Ulundi. Buller was given the task of reconnoitring a good spot for the combined force to take up position in what was expected to be the final battle. He was also ordered to ascertain the Zulu numbers and plan of attack. As the force approached Ulundi Buller rode ahead, enticing the Zulus to attack. Lord Chelmsford's report sets out graphically the part he played:

> "Lieutenant-Colonel Buller crossed the river by the lower drift to the right of our camp, and was soon in possession of the high ground on our front…The object…was to advance towards Ulundi, and to report on the road and whether there was a good position where our force could make its stand if attacked. I was also anxious, if possible, to cause the enemy to show his force, its points of gathering, and plan of attack. [Buller] completely succeeded in the duty entrusted him. Having collected his mounted men…from the thorny country near the river, he advanced rapidly towards Ulundi….he was met by a heavy fire from a considerable body of the enemy lying concealed in the long grass around the stream. Wheeling about, he retired to the high ground…where he commenced to retire by alternate positions of his force in a deliberate manner. The Zulus were checked, but in the meantime large bodies of the enemy were to be seen advancing from every direction, and I was able with my own eyes to gain the information I wished for as to the manner of advance and points from which it would be made….Though the Zulus advanced rapidly and endeavoured to get round his flank, Lieutenant-Colonel Buller was able to retire his force across the river with but a few casualties. He informed me of a position which, on the following day, my force occupied, and which subsequent events showed was admirably adapted for the purpose I had in view."[50]

The final confrontation took place on the plain before Ulundi, with the British forming their famous hollow square, shielding the guns that were to decimate the attackers. Once again Buller led the way, drawing the Zulus onto the guns, which inflicted heavy casualties and stemmed the attack. He then led his cavalry out to pursue the remnants of the defeated Zulu army at the end. Wood, in his dispatch on the battle, wrote:

> "Colonel Buller gave us such aid as has seldom been afforded by light cavalry to a main body of troops."[51]

Garnett Wolseley had been sent out from England to replace the unfortunate Lord Chelmsford. He was anxious to retain Wood and Buller, but both men were exhausted. Buller continued to suffer from a wound that would not heal, and was covered with sores from his sixteen months without relief in the field. Reluctantly, they were let go. Buller sailed from Cape Town on the *SS German* on August 5, arriving in Plymouth on August 26. When he returned to his home at Downes his fellow-townsmen turned out in force with flags to welcome him, and a month later he was honoured by the county at a dinner in Exeter.

Wood and Buller were then invited to Balmoral to meet Queen Victoria. The Queen took an instant liking to Buller, finding him very modest. This affinity was to stand him in good stead later in his career. After presenting him with his VC the Queen wrote:

> "Colonel Buller is reserved and shy, with rather a dry, gruff manner. He also, though naturally averse to talking, told me much that was very interesting. He is very downright when he does speak and gives a very direct answer…Col Buller is very modest about himself, saying he had got far too much praise."[52]

Buller is quoted as replying: "If I am not to tell the truth to my sovereign, I don't know to whom I am to tell it."[53] As a consequence of this visit Buller was asked to see the Prime Minister, Disraeli, at his home, Hughenden Manor.

Controversially Buller refused to attend, as Disraeli had refused to see Lord Chelmsford, even though the Queen had asked him to. Buller saw this refusal as a slur on his chief (which it was), and although he did not think that highly of Chelmsford he was forever loyal to his superiors in the army. Other honours bestowed on Buller included promotion to Brevet Major and a C.B.(Commander of the Bath). The Queen appointed him as an Aide de Comte, which brought with it the rank of Colonel.

Later Buller was to meet Cecil Rhodes, who admired him:

> "Cecil Rhodes told me that he had wished to make my acquaintance because I am the only English officer who could manage Colonists...as far as I knew the way to manage them was by deference and flattery...you cannot drive them but you can lead them by the nose."[54]

Buller's sojourn at home was to be short-lived. Early in 1881 he was posted to the second battalion of his regiment serving in Afghanistan. He was still a Captain in the 60th Rifles, although in the army he ranked a full colonel. This anomaly was not uncommon in the complicated regimental system, but was embarrassing in this instance. The Duke of Cambridge, advisor to the Secretary of State for War stopped him from going to Afghanistan. For a few months he acted as Quarter-Master General, first in Scotland and then at Aldershot, army headquarters.

Deskwork did not suit him. Soon he was pleased to be on his way back to South Africa. He was ordered to go there as Deputy Adjutant and Quarter-Master General, on the staff of Lieutenant-General Sir Leicester Smyth. The Boers were showing signs of rebelling against the annexation of the Transvaal, and threatened the British garrisons in that territory. Following skirmishes during which fire was exchanged between the Boers and the British garrisons, the first set piece confrontation took place at Majuba Hill, on the border of Transvaal and Natal. As described in the introduction, the British attempt to enter the Transvaal from Natal resulted in a disastrous defeat, with the officer commanding, Colley, being killed.

Landing in Cape Town on the day of the battle for Majuba, February 26, 1881, Buller heard of the defeat, and Colley's death. He was very concerned. Writing to his sister, he perceptively remarked:

> "British rule in South Africa hangs in the balance, and one more disaster it will take us all we know to set it fairly up again. However, I shall not have come out here for nothing at any rate, as this Transvaal business seems likely to be a pretty big one."[55]

By March 6 he was in Pietermaritzburg, and by the 13th he had joined Wood in Newcastle, northern Natal. Both he and Wood were anxious to confront the Boers. Wood had 14,000 men under his command, and considerably greater experience of fighting in South Africa than the unfortunate Colley. On March 23 came the orders from London to agree a peace treaty with the Boers. Wood had conducted long and difficult negotiations with Kruger; now the British Government was prepared to give in to all the Boers' demands. Buller was dubious about the consequences:

> "Time only can show what will be the result. Of one thing I have no fear, and that is that we shall beat them when we do fight. Still, I hardly think that we shall beat them as easily as we ought to. No one can believe what an importance a first success is to a force, and our force has had three heavy defeats, while the Boers of course are elated by three successes."[56]

Buller was against the peace treaty. "I like the Boers," he wrote, "and am glad to see them get their country back, but I do not think that either the time or the manner of the settlement arrived at was fortunate."[57] He remained concerned that the regaining of the Transvaal would encourage the Boers to think in terms of dominating the whole of South Africa. In this suspicion he was right.

A Natal newspaper gives us a glimpse of the figure Buller cut at this time:

> "A tall, muscular, wiry-looking man, with bronzed face and grizzly beard…This was Colonel Buller, the Devonshire soldier, the hero of Zlobane [Hlobane], Kambula, and Ulundi…the crack commander of Cavalry irregulars, a brave officer, a true gentleman, and one who won the esteem and respectful admiration of those he commanded, and those who knew him only by reputation."[58]

Between March 1881 and the end of the year Buller was stationed in Pietermaritzburg. The position remained uncertain while the details of the peace treaty were worked out. He was concerned that the Boers would choose this opportunity to carry the fight into the territories adjacent to the Transvaal, Natal being the obvious choice.

The Boers struck a hard bargain. They were encouraged by the attitude of the British government, which seemed to be eager to settle the details and be rid of the embarrassment caused by their surrender to the Transvaal Republic's demands, It was clear that they did not want war. The Boers felt they could "ask for anything"[59] Finally Gladstone was pushed too far and in October put his foot down. Either the Volksraad ratified the Convention or they would lose their self-government. Agreement was reached on October 25.

With the treaty finally ratified, Buller was relieved. In a prescient letter to his sister he remarked:

> "…I really like a good many of them [the Boers], besides that they have in the long run justice on their side. It would also have been a war from which little credit could be gained, and which would have been an unpleasant one to fight out; for as the Boers had no strategical point the occupation or destruction of which would render a continuance of the struggle hopeless, we should have had to reduce them by harrying their farms and burning their homesteads: cruel work at the best of times and very cruel against a much-married and much-scattered population like the Boers."[60]

chapter 4.
EGYPT AND IRELAND.

BULLER.

BULLER LEFT South Africa on December 6, pleased to be returning home. There he was immediately thrown into the busy life of Downes, and for seven months did little else but manage the estate. He renewed his acquaintance with an old friend, Lady Audrey Jane Charlotte Howard. Previously she had been married to Buller's cousin, the Honourable Greville Theophilus Howard, son of the 17th Earl of Suffolk. They had had four children between 1875 and 1878, Howard dying in 1880.

Buller and Audrey married on August 10, 1882. His wife was five years older than he was. He treated her children as if they were his own. The couple spent the first part of their honeymoon in Belgium and Holland but this sojourn was cut short by a call to arms. The global scramble between major European powers for influence in Africa had come to focus on Egypt, whose finances were in chaos due to the extravagance of the Khedive, Ismail Pasha. He was saved from bankruptcy by selling his Suez Canal shares to the British for £4 million, a huge sum in those days.

When the Khediv died, the army mutinied and took authority for the state. Britain could see that access to the Suez Canal was now in jeopardy, and the situation could not be allowed to continue. A force under Garnet Wolseley was assembled. First the forts at Alexandria had to be silenced, as the British fleet lying in that port was at risk. When this was successfully completed on July 11 an invasion force of 9,000 men was assembled at Ismailia on the west bank of the Suez Canal.

On August 21 Buller, on his honeymoon at The Hague in Holland, received a request from Wolseley to join him in Egypt. If his mentor required him, Buller must respond. This was a request both Buller and his wife felt he could not refuse. They returned to England the same night, and within the week he was at Port Said.

Wolseley appointed Buller as Chief of Intelligence. The Egyptian army held a strongly entrenched position thirty miles west of Ismailia commanding both the railway to Cairo and the Sweet Water Canal, on which Ismailia depended for its water supply. On August 24 the British force without too much resistance secured a crucial lock on the canal.

Buller landed at Port Said on August 27. He does not seem to have been worried by the impending conflict. He wrote to Audrey:

> "You must not distress yourself, as these blessed Egyptians do not fight well and shoot very badly. I cannot think this will be a long business. Indeed I cannot see why it should last more than the month I told you of."[61]

He arrived in Ismailia on September 1. Over the first ten days he embarked upon a series of exploratory sallies at considerable risk to himself, during which he was able to pinpoint with remarkable accuracy the deployment of the Egyptians. Thus when the British moved forward by night the timing and location of their assault was remarkable accurate. Attacking at dawn, they were able to rout the enemy with ease. Within a day they had captured Cairo at the cost of 9 officers and 48 soldiers killed.

Buller, always up for a fight, had taken a leading part in the attack. He wrote to his wife about

> "...thirty-five minutes' sharp fighting" - something which he was ashamed to admit he "thoroughly enjoyed."[62]

In a later letter, having had time to think about the skirmish, he reiterated these sentiments:

"I did not somehow feel at all as if I were likely to be shot. It really was very odd. I felt like two people; when I thought of the coming fight my spirits rose and I felt so happy, and then I thought of you and that you might be made miserable, and I felt that it was really wicked to be glad there was going to be a fight. I do believe that it is very wicked and very brutal, but I can't help it: there is nothing in this world that so stirs me up as a fight. I become just as if I were aerated. I always feel very much ashamed of myself afterwards, but I cannot help it."[63]

Within six weeks Buller was back in England, enjoying a belated period of companionship with his wife. It was not until July 1883, some ten months later, that he was posted as Assistant Adjutant-General to headquarters at the War Office in London. During his time off at his Devonshire home his daughter, Audrey Charlotte Georgiana, was born. Buller had always been fond of children. He did not always show it. He wrote: "The baby is decent and an addition to the household; I am told I ought to admire the Rose of Devon [a prize heifer], but I prefer the baby."[64] For a man of the country, who had always taken great pride and satisfaction from his estate, this was praise indeed!

With the capture of Egypt Britain assumed responsibility for that country. Reforms were urgently required. The British resolved that the way forward was to develop institutions in Egypt that would allow the country to progress once more to responsible self-rule. However, the most pressing problem was the troublesome province of Sudan, a vast area under revolt led by a religious fanatic, Mohammed Ahmed, known as The Mahdi. The Mahdi's followers heavily defeated an Egyptian force led by General Hicks, a retired Indian officer, in November 1883. General Charles Gordon was sent to Khartoum by the British to supervise an orderly withdrawal from the Sudan.

It was apparent by this time that much of eastern Sudan was under the control of the rebels, and British forts at Tokar and Sinkat were in danger of falling. Despite a relief column being sent from Egypt, the garrison at Sinkat was annihilated. Reluctance to become involved in what was seen in Britain as an internal struggle gave way to outrage, and it was decided to send a force made up of troops already in Egypt and a battalion on its way home from Aden to rescue Tokar and pacify eastern Sudan. Buller was appointed to command one of two brigades formed by this force. Within a week he had sailed for Egypt, and by February 27 he had landed at Trinkitat, the closest point to the rebel forces.

When the enemy was engaged a sharp fight ensued. Although the British were victorious, and forced the Arabs back, it was no rout, and casualties were high on both sides. Buller, now a General, rued not being able to participate in the battle. He reassured his wife: "I told you I should be quite safe. I shall never have any more of that fighting, I am afraid!"[65] The troops returned to Trinkitat and embarked for Suakin Moving inland, they encountered the enemy at Tamai. The Arabs put up stout resistance, and at one stage in the battle Buller's infantry, formed in the famous square used traditionally by the British army, showed signs of unsteadiness under the pressure of a dense mass of the enemy. He immediately rode to the front of his men and rallied them. This proved to be the turning point. Although the enemy massively outnumbered the British, their losses were so great that they finally turned and fled under the steady fire. A book written after the battle, 'In the Soudan,' referred to this incident:

> "Buller had his men well in hand, just as if they were at a review. He commenced firing volleys. The Arabs, who were in irregular formation, and from three to ten deep, came along at a run, and it was just like a big black wave running up a beach. It began to break on the crest, the white foam being represented by the men that fell simultaneously with every volley, and the wave began to grow less and less the more it neared the square. Within 259 yards it nearly ceased, and not one man could get near enough to use his spear."[66]

An interesting anecdote from Buller's service in Egypt illustrates neatly his strength of character. While on a river steamer negotiating dangerous water in one of the higher cataracts of the Nile, Buller and Sir Charles Beresford obstinately argued about which was the proper channel to take. Finally Buller prevailed, and the steamer passed through the channel safely. "You see I was right," said Buller, "mine was the proper channel." "That was mine too," replied Beresford calmly, "I only recommended the other because I knew you would go against whatever I said."[67] Buller's stubbornness was both a strength and a weakness: his strong views inhibited subordinates from voicing their opinions or making suggestions. On the other hand his single-mindedness often carried the day.

This was the last engagement of that particular campaign in Egypt and the Sudan. On April 1 he embarked upon the *S.S.Utopia* and arrived in London a fortnight later. His part in the fighting had been noticed. General Stephenson, commander of the troops in Egypt, wrote to the Duke of Cambridge: "Buller seems to have handled his Brigade admirably, and by keeping its formation compact, and delivering a cool and steady fire, sustained hardly any loss, and effectually prevented the enemy from getting too near." General Graham concurred that Buller "…by his coolness of action, his knowledge of soldiers, and experience in the field, combined with his great personal ascendancy over both officers and men, has been most valuable."[68]

Unfortunately it was soon evident that the Suakin campaign had done nothing towards improving the situation in the Sudan. By the time Gordon arrived at Khartoum, most of the Sudan was in the rebels' hands, and the garrison at Khartoum was coming under severe pressure. Contrary to his orders Gordon decided that it would be wrong to withdraw the garrison and abandon the country to the Mahdi, who was not a public-spirited freedom fighter but a bloodthirsty fanatic. He asked for reinforcements and put forward plans for a counter-attack.

Gladstone remained determined not to be involved in colonial ventures, but came under severe pressure in Parliament. Baring, from Cairo, and Wolseley, backed Gordon's appeals for help. The Cabinet resisted these pleas until late summer 1884. Then the Secretary of State for War, Lord Hartington, making it a matter of confidence in the Cabinet, persuaded the Government to rescue Gordon.

It was decided that Wolseley would be in supreme command, with Buller as his Chief of Staff. Wolseley had asked for Buller, informing the Duke of Cambridge that "The longer I live, the more I realise how very very few men there are with brains so organised as to enable them to look at affairs from a war point of view. It is a…rare gift….Sir Redvers Buller has it."[69]

As Chief of Staff Buller's main responsibility was to marshal resources and ensure both men and their means of transport were in the right place at the right time, not an easy task in chaotic Egypt. Wolseley swiftly assembled a strike force of 10,000 men in Cairo. Supported by Buller, he proposed that the force advance up the river Nile as far as they could go by railway and steamer to the head of the Second Cataract, approximately 800 miles from Cairo. From there boats with a very shallow draft carrying twelve men each would be used. In October the expedition crossed the southern border of Egypt into Sudan.

Progress up the Nile proved to be slow, and messages from Gordon indicated that he would not be able to hold out for much longer. It occurred to both Wolseley and Buller that the only way to accelerate the relief would be to send a column across the desert on camels. Wolseley wanted to accompany the column, but was overruled by the Secretary of State. Command was handed to General Stewart. The going was arduous, and water in scarce supply.

At the wells of Abu Klea Stewart found the enemy waiting, and a desperate fight ensued. 18 officers and 140 men were killed before the Arabs could be driven off, but now the column faced recurring attacks from large forces. Both Stewart and his designated successor, Colonel Burnaby, were killed. Command passed to Sir Charles Wilson.

Wilson set off for Khartoum in two steamers, but when he arrived it was to learn that Gordon had been killed two days earlier, and the town had been taken. Falling back, he suffered a number of mishaps. When it became obvious that his advance had stalled and his force was in some difficulty, Wolesley was asked to take command of the remainder of the desert column, augmented by fresh reinforcements.

Buller was sent forward by Wolseley to help. He reached Gubat, where the column was situated, in the second week of February, 1885. He found the position perilous. The force was dispirited and lacking firm leadership. The fort was overcrowded, isolated from the main army, which was 200 miles away across the desert. The post was threatened by the Arab hordes, which were buoyed up by their victory at Khartoum. Buller's own despatches show that he vacillated over whether to attack the Arabs, as Wolseley had instructed, or retreat. He finally decided that retreat was the only practicable alternative. This was effected at dead of night without casualties. The desert column was restored to the main body of the army successfully.

Recognition that the British would not be able to control the Sudan followed. The Mahdi was to be left alone, and the front line consolidated in the Nile Valley. The British Government, with one eye on the threatening situation in Afghanistan, had no stomach for a prolonged campaign in such difficult conditions.

Buller returned home in October, his reputation greatly enhanced. Wolseley had marked him out as "the coming man in the army."[70] His work as Chief of Staff had been exemplary in trying circumstances. His administrative and organisational skills were of the highest order. His coolness and courage under fire marked him out as an outstanding fighter and his extrication of the desert column, when others had failed, his crowning achievement. Nevertheless critics have pointed out that his indecision at Gubat was the first example of his unease with the responsibilities of overall command.

He returned to the War Office, remaining there from November 1885 until September 1897, by which time he was Adjutant-General.

In August 1886 he was given a special assignment to help quell disturbances in Ireland. Bands of men were roaming the countryside in Kerry, Cork and Limerick demanding arms. As Special Commissioner he was given control through the police force and divisional magistrate to put a stop to these activities. This required reorganising a demoralised constabulary that had been grappling with the problem for seven years. Initially he was resented by the police force, particularly when he started making changes. However, his total fearlessness, despite threats to his life, and willingness to engage with his men quickly won them over. The historian Edmund Gosse noted:

> "Within a single fortnight they had all rallied round him, and one man expressed the general feeling in declaring 'there is not a policeman in the county of Kerry who would not lay down his life for Sir Redvers.'"[71]

Barely a month after he accepted the assignment, twenty-four of the miscreants had been arrested. Much of his success was attributed to his popularity with the country folk, who provided valuable intelligence. He travelled extensively, learning about the country. By the end of October he could claim that his assignment was successfully concluded, and that the local police could be left to cope. In November he was appointed Under-Secretary for Ireland in Dublin, where he served for nearly a year.

He was recalled to London under something of a cloud. Lord Carnarvon, who had been Lord Lieutenant in Ireland but now sat in the House of Lords, had been critical of the military in Ireland. Lord Cadogan had complained that rebels living in the villages had not been ousted. Carnarvon felt that unrest among the Irish could have been dealt with swiftly and effectively. Buller, whose responsibilities included security, took issue. His letters to Carnarvon at the time reflect many facets of his personality: his short fuse and sense of certainty in himself, and his concern for his men above all else:

> "...it is of course impossible to make 4 men live at the same time in 6 places....Had you not been the Speaker in the House of Lords on Tuesday I should have caused a letter to be sent to The Times defying you to prove that you ever did what you say you did when Lord Lieutenant, or that it was a simple matter to break into strongly fortified stone buildings defended by desperate men without either using means that could hardly be supported, or causing loss of life....Lord Cadogan of course knew nothing and his reply was idiotic, but it is the fact, that the... utterly misleading statements made by you is always allowed to go unchallenged and uncontradicted when dozens of people are in a position to know better, that makes the Govt. of Ireland so difficult."[7272]

In another letter to Carnarvon a few days later, he vented his anger again:

> ".... Irish officials have become gradually demoralized and seek in all things to evade responsibility...I have tried to remedy this by insisting on the officials accepting a proper share of responsibility, and secondly by defending them directly and indirectly whenever or by whomever they are attached.....All I can say is that I disagree with you in toto and I believe your military friends would also if they knew the facts. There is a state of things in Ireland which never occurred before and was not dreamt of when you were Viceroy. A series of....houses are carefully and thoroughly fortified and defended by desperate women with boiling water, hot lime, gaff hooks. Each house is a small fort....Whether we should be justified in blowing up each in a house full of women with ...explosives is a matter of policy, my view is that it would most probably blow up any Government who sanctioned it...the possibility that to take 31 fortified houses (not half a dozen cottages as you

say) without the use of some sort of explosive is not, and cannot be made, 'an affair of hours.'"[73]

Wolseley was anxious to have him back at the War Office. His spell there enabled him to gain a knowledge of the army and the workings of the War Office that was not matched by anyone else in service.

During this time he issued a new Drill Book, rewrote the manual of Military Law and established the Army Service Corps. This last achievement led to the claim that he ranked among the greatest builders of the British Army as it appeared before the start of the First World War. The essence of the Corps was to link transport and supply together and make them an integral part of the Army. Hitherto these services had been under civil control, either the Treasury or civil side of the War Office. They were hidebound by bureaucracy, effectiveness measured by cost control and administration rather than results. Major deficiencies during the Crimean War led to a Royal Commission that accurately identified shortcomings, but no action had been taken to improve the service.

Buller's reform transformed the service. Integrated into the Army, it became responsive to its needs, and attracted officers of talent, ability and ambition. The performance of the Corps during the Boer War was to be testimony to the improvements made.

chapter 5.
PREPARING FOR WAR.

BOTHA.

BETWEEN 1886 and 1894, Botha gained valuable experience as Veldcornet in Vryheid. This was a post of some importance, for he administered the military roll, assembling men liable to serve in times of war. He also acted as Collector of Taxes. In 1897, showing a desire for political influence, he stood for election to the Transvaal Volksraad, the administrative body in Pretoria. Facing a more experienced candidate endorsed by the leader of the Volksraad, Botha won a sensational victory. From being a homestead farmer in Natal he now identified himself as a member of the Boer republic that was to be at the heart of conflict with the British. He was obliged to resign his Veldcornetcy and hand over his farming to managers. From then on he lived for six months of each year in Pretoria.

When Botha joined the Volksraad Paul Kruger, who ran it like a personal fiefdom, dominated it. A deeply religious man, Kruger used quotations from the Bible to make his points. His reaction to any disagreement with his views was to storm at the person raising the objection in the expectation that this would succeed in dismissing it. If that did not work, he would quote from the Bible in support of his view. The devout members of the Volksraad knew better than to question his references.

During this time Botha added to his farming interests. In 1897 he bought a part of Uitzicht, neighbouring his principal farm, Waterval. His assets at this time were estimated to be worth £30,000. In 1898 he added a part of Kalbasfontein, and a farm called Yorkshire. He was financially independent, the owner of 16,000 acres of farmland. His interests also included 1,800 acres containing coal, and a contract for the construction of a railway line from Vryheid to the Buffalo River. These investments proved to be very profitable.

In 1897 the young Louis Botha was making his mark in the Volksraad. Pre-eminent among its youngest members, he challenged the accepted practices which Paul Kruger's dictatorial ways had imposed. Unlike the strictly Calvinistic Afrikaans elders, he enjoyed dancing, playing games and having a drink with his colleagues. He could see that Pretoria itself was evolving as a metropolis. The influx of foreigners in search of their fortunes in the goldfields had added a cosmopolitan element to the town. Fine buildings were springing up, and the influence of the English affected the cultural life.

Sessions at the Volksraad lasted from February to October. Piet Joubert, who was one of the founding fathers of the Transvaal Republic, led the opposition to Kruger. He had been elected Commandant-General of the Boers and had led them to victory at Majuba. Paradoxically, he was a pacifist who hated armed conflict, but as a father of his people he felt his responsibilities keenly. He was not anti-British, and longed to see all sections of the community live in harmony. He was to be an important influence on Botha.

From his first day in the Volksraad Botha played an active part in the proceedings. He became frustrated with the petty-mindedness of many of its thirty members, and advocated delegating trivial issues to the executive. With Joubert, he criticised Kruger for not punishing bribe-takers, and did not like the President's dictatorial ways. Kruger would often threaten to resign if he did not get his way in the Volksraad, and on one occasion Botha, boldly opportunistic, dared to move that it be accepted. A debate followed (which Botha hugely enjoyed), before Kruger withdrew his threat.

Most importantly, participation in the Volksraad brought Botha into contact with people of influence and ability outside his normal circle of friends. One of these was the young Jan Smuts, a brilliant Cambridge graduate, who had been appointed State Attorney in the Transvaal at the age of twenty-eight. Eight years Botha's junior, Smuts was the second son of a prosperous farmer in the rich Malmesbury area of the Cape. His early years were spent on the farm, and it was only when he was sent to a boarding school at the age of ten that he learnt to read. From then on he was a voracious reader, and was the star student at Victoria College, Stellenbosch. There he met Cecil Rhodes when the great man came to address the students. Smuts was chosen to reply on behalf of them. His speech made an impression on Rhodes – enough for him to be remembered when they met again several years later.

Rhodes, in turn, made an impression on Smuts with his vision of a united Africa, one nation under the British Empire. Despite his rural, Afrikaner upbringing the young Smuts was far-seeing enough to recognise the realities of the future in Southern Africa. A scholarship took him to Christ's College, Cambridge in England where he gained a first class law degree. After being called to the bar in London he returned to Cape Town in spite of tempting offers to further his career in England. Rhodes was by then Premier of the Cape, and intent on reconciling the Dutch and English communities, a project to which Smuts lent powerful assistance.

Smuts and Botha were to form a life-long friendship that was to shape the future of South Africa. They were uniquely matched. Botha, though not well educated, possessed intuitive good judgement and was sensitive to the people's needs. He enjoyed meeting and talking to people. From the moment he entered political life his door was open to anyone who wished to approach him. Smuts was not good with people. He did not suffer fools gladly, and was impatient with slow-witted colleagues. However, with his rapier of a mind and attention to detail, he turned Botha's dreams and vision into action. They needed each other in order to achieve their aims. Botha instinctively brought to statesmanship common sense, breadth of view and judgment. Smuts brought, with his learning and legal training, a brilliant intellect and an alert and lucid mind.

Smuts was obsessively loyal: on his appointment as State Attorney he devoted himself to Kruger. Soon he was to move that attachment to Botha, whom he served thus for the rest of his life. Both men moved their main residences to Pretoria, and the families lived near to each other. However, Smuts supported and looked up to Kruger, while Botha, more independently minded, could never do that. Botha did not read much, and could not come to terms with Smuts' lack of interest in games. Smuts was totally bilingual; Botha almost always spoke in Dutch or

Afrikaans. Botha was slow to come to decisions, but had unlimited patience, a persuasive manner and willingness to discuss issues with anyone. Smuts preferred making decisions himself with a minimum of consultation. He had a remarkably quick mind and huge drive.

Botha was opposed to the dynamite monopoly, one of many concessions granted by Kruger to his compatriots. In 1892 a Hungarian adventurer, Hugo Nellmapius, persuaded Kruger that a useful way for the state to raise money was to sell monopoly concessions to independent businessmen. A number of concessions were sold on key supplies, some for a considerable length of time,. Soon this led to widespread corruption. The British were particularly concerned about the dynamite monopoly, as its terms excluded British dynamite. A French consortium bought the concession and continued to import dynamite duty-free.

The Volksraad was in uproar. Nobody had a clear idea of the best line to take. The monopoly was designed to encourage local manufacture, but adequate supplies were not yet available. Following an acrimonious debate the monopoly was cancelled. The government took over the monopoly and contracted with the English, French and Germans to supply it for fifteen years. By 1898, with the help of the French and Germans Kruger had built up in Johannesburg one of the largest explosive factories in the world. He argued that not only did it give the Transvaal the local supply source it needed, but it created firm allies with the two European powers. Critics pointed to the considerable revenue flowing back to Europe.

Then, on August 21, 1899, Botha made a speech in the Volksraad in which he changed his view. Having looked into the contract, he was convinced that no court of law would agree to the annulment of the dynamite monopoly. There was amazement and much criticism of this u-turn. The President of the Orange Free State, Marthinus Steyn, pressed Kruger to cancel the concession. He was concerned that Lord Milner would use the continuation of the monopoly as a casus belli. Eight years later a criminal case was brought against a blackmailer who threatened to reveal that Botha had received £2,000 from the Dynamite Company on the day the vote was taken to continue the concession. It was never proved.

The subject of Uitlanders' rights arose again. By 1897 there were so many of them in the Transvaal that lack of political representation had become a major issue. Driven forward by the mine magnates, who wielded considerable influence in London, the question demanded attention. Albert Milner, the new Lieutenant-governor of the Cape with responsibility for Britain's colonial interests in South Africa, entered discussions with Kruger. Kruger was reluctant to embrace change and resistant to the claims of the Uitlanders. As Edmund Garrett editor of The Cape Times wrote after a lengthy interview with Kruger:

> "...neither Kruger nor his 'old burghers' wanted to accept 'foreigners' as full citizens. As they saw it, allowing the franchise would have given the Uitlanders so much say in the government of their country that far-reaching changes would have been introduced against their wishes. These changes would have almost certainly affected the burghers' way of life, and might well have threatened Kruger's position as President."[74]

As described in the introduction, the discussions dragged on, neither side trusting the other. The concessions offered always had provisos attached to them which virtually guaranteed the other side would reject them. In addition to the Uitlander question, there was a fear in British political circles that other major European powers, notably Germany and France, were attracted to the mineral wealth of South Africa. Milner, a convinced imperialist, believed the only solution for South Africa was British dominance. The pressure exerted on an obdurate Kruger was bound to lead to a breakdown in negotiations, which finally occurred. On October 11, 1898 an ultimatum issued by Kruger demanding that British troops be withdrawn from the borders of the Transvaal Republic, and outstanding questions referred to arbitration, was rejected out of hand by Milner. War became inevitable.

Botha and Smuts were to be drawn closer together by the threat of war. On September 6, 1899, a debate took place in the Transvaal Volksraad to consider Milner's proposals. Botha, opposed to a war, attempted to persuade Kruger to compromise with Milner. Botha and other progressive members of the Volksraad wished to avoid armed conflict at all costs, and urged Kruger to make further concessions. Once it became evident that war was inevitable, however, Botha threw his weight behind Kruger. He still favoured a defensive, non-aggressive stance, but opposed any steps that would threaten the republic's independence.

He now recognised the die was cast. He addressed the assembly:

"The Transvaal has done all it can in order to preserve peace, but I think that we have now gone far enough. Already it is being said: the Boers are afraid. We have yielded, yes, and we have gone very far because we want peace, but not on account of any fear."[75]

BULLER.

Since June 1899 discussion among the political and military elite in London had been on one topic: war preparations. The British Army was not ready for a major conflict in South Africa. Its forces were spread across the empire, and a sizeable contingent would take time to assemble. Of a total army consisting of 316,000 regular soldiers and reservists, permanent garrisons in Britain, India and Egypt left a mere 70,000 men available for other overseas duties. The army budget had been restricted to £20 million, resulting in shortages of supplies, artillery and cavalry. The Boers could mobilise 35,000 men immediately, and could call on a further 19,000 if required. There were less than 10,000 British troops in South Africa. If the Free State militia agreed to enter a war alongside the Transvalers the Boers had a force that could rapidly overrun Natal and possibly capture the vital port of Durban.

All was not harmonious in the War Office in London. Wolseley had been appointed Commander-in Chief in preference to his rival, General Frederick Roberts. Wolseley's reputation had been made in Africa, Roberts' in India. Both were brilliant field commanders and fearless soldiers. Around them had coalesced the senior officers of the British Army, in two "rings" – the Africa ring and the India ring. No love was lost between the two groups, who constantly vied for advantage within the army.

The Secretary of State for War was Henry Charles Keith Petty-Fitzmaurice, fifth Marquess of Lansdowne. Extremely wealthy, he was a member of one of the patrician families of Great Britain, with properties in England, Scotland and Ireland. Unfortunately his abilities did not march his status. He was hard working and clean living, but dull and unimaginative. Lansdowne was an admirer of General Roberts, and did not like Wolseley. The distance between the two men was broadened when Wolseley bombarded Lansdowne with demands that the army be mobilised and increased in size. It was his considered opinion that a further 10,000 men were needed in South Africa immediately. And that was merely the start: an essential emergency measure. Lansdowne was under pressure from the Chancellor of the Exchequer, Sir Michael Hicks Beach to save money. General political opinion was still that there would be no war in South Africa, so Lansdowne did nothing.

Lieutenant-General Sir William Butler was the most senior British officer in South Africa and Governor of the Cape. He had offered no ideas for plans of defence, and appeared not to be in touch with events as they progressed. He was not highly regarded, and clearly not able enough to lead the British forces should war break out. The total size of the British force in South Africa numbered 8,456 men. It was necessary to appoint appropriate men to command. Butler was recalled.

Major-General Sir Penn Symons, a brigadier from India, was appointed to command the forces in Natal. He had a reputation for impetuosity. In his first communique from Natal he reported that 2,000 extra troops would make Natal secure. This was in stark contradiction to Wolseley's request for another 10,000. After consideration he later amended his request to 5,600 men, still less than the 10,000 that Wolseley thought were needed.

The question of who would assume overall command was quickly settled. Wolseley proposed that Redvers Buller be sent as soon as possible. A measure of the esteem in which Buller was held at the time can be seen in a newspaper article of October 15, 1898:

> "Sir Redvers Buller, who entered on his duties as Commander at Aldershot this week, is a good soldier, and has earned his promotion by sheer hard work and good service. He has fought in most of our wars from China to Canada, and from the Cape to the Soudan, and he has proved himself a good administrator as well as a good fighter. Nor is he a mere martinet, who regards men only as machines invented for the purposes of obeying orders. It is almost forgotten now that during the worst of the Land League troubles in Ireland, Buller was sent over to impart the necessary amount of military rigour into the civil administration…But he soon showed that he had a heart and a head, and he gravely offended the Irish officers by telling them that

law and order could not be built up in Ireland any more than in Egypt on injustice and extortion. His services were quickly dispensed with by the Government. But his name is remembered in Kerry as that of a just and strong man."[76]

As Buller was a protégé of Wolseley the animosity which Lansdowne felt for Wolseley applied to Buller as well. Buller was blunt and tactless; Lansdowne told him he found him hard to work with. Buller had many Boer friends from his previous time in South Africa, and Lansdowne privately considered him pro-Boer. He would have preferred to have as Commander-in-Chief General Roberts, who had distinguished himself in India and Afghanistan, but Wolseley was very popular in England and was the man in possession of the top job. After Wolseley, Buller was regarded as Britain's most distinguished fighting general. If Wolseley was not to go, it was almost inevitable that Buller, as Adjutant-General and right-hand man to Wolseley, would be appointed.

Buller saw Lansdowne at the minister's private residence in the spring of 1899. Lansdowne told him he had been selected as the best officer to hold the chief command. Buller's response was both direct and honest, and revealed a certain lack of confidence:

"I said that I had never actually held an independent command, that a war in South Africa, if one really occurred, would be a big thing, and....I thought a stronger combination, and a better one for the Army... would be Lord Wolesley as Commander-in-Chief and myself as...Chief of Staff....I said that I always considered I was better as second in a complex military affair than as the officer in chief command. So far as knowledge of detail, power of organization, tactical knowledge, and capacity for handling the three arms, and for getting men to fight for me in the field, I thought I could fairly say that I could hold my own with any other officer in the Army; but that the command of such an expedition would be a big thing, and though I did not in some respects doubt my own capacity, yet the facts remain that....I had never been in a position where the whole load of responsibility fell on me, alone....6,000 miles from home. That I was combatant by nature, and that, if difficulties arose, I should, I knew, be too apt to plunge into the actual struggle."[77]

Lansdowne waved these objections away, and to Buller seemed less than concerned by the potential challenge presented to the British Army in South Africa.

The Liverpool Mercury shared Buller's misgivings. In a prescient article in September 1899, it commented:

> "There is not much enthusiasm in any quarters at the appointment of Sir Redvers Buller to the chief command in South Africa if war takes place. He did not show much strategic genius at the late manoeuvres, where it was intended that he should win, and where he was sadly beaten by a more wily or more ingenious antagonist....It is said in some military circles that if the present crisis ends in war Sir Redvers will not really be the general sent, but he is held in too high esteem at the War Office to be subjected to what would really be an insult. Nevertheless, the feeling is that he is not by any means the man who should have been placed in chief command at the Cape."[78]

Buller had given strategy some thought. He had three alternatives: to advance due north from Cape Town through the Orange Free State; north west from the port of Durban through Natal; or due west from Delagoa Bay in Mocambique. The third of these alternatives offered the shortest route, but the Portuguese, who ruled in Mocambique, were unlikely to agree. Advancing through Natal the British force would be faced with hills and mountains that were formidable barriers and offered the mobile Boers many opportunities for guerrilla warfare. By far the simplest would be through the Orange Free State, a high, relatively flat plain which would allow the British with their superior numbers to sweep forward unimpeded. The problem was that the Orange Free State was an independent republic, and had not yet declared its allegiance.

The Transvaal exhorted its brother republic to enter the fray on its side, but President Steyn of the Free State did not necessarily agree that his republic was affected by the looming conflict. Buller therefore identified the position of the Free Staters as crucial. If it did not enter the war on the side of the Transvaal, and was prepared to stay out of the war, then an attack on Pretoria from the south via Bloemfontein would be straightforward. In addition, if the Free Staters remained neutral the force that the Transvalers could deploy in Natal represented less of a threat.

Lansdowne felt that an advance through the Free State was out of the question. Buller insisted that

> "The Government of the Orange Free State must be compelled to declare itself actively on one side or the other."[79]

A discussion of numbers followed. Buller agreed that the size of the force proposed would be sufficient "if the object of the Government was merely to attack the Transvaal, but I added that that object was to my mind an impossible one."[80] At this time the forces he would command in South Africa numbered less than 10,000 men with three batteries of field artillery, and support services. The Transvaal Boers could field 25,000 burghers. The Free State had 15,000 men at its disposal; if they were to join the Transvalers, Buller would be facing a formidable foe. Yet the War Office was in no hurry to send reinforcements. Intelligence reports suggested that the Boers would confine themselves to small, cross-border raiding parties.

Buller went straight from the meeting with Lansdowne to see Wolseley. His old mentor had suffered a serious illness in 1897, and appeared somewhat vague, so Buller received no help or advice from him. A colleague, Colonel Neville Lyttleton, present during the meeting, was alarmed. Buller "expressed very strong objections to accepting the command, said he was sick of South Africa, and if he was forced to go out would come away as soon as he could."[81] On the eve of sailing Buller made clear his regret that Evelyn Wood, his mentor and commander at Kambula, had not been offered the job: "I have always looked upon this as Evelyn's journey....I think he would have done it better than I shall, but I shall try my best."[82] Wood was by now over sixty, and considered too old for the task.

Negotiations between President Kruger and Governor-General Milner in South Africa had led to a lingering uncertainty. Each time they broke down war loomed but then fresh terms would be offered. The British cabinet was reluctant to commit the extra troops requested while peace was possible. They were warned that the sending of reinforcements could provoke the Boers into war. Finally, when it appeared that war was inevitable they agreed to the 10,000 men for whom the generals had called.

BOTHA.

The Boers were now ready. They had foreseen this outcome. The Jameson Raid and the attitude of Milner made it obvious that a showdown was imminent. They stocked up with the latest armaments from Europe: Creusot and Krupp field artillery from France and Germany respectively, Maxim guns and 37,000 Mauser rifles, accurate over 2,000 yards. They imported 80 million rounds of ammunition. Their equipment was superior to the British armaments. In addition they could call upon between 50,000 and 60,000 men, some mere boys, prepared to fight. They held a numerical advantage over the British and Colonial forces, who numbered 22,000 at the outbreak of war. More than a quarter of this force had been locally recruited and was largely untrained. On the Boer side a system of conscription placed upon every male between the ages of sixteen and sixty the obligation to serve in the military when called upon to do so by the state.

The position of the Orange Free State had been resolved in favour of the Transvalers. President Steyn of the Free State had given Kruger private assurances that if war became inevitable his republic would support the Transvaal. Steyn had done everything he could to reconcile the two sides, without success. He held out from entering the war even after the Transvaal had mobilised its troops. It seems that a threatened revolt among his own burghers led by Christiaan de Wet finally persuaded Steyn that he had no alternative. On October 9 the Free State declared their support for the Transvaal's offensive.

BULLER.

In London the politicians were not yet taking the threat of a full-scale war seriously. With a long history of military dominance over its overseas possessions, it was assumed that any armed conflict with the Boers would be short-lived and one-sided. Thus necessary preparations were both tardy and desultory. In fact, British supremacy on the battlefield was somewhat illusory. Most of their wars had been fought against backward nations, poorly equipped and badly trained. The quality of the common soldier in the British Army was suspect. Recruited mainly from the lower classes, many were stunted by poverty. Most were in their late teens when they joined the army.

Buller was left out of all the discussions in preparation for war. He was not allowed to communicate with anyone other than Lansdowne on the subject, and was kept ignorant of the logistics. Buller noted: "No Council of War was held (before August 15), no plan of campaign was adopted, no regular military preparations were undertaken."[83] The British Government continued to show every sign that they believed war could be avoided.

With 8,000 additional men on their way to Natal, a more senior officer than Penn Symons was required there. The man chosen was Lieutenant-General Sir George White, the sixty-four-year-old Quarter-Master General at the War Office, a member of the group of officers associated with Lord Roberts. With him went two of Roberts' keenest supporters, Colonel Ian Hamilton and Sir Henry Rawlinson.

Buller was becoming alarmed at developments. His knowledge of the Boers was greater than anyone else involved, and he now wrote a private letter to Lansdowne urging him to send more troops to Natal.

> "…if the Boers are bold….they have now the chance of inflicting a serious reverse upon us in Natal…. should they do that every day saved in the sending of reinforcements would be worth its weight in gold."[84]

He cautioned that it was essential White should not push his force too far forward when he arrived in Natal. He must stay on the defensive south of the Tugela River. Buller knew the terrain well, and was aware that Ladysmith lay in a natural bowl surrounded by hills. To establish a garrison there, so far in advance of supporting troops to the south, would be to invite disaster. Lansdowne brushed aside all Buller's appeals.

When White landed in Cape Town at the beginning of October he found Milner in a very nervous state. From the start Milner had been worried that hostilities in the two independent republics would provoke the Boers living in the Cape Colony, so far docile, to rise up against their British rulers. The Boers had assembled large forces on the frontiers of both the Cape Colony and Natal. An ultimatum from them was expected daily.

White advised London that war was imminent. He reported that the north of Natal was threatened by Free Staters massing near the Drakensberg, with Transvalers to the north, east and west. He singled out a small advanced British force in Glencoe that could become isolated. He wanted it to retire to Ladysmith. Penn Symons had decided on his own authority to advance a brigade to Dundee, close to Glencoe and seventy miles north of Ladysmith, dangerously dividing his force.

White lost no time in heading for Natal. To cut the journey time he took the train from Cape Town to East London, where he sailed in the steamer *Scot* for Durban. On the way the number of armed men he saw by the railway side, showing aggression, shook him.

It does not appear that White consulted Buller before leaving, as Buller's appointment was not yet public at that time. Once he arrived in Natal White again identified the exposed position in northern Natal as constituting a risk, but was advised by the Governor of Natal that if the British were to show any weakness – for instance by falling back on Ladysmith – the Zulus, 750,000 of them in Natal and Zululand, would be encouraged to make trouble. Loyal whites would be discouraged and the disloyal in Natal and the Cape Colony would be encouraged to join the Boers. White therefore allowed Penn Symons to remain where he was.

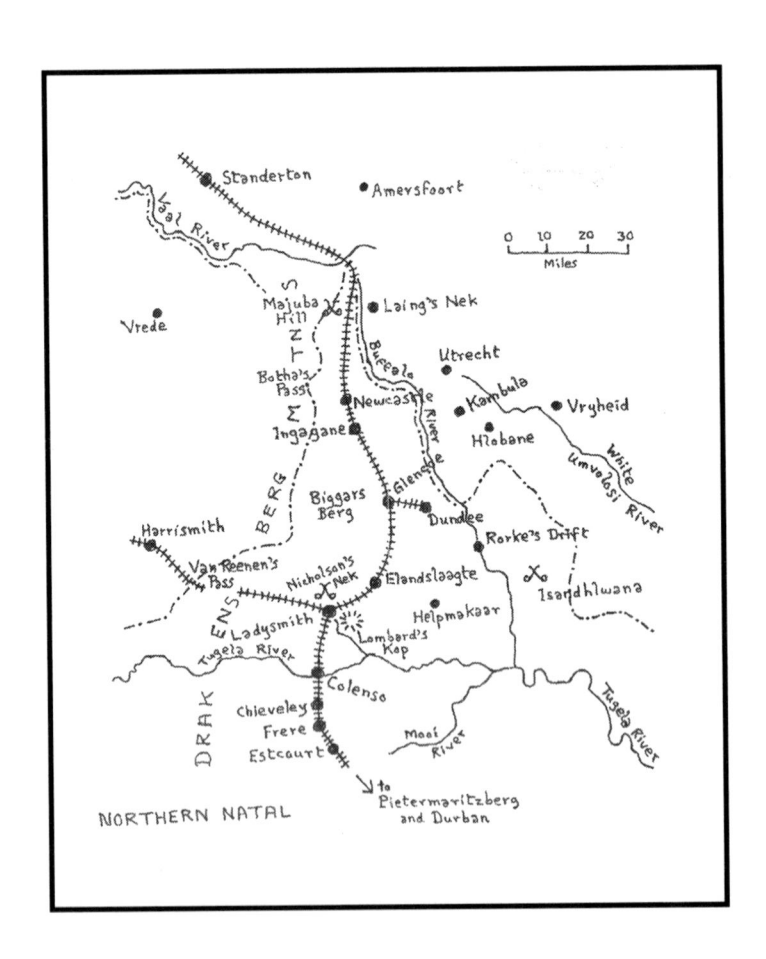

chapter 6.
LET BATTLE COMMENCE.

BOTHA.

THE BOERS resolved to take the fight to the enemy. That meant invading one or both of the two crown colonies. Smuts envisaged a pre-emptive strike into Natal lead by General Joubert and another into the Cape with General Cronje. However the Republican leaders' strategy was to protect their independence in a defensive manner, invading British territory only to the extent to which it was necessary.[85] It is argued by Thomas Pakenham and other commentators that had the Boers been able to advance in September rather than several weeks later, they would have overrun Natal before the British could assemble a sufficiently large force to resist them. Buller commented at the time that the wily Kruger had delayed attacking Natal until there was sufficient spring grass to feed the Boer horses.

The Boers were more prepared for war than the British. They could mobilise in a few days. In both the Transvaal and Orange Free State every man between 16 and 60 was obliged to do unpaid military service if called upon. He was required to report for duty with 10 days' rations, a rifle and 30 rounds of ammunition. Each district within the two Boer republics (twenty-two in the Transvaal and nineteen in the Orange Free State) provided one commando under a commandant elected by his peers. Commandos varied in size from 300 to 3,000 men. No uniforms were issued: the men fought in their everyday clothes. Travelling light and with agile horses they could be moved rapidly to the point of conflict.

The Natal border, so accessible from Pretoria, represented the nearest and easiest point of attack. Within a day the commandos had moved. Trains carried them south-east with their horses, baggage and ammunition. Observers watched six miles of bullock wagons with canvas covers winding down the passes of the Drakensberg into Natal. At Volksrust, on the border, they joined men who were waiting, prepared, for the outcome of the ultimatum. Soon the small town was humming with activity and excitement.

General Joubert was in command of the Boer forces; Lukas Meyer, Botha's old friend and mentor, was Assistant-Commandant-General. Louis Botha was Veldcornet in the Vryheid commando. Originally a title given to a local official responsible for military, administrative police and judicial matters, it came to be the equivalent of a captain in the army.

Botha was now among men he had known all his life. It was also a time of sadness for him: many of his sisters had married Englishmen. Reluctant as he was to wage war, his spell on the Volksraad had persuaded him to identify completely with the Boer cause. He was ready to fight, and perhaps die, for that cause. He believed that a swift, daring attack would catch the British unprepared and could sweep them out of Natal. The British force in Natal was estimated at about 13,000 men. The Boers numbered 14,000, and could rely upon a further 6,000 Free Staters, moving up along the Drakensberg mountain range. The Boers knew that the British were bringing reinforcements from other parts of the world, and would soon be augmented by troops landing at Durban. If they could take Durban before these troops landed, and control the port, the war would turn decisively in their favour.

The sixty-eight years old Boer general, Piet Joubert, was a very conservative man. He hated the thought of men dying in battle, and he had not yet accepted fully the fact that he was at war. He saw his role as essentially defensive, to protect the Transvaal Republic, and was reluctant to take the initiative.

Nevertheless on October 13, 1899, the Boers advanced to the Buffalo River near Newcastle on the Natal border. Through the pouring rain they looked across to the land they believed had been taken from them by the British; now they would reclaim it. One of the leaders wrote:

"amid enthusiastic cries we began to ford the stream...the cheering and the singing of [the national anthem] were continuous, and we rode into the smiling land of Natal full of hope and courage."[86] They discovered that the British had not destroyed a single bridge or tunnel, and were not guarding any of the passes. The way was clear for the Boers to press forward. In a way this lack of insight epitomised the British approach. It was thought the war would not last long, and they were reluctant to destroy an infrastructure they would later have to reinstate. Without resistance the Boers occupied Laing's Nek, the key hill on the main road between Johannesburg and Durban. Botha, leading part of the Vryheid commando, crossed the Buffalo River at Dejagersdrift on a reconnaissance mission, and captured six border policemen, perhaps the first enemy prisoners of the war.

BULLER.

The Government of Natal was also ready. The commander of British troops in Natal, Major-General Penn Symons, had requested an additional 5,600 men to augment the existing force of 6,000. By the middle of October three cavalry regiments, four battalions of infantry and three batteries of artillery, had arrived in Durban from India: 5,652 men, 2,252 horses, 18 field guns and 7 machine guns. The reinforcements arrived too late to occupy the key position of Laing's Nek, but Penn Symons had already crossed the Tugela and established a garrison in an advanced position at Dundee. He was familiar with the area, having fought in the Zulu War of 1879. He was under instructions to protect the extensive coalfields that existed in the area.

Lukas Meyer was given the task of attacking the British garrison of four thousand men at Dundee. He had under his command two and a half thousand burghers and four guns. Louis Botha accompanied Meyer as his second-in-command. The first experience of warfare came as a shock to many of the burghers. They were, in the main, farmers who normally lived an isolated and independent existence, and were not used to taking orders.

News soon reached Dundee that General Joubert's army was on the move from the north, where Mpati, the highest hill in the area, was visible from the town. The thought that a rabble of farmers with no proper army would challenge the strong garrison seemed absurd to the

British. Perhaps for that reason the garrison at Dundee left two hills to the east and north-west of the town – Talana and Mpati – unguarded. The Boers brought with them a formidable arsenal of field guns: 2 heavy six-inch Creusots and 16 Krupps. When at 5.30 a.m. on Friday, October 20, the Boers appeared on Talana and commenced a bombardment of the town with their French Creusot artillery pieces, the British were unprepared for an onslaught. The first engagement of the war had started. Penn Symons trained his own guns – a total of eighteen - on Talana and started to pound it, but the guns did not have the range to reach the summit.

Unused to the military disciplines required, nearly one thousand of the Boers immediately broke away and fled towards the north. Penn Symons moved his guns nearer to Talana in order to reach the summit, and under the covering fire sent out three columns to confront the Boers. The Boer artillery fire had started to slacken by the time the infantry reached the foot of Talana. Penn Symons, steeped in British military training, believed in close order attacks and concentration of firepower. He would concentrate his forces in the few hundred yards covered by stone walls and trees directly below the summit of Talana and aim to deal a knock-out blow. In the wild hills of Natal, faced by Boers skilled in accurate rifle fire, these were poor tactics. Once in range of the Boer rifles, the British infantry were surprised at the intensity and accuracy of their fire. They were pinned down behind stone walls, unable to move. Penn Symons himself took the lead over the wall and was immediately struck in the stomach, a wound of which he died a few days later.

Nevertheless Penn Symons had provided the impetus required, and the British stormed the hill, though at heavy cost. The battle lasted less than five hours. At the top they found that Boer resistance had melted away. Both sides claimed victory: 23 Boers were killed, 66 wounded and 20 missing; 41 British were killed, and 185 wounded. Arthur Conan Doyle was serving as a volunteer doctor in a field hospital near Bloemfontein. At the same time he was writing pamphlets in support of the British. He called the Battle of Talana Hill "..a tactical victory but a strategic defeat."[87] There is now an outstanding museum on Talana Hill, showing graphically how it was won and lost.

The main British army in Natal was situated at Ladysmith, on the main road south from the Transvaal. The third largest town in Natal, it was predominantly a centre for the farming community with a railway station and two parallel streets lined with tin-roofed houses. At the centre was the Town Hall distinguished by a baroque clock tower. (Much of the centre of Ladysmith remains the same today). Near it was the wooden-canopied railway station, the reason for Ladysmith's existence. This was a key railway junction between Durban and Johannesburg. In this dusty, unprepossessing place the British, thirteen thousand troops with the paraphernalia that goes with a marching army, established their base. Bell-tents sprouted up on any available piece of flat ground. Every hour trains steamed in from the south carrying stores, tents and medical supplies. Forage was required for three thousand horses, mealies for the African drivers and grooms.

Here White set up his headquarters. Sixty-four years old, he was a country gentleman from Ireland who had worked his way laboriously up the ladder of promotion. He was not considered to be among the brightest prospects in the British Army, but he had seen action in India and Burma, where he was awarded the Victoria Cross. A lame leg, the result of a riding accident, handicapped him. He is quoted as saying: "It is good enough for anything except running away."[88] Most seriously, however, he knew nothing of Africa before he landed at the Cape on October 3. His appointment did not meet with everyone's approval in London, but it was felt that he would do until a better qualified Commander-in-Chief could be sent to South Africa.

In order to gauge the strength of the Boer force on October 22, the day after the battle of Talana, he sent forward the Imperial Light Horse, consisting mainly of Uitlanders, under the command of Major-General John French, to Elandslaagte, north of Ladysmith. There the enemy was reported to have cut the railway and telegraph lines leading to Dundee. An armoured train accompanied the cavalry with six guns from the Natal Artillery and 400 men from the Manchester regiment. French discovered that the Johannesburg Commando, a Boer unit, had occupied the station with around one thousand men. This presented French with an opportunity to destroy the Commando if he could muster sufficient infantry, and restore the links to Dundee. Men from the Gordon Highlanders and the Devonshire regiment were sent forward from Ladysmith, under the command of General Ian Hamilton. French now had at his disposal 1630 infantry, 1314 cavalry and 552 gunners with 18 field guns.

Although Elandslaagte is situated on level veld, just to the south of the town there is a horse-shoe shaped bit of high ground, culminating in a kopje or hillock that rises about 300 feet above the veld. The Boers took up their position here, and although they possessed only three guns they were modern Krupps, more than a match for the outdated British guns. French was forced to withdraw his guns to save them, but he thrust forward the infantry. Hamilton deployed his men in extended order, contrary to the standard British close formation – a tactic that was to be used increasingly as the war progressed. The superior Boer position on the kopje made Hamilton's job very difficult, and the British incurred heavy casualties at first. At 4.30 p.m. a severe thuderstorm swept the battlefield, obliterating everything. Seizing their chance, the British infantry charged the hill and drove the Boers back. When they crested the ridge and realised that victory was theirs, they raised their helmets and shouted "Majuba! Majuba!"[89]

Now came a stock feature of British military tactics: the cavalry charge. For the first time in this war the British cavalry were able to sweep forward onto level ground as the Boers retreated. Unprepared for the onslaught, the Boers were jogging back the way they had come when 400 Dragoons and Lancers fell upon them in the twilight with sabres, lances and revolvers. Cries for mercy went unheeded. Previously the Boers had tricked the British by waving white flags and then shooting at their enemy at close quarters. So attempts to surrender were ignored, and in any event the orders were to take no prisoners. The result was a bloodbath and the first decisive British victory of the Boer War.

BOTHA.

There remained a number of Boers in possession of Mpati Hill, in a position to dominate Dundee and perhaps inflict serious damage on the British garrison, now licking its wounds. It has been argued by Boers who were there, among them Deneys Reitz that the town lay at the mercy of the Boers, and that a swift raid would have swept the British garrison away. Botha, who had assumed command when Lukas Meyer was taken ill, was anxious to press home his advantage, but the commandos on Mpati had not communicated with him, and he did not know the real state of affairs there. The wholesale defection under the initial British barrage did not augur well for Boer resolve this early in the war, and Joubert's natural cautiousness was against risking a foray into the town.

The Boers having retreated from Talana did not move forward again.

The next morning General Erasmus, in charge on Mpati, sent scouts forward. To their amazement they found the camp in Dundee deserted. Lighted candles in the tents had given the impression that the camp was still occupied. Although the British had, technically, won the battle of Talana, they were instructed to fall back to Ladysmith, as General White believed them to be dangerously exposed in Dundee to the advancing Boers. Only the British wounded, and the dying Penn Symons remained. General Yule, who had assumed command from Penn Symons, had found an unguarded valley through which he took his troops in retreat back to Ladysmith. Dundee was plundered unmercifully by the triumphant Boers.

Jacobus De la Rey, an experienced soldier fifteen years older than Botha, was considered the leading military thinker on the Boer side. When Botha was in Pretoria at the Volksraad he lodged with De la Rey's daughter and husband, and came to know the family well. Before the war commenced Botha learnt military strategy from De la Rey. When the battle of Talana ended De la Rey, who had been following it closely although he was with Cronje's column in the Orange Free State, was critical of Meyer and Botha. He believed that no Englishman should have escaped from Dundee.

BULLER.

The morning after the victory at Elandslaagte, French marched his force back to Ladysmith. British failure to destroy the main railway line to the north had enabled the Boers to bring reinforcements up from the Transvaal rapidly. A token force of colonial troops had been left to defend Ladysmith, and Boers were in evidence at several points above the town. If they were not stopped from advancing south there was a real danger that the Boers could sweep all before them down to the port of Durban. White sent an urgent request for more artillery: he was being seriously outgunned. The tardiness of war preparations in Britain was now exposed. To supply additional artillery from London would take a minimum of three weeks, and probably a good deal longer.

A colourful figure now made a singular contribution to the build up. Captain Percy Scott, captain of the cruiser HMS *Terrible*, arrived in Simons Bay, Cape Town on October 14. A splendid Victorian figure with a waxed moustache and beard, he was an original thinker who did not disguise his disdain and contempt for his masters in London. He did things his way. An expert on artillery, he was instrumental in making significant progress in the accuracy of naval guns. In due course he was to rise to be one of Britain's greatest admirals.

The news from Ladysmith caused Scott to appraise the situation. Boer artillery was modern, and outranged the rather antiquated British pieces facing them. Guns were something Scott knew about. His ship was armed with powerful, long-range guns. Why not use them on shore? They were fixed to the deck, but could be removed. The 12-pounder, 12-hundredweight guns would be formidable weapons against an army in the countryside. He found wagon wheels and axle-trees, and within twenty-four hours had highly mobile, large, long-range field-guns. Having achieved this successfully, he looked at the two massive 4.7 inch turret guns. They were removed from the ship and mounted on four pieces of timber each, 14 feet by twelve inches in the form of a cross.

The military authorities, however, lacked Scott's sense of urgency and rejected his help. By October 25 White was signalling urgently for help. Finally Scott was listened to. Two 4.7 inch guns and four long 12-pounders were shipped to Durban on *HMS Powerful*. There they were immediately entrained for Ladysmith with a contingent of sailors. They arrived in Ladysmith forty-eight hours before the garrison was cut off from the outside world.

Botha was later to tell Scott:

> "If it wasn't for your guns, the Vierkleur [the 'Four-colour' Boer flag] would have flown over Durban."[90]

BOTHA.

Botha, meanwhile, set out in pursuit of the British retreating from Dundee. He came upon the rearguard floundering through thick mud and swollen rivers but could not prevent the main body of the garrison reaching Ladysmith on October 26. With the arrival of the retreating Dundee garrison White had at his disposal 12,000 men and seven batteries of artillery, mountain guns and Maxims. The Maxim machine gun, invented in 1884 by an Englishman, Sir Hiram Maxim, fired 600 rounds per minute, 30 times the rate of a conventional, breach-loading rifle.

Not for a moment did he think that his force would be besieged in the town, though even a cursory survey would have shown that the position was extremely vulnerable. The town was located in a natural bowl surrounded by hills and dependent upon a single railway track for supplies and reinforcements from the south. White reasoned that only fifteen miles south of Ladysmith the terrain levelled out into a verdant plain, providing him with an easy retreat if necessary. He was still confident that a frontal attack on the advancing Boers would result in victory. What he had not foreseen was that Ladysmith was north of the Tugela River, a swift-flowing and broad torrent with tangled undergrowth on the banks. This not only presented something of a barrier to crossing, but also afforded cover to the enemy. Buller was by then appointed as Commander-in-Chief. He knew the terrain well of course, and had earlier sent messages to White urging him not to venture north of the Tugela.

Meyer and Botha arrived outside Ladysmith on October 29. Their leader, Joubert, and the Free Staters joined them there, bringing the total Boer force to 8,000. The Boers were able to take up a strong position to the north, overlooking the town. They also commenced an encircling movement, aiming to surround the town. Anxious to engage them before the siege was complete White sent forward two brigades during the night of Sunday, October 29 to attack the Boer stronghold he had identified four miles north of the town on Pepworth Hill, a large conical hill near Rietfontein. There the Boers could be seen building a gun platform for one of their heavy guns. The British strategy was first to mount an artillery barrage to soften up the enemy, then the infantry would charge.

At four a.m. a fierce artillery duel commenced at Modderspruit. Botha was heavily involved in this exchange, taking command of Meyer's commando when his mentor became ill. It was evident that the Boers had superior firepower, and the advancing British troops took heavy losses, caught in a cross-fire. The mobile, mounted Boers harried the infantry.

The British suffered a serious setback during the night, which was very dark. Advancing through a defile, a narrow gorge, the Irish Royal Fusiliers came under fire and boulders were rolled down the hill. Close behind them the leading mules, drawing guns, panicked, wrenched themselves free and turned, squealing. Within minutes the entire pack was thundering down the hill onto the Gloucesters, who were following the Fusiliers. Many of the soldiers were knocked down in the rush. In the darkness this sudden mass movement was interpreted by the Irish as a Boer commando raid. Firing haphazardly, they were forced to retreat in some disorder as the mules had carried away their reserve ammunition. They had no option but to retire back to Ladysmith.

Botha was credited with the strategy that led to Boer success. The so-called Battle of Ladysmith had been a fiasco for the British: no clear plan of action, no flexibility when the first attack failed. Casualties were 200 Boers and 1,266 British. Many of the Boer horsemen were eager to advance among the disorganised, retreating British troops, but Joubert held them back. He maintained a steady policy of defence, preferring to resist any attempt by the British to move on the Transvaal than risk a pitched battle in Natal.

Ladysmith was now surrounded. On Tuesday, October 31, 1899 the Boers cut the railway line to the south and at 2.30 p.m. the telegraph line went dead. The siege of Ladysmith had begun.

chapter 7.
BULLER TAKES OVER.

BULLER.

BULLER LEFT for South Africa on October 15, 1899, aboard the *Dunottar Castle*. He was fifty-nine. A huge patriotic crowd saw him off. Some perched on the top of railway carriages, others climbed the iron work of cranes to get sight of the great man. They sang "Rule Britannia" and "For He's a Jolly Good Fellow." The baggage loaded onto the ship was impressive. Black tin trunks, sword scabbards, polo sticks – even a bicycle. Buller's two war-horses, Ironmonger and Biffin, went on.

Buller was not a polished public speaker, and did not enjoy being in the limelight. His gruff, short speech of thanks at the head of the gangplank included the sentiment that he hoped he would not be away for long.

An extremely shy man with a profound distrust of the press, he shunned the other passengers during the voyage. His reticence drew some criticism, but he had much to ponder. He was full of foreboding. Such was the British army's state of unreadiness that it was desperately short of field artillery and transport.

There was concern in London that, were Africans to become involved in the conflict, particularly bearing arms, the consequences could be dangerous for both Boers and British. The complexities of assessing the Africans' loyalties further clouded the scene. It was therefore decided by the British that the Boer War was to be a "white man's war," thus excluding the indigenous soldiers in the experienced Indian Army and any involvement under arms of the Bantu and Coloured races in South Africa.[91]

Buller had always got on well with the Boers, and did not fancy the idea of fighting them. He did not underestimate the difficulties of fighting a war so far from home against a skilled enemy fighting for their livelihoods. He wrote:

> "...it was plain to me that the war could only be carried to a successful conclusion by the actual conquest of every armed man in the field; and this task promised to be doubly difficult owing to the extreme mobility of the enemy."[92]

For much of the voyage to the Cape his ship was out of communication with London and South Africa. At Madeira, he received two telegrams: the first informed him of the Boer invasion of Natal and their convergence on Ladysmith, and the second the isolation of Mafeking and Kimberley, where the garrisons were besieged. Nearer the Cape, on October 29 they sighted *The Australasian*, a troopship bound for England. From its deck a large blackboard was held up. It read "BOERS DEFEATED. THREE BATTLES. PENN SYMONS KILLED." Succinctly this summed up the Boer offensive at Dundee and the subsequent skirmish at Elandslaagte. Buller's aides were disappointed. A staff officer remarked: "It looks as if it will be over, sir." Buller's response was: "I dare say there will be enough left to give us a fight outside Pretoria."[93]

At 9.15 p.m. on October 30 the *Dunottar Castle* steamed into Cape Town harbour. That evening Buller learnt of the retreat from Dundee, the fiasco of the Battle of Ladysmith and the siege that followed. The citizens of Cape Town had not heard this news yet, and the atmosphere in the streets was ebullient. The next morning Buller disembarked and rode in an open landau to Government House through enormous, cheering crowds waving flags. His reputation, his achievements, his previous heroics in South Africa, gave him the image of the essential British leader.

He found the Governor-General, Alfred Milner, in a high state of anxiety. Milner had provoked the war, believing British military superiority would soon prevail and solve his problems with the breakaway states. This simply had not happened. The country was in a state of uproar. The news from Natal was not good. White had reported that he could not move out of Ladysmith. The Free Staters had joined the Transvalers in resistance to the British. Milner's main concern now was that the Cape Province, hitherto peaceful and loyal to the Crown, would rebel. Two-thirds of the settlers in the Cape were Afrikaners. Milner was also terrified that White would surrender and leave the way open to Durban. If Durban fell, the blow to British credibility would be severe. Natal would be lost.

The situation was even worse than Buller imagined. With the war in full swing, British reinforcements were urgently required. The Boers had already been given a clear run for a month, and time before that to prepare and arm. Only a defensive mentality and reluctance to take too many risks had prevented the Boers pushing on towards Durban. The naval presence in Durban, and use of ships' guns, had now secured the town. The need for British guns was acute. Three batteries of artillery had been ordered on September 8, but only left England on September 25. They were on two very slow, old ships, the *Zibenghla* and *Zayathla*. Both immediately encountered mechanical problems. The *Zibenghla* finally left the Mersey on October 7; the *Zayathla* had sailed on September 29. It took both of them until the last week of October to reach Cape Town, a week longer than faster ships. It was said that cheapness was a factor in choosing such slow ships, but whatever the reason it exhibited a disregard for the seriousness and urgency of the situation.

These mistakes were repeated with the mobilisation of infantry. Instead of preparing for war in the summer, it required the Boer invasion of Natal to stir the politicians. The call-up of reservists needed the consent of Parliament, and to convene Parliament notice was required. The necessary consent was given in early October and mobilisation commenced on October 7. Unfortunately, sufficient transportation was not yet available. The first troops finally arrived in Cape Town on November 9. The expeditionary force, in total 50,000, was the largest ever to leave Britain. Of this total only 4,600 men were mounted. This represented the smallest proportion of cavalry in any European army. Bearing in mind the nature of the terrain, and the mobility of the Boers, almost all of whom were mounted, this placed the British at a severe disadvantage in the field.

All Buller's advice on tactics in Natal had been ignored by his superiors in London, and by White. Buller had not wanted his Natal contingent under White exposed to risk until the situation could be properly assessed. All through July and August he had bombarded the War Office with warnings for the Natal force not to venture north of the Tugela. The terrain was well known to him from his previous visits. His concern was that any advance into northern Natal without adequate support would expose the British force to being isolated. When he learnt of the Dundee garrison and White's position at Ladysmith he feared the worst. Against his advice White's advance to Ladysmith had resulted in a large part of his resources being bottled up and under siege. It was not only Buller who criticised White. The Commander-in-Chief in England, Wolseley, testifying to a War Commission after the war, said:

> "If I was in command of such a force as was then in Natal, and hearing at that time – because they did – that there was a large force of the enemy coming for me, nothing in the world would have induced me to stay in Ladysmith. I would have burnt my supplies rather than have stayed there. I would have fallen back to the next line which was Colenso, and behind the river."[94]

To make matters worse, none of the normal precautions in preparation for a siege had been taken in Ladysmith. White had not believed that Ladysmith would be isolated. As a result he did not evacuate non-combatants. Women and children remained resident there; the sick had not been moved. The Boers had been allowed to take up positions around the town and finally cut the route south. Now the British were surrounded. The need to relieve the town was made more urgent by these mistakes. Fortunately the Boer tactics, as in other sieges at Kimberley and Mafeking, were to remain passive. They did not at once attack the town or seek to capture it. They sat and waited, preferring a defensive mode.

Buller had predicted this. From his knowledge of the Boers during his earlier visit to South Africa he had seen how they were reluctant to take risks by venturing into the attack. The Boers observed a strict routine. They seldom mounted any bombardment before breakfast, paused for lunch, hardly ever fired in the evening or when it rained. They did not fight on Sunday.

White's forces represented the cream of the British contingent in South Africa: experienced, professional soldiers and cavalry. The besieged garrison numbered 572 officers and 12,924 men, of whom about 10,000 were combatants – a serious loss to Buller's preparations. Civilians and helpers brought the total besieged in Ladysmith to just over 20,000. In anticipation of a siege substantial stores had been assembled: 979,000lb of flour, 173,000lb of tinned meat, 142,000lb of biscuits, 267,000lb of sugar, 23,000lb of tea, 9,500 lb of coffee, 3,965,000lb of maize 1,270,000lb of oats, 932,000lb of bran and 1,864,000lb of hay. In addition there were 9,800 horses, 2,500 oxen and hundreds of sheep. The one glaring deficit was in ammunition. There was not enough for field guns or rifles, which inhibited any positive action.[95]

Both sides believed the siege would be a short one. The Boers underestimated the garrison's reserves; the British knew a significant relief force was on its way. White would not release General Archibald Hunter, who had been designated as Buller's Chief of Staff. With his intelligence and experience, Hunter would be sorely missed. Hunter was a seasoned field officer who not only led his troops well, but also had the capacity to think and plan ahead. He had served with distinction in Egypt, participating in the expedition to rescue Gordon at Khartoum. He had arrived in Natal shortly before war broke out. White also retained supply officers with all their records and ciphers, and the entire intelligence staff. Thus Buller was flying blind. He demanded that White release Generals French and Haig to serve with him. They were to prove valuable during the siege. His original plan was in tatters. Reinforcements were urgently required in Natal.

The town of Kimberley, close to Bloemfontein but actually in the Cape Province, had been isolated and besieged by the Boers. To complicate matters Cecil Rhodes, previously Prime Minister of the Cape, had dashed to Kimberley in order to protect his valuable diamond interests, and was now cooped up there. He placed daily pressure on Milner to relieve the siege. Otherwise, he warned, they would soon be forced to surrender. With him would go the diamond fields. Milner felt compelled to send help immediately. Kimberley would have to be relieved before a main thrust northward through Bloemfontein could commence.

Originally it was planned that the British forces would advance north via three railway lines from Cape Town, Port Elizabeth and East London. They would cross the Orange River independently and converge on Bloemfontein, the capital of the Orange Free State. If they could defeat the Free Staters, the way would be open for a rapid, concerted advance on Johannesburg and Pretoria. Sieges at Ladysmith, Kimberley and Mafeking in the Transvaal caused Buller to reappraise this strategy. A large proportion of the Boer force was engaged in relatively passive sieges. Should these towns fall, the Boers would be freed to resist the British else where.

Buller saw Natal as his priority. There was virtually no defence between Estcourt and Durban: if the Boers were to take Durban they would control Natal. The port would enable them to obtain assistance from overseas. Many European sympathisers, particularly in Germany, were poised to provide help if it could be arranged. Milner, his concern centred upon the Cape Colony, was prepared to sacrifice Natal. This would mean 12,000 British prisoners and submission of the colony's inhabitants, nine-tenths of whom were of British origin.

Buller disagreed. He consulted the generals assigned to him: Clery, Lyttleton and Hildyard. Unanimously they urged Buller to take personal command of the relief of Ladysmith. Buller concurred. He felt that Ladysmith had to be relieved. Until this happened he could not reasonably expect much progress towards Pretoria. The garrison at Ladysmith could last for two months at the most – not long enough for Buller to relieve Kimberley and still deploy forces to Natal. The original plan, to sweep north from Cape Town through Bloemfontein to Pretoria was no longer feasible for the present.

By November 4, six days after his arrival, Buller was ready to implement his decision. He would divide the Army Corps between Natal and the Cape. Fortunately the Army Corps, numbering 50,000 men, was beginning to arrive in Cape Town by ship. Volunteers from other parts of the British Empire – India, Canada, Australia – were also arriving. A group of Texan muleteers imported their mules and stayed to fight in the South African Light Horse.

A relief column under the command of Lord Methuen was detailed to march north immediately towards Kimberley. Lieutenant General Sir William Gatacre, who was to have commanded a division of the Army Corps, was given a brigade and ordered to defend the north and central Cape against incursion, and to hold down any incipient rebellion. Buller recognised that should he go to Natal it would be difficult for him to maintain overall command in South Africa for any length of time. The relief of Ladysmith would need to be achieved swiftly. On November 8 General French, having left Ladysmith before it was finally surrounded, arrived in Cape Town and was able to brief Buller on the latest events. Buller's response was immediate:

"Was I to sit with my hands crossed waiting for troops, while Natal was overrun…or should I scrape up what forces I had and try at any rate to protect Natal, and relieve the pressure on Kimberley and Ladysmith? I had no doubt which alternative to adopt."[96]

On board the *Dunottar Castle* was a young reporter, Winston Churchill. He foresaw "…a fierce, certainly bloody, possibly prolonged struggle lies before the army in South Africa."[97] Churchill's urgent aim was to reach Ladysmith before it was cut off. He worked out that by travelling by train to East London and catching a small coaster from there to Durban he could save three days on colleagues who remained on the *Dunottar Castle*. He was lucky: his was the last train allowed through to the eastern Cape before hostilities closed the line. The train ran via De Aar along the southern border with the Orange Free State, close to the Boer forces, and ran the risk of being intercepted. Nevertheless he reached East London safely. The 100-ton steamer he boarded there, the *Umzimvubu*, endured a very stormy passage to Durban, which it reached at midnight on November 4.

In Durban Churchill learnt that Ladysmith was cut off. He visited soldiers wounded at Elandslaagte in hospital. One told him: "All these colonials tell you that the Boers only want one good thrashing to satisfy them. Don't you believe it. They mean going through with this to the end."[98] He immediately set out for northern Natal. Pietermaritzburg, "a sleepy, dead-alive place"[99] was busy fortifying itself with wire encircling the town. He was impressed with the "composure of the civil population."[100]

BOTHA.

Meyer's health continued to deteriorate, and he was given leave of absence. Botha was appointed in his place temporarily. This was a popular appointment: he had shown great skill in handling his men and had a natural empathy that was appreciated. Moreover, despite a complete lack of military experience before the war commenced, he seemed to possess an instinct for the correct tactics in the field that was quickly seen by others on the Boer side.

On November 9 the Boer commandants held a council of war at

Modderspruit, a few miles east of Ladysmith. What the British did not realise was that the Boer strategy, and the professed aim of both Kruger and Joubert, was essentially defensive. To defend their homeland – the Transvaal – was the objective. If that meant confronting the British in Natal, so be it, but such a confrontation was to stop the enemy advancing into the Transvaal, nothing else. Joubert is reputed to have said: "When God holds out a finger, do not take the whole hand."[101]

Joubert wished to keep White bottled up in Ladysmith and prevent his force breaking loose. Not only would this take immediate pressure off the Transvaal, but it would also preoccupy any rescuers moving up from Durban, on the coast. Joubert was under no illusion about the reinforcements now on their way to South Africa. He was concerned about the morale of his own men. They had fought magnificently so far, but casualties had been quite heavy, and the Boer soldiers were not professionals. The best were farm boys, living on their wits and awareness of the countryside; the rest were the lower order from the towns springing up in the Transvaal, unused to fighting. He could not be sure his army would not melt away and return home when the going got tough.

A message to Pretoria from him illustrated his concern;

> "The men come to me in streams asking for permission to go home. Although I refuse them permission every time, the number of burghers is melting away. The officers themselves…set the example in going off home. Every morning I receive such serious complaints about the melting away of the burghers and disobeying my orders, that I shudder at our situation. Unless the government publishes an order to send back the absent burghers immediately, I shall shortly have no commandos at all."[102]

Instead of attempting to take Ladysmith he therefore proposed to contain the British and wait to see what happened.

Botha could see that there was a unique opportunity to sweep the British out of Natal before the reinforcements arrived. A swift raid south of Ladysmith could overrun Pietermaritzburg, leaving the road to Durban and its priceless port open. He reckoned that the garrison at Estcourt numbered 3,000 men. A much greater number were known to be on their way to Durban. For once, Joubert was amenable. Action appealed to his hesitant army: a long drawn out stalemate at Ladysmith would affect morale adversely. The Free Staters informed him that they would not venture across the Tugela. Their cause was not the same as the Transvalers, and they were reluctant to be seen to be invading Natal.

Joubert, however, had 1,500 Transvaal burghers at his side, and a dashing young commander in Louis Botha to inspire them. On Monday, November 13 Joubert's forces circumvented Ladysmith by moving around it to the west and fording the Tugela River. With him, despite their commandant's decision, rode 500 Free Staters. At Colenso they laid dynamite under the bridge before sweeping on towards Estcourt.

By the evening of November 14 the Boers had reached Chieveley, twenty miles north of Estcourt. Botha knew this part of the country intimately, having been brought up not far away in Vryheid. He realised that the lifeline for the British was the railway from Durban to Ladysmith, and his intention was to attack the armoured train north of Chieveley. The British relied heavily on the railway for moving supplies and armaments, and for patrols. The disadvantage was that the train was helpless against field guns.

By November 6 Churchill was in Estcourt, forty miles from Ladysmith, seen as "the front." The Boers had taken the only significant town in between, Colenso, sitting on the southern bank of the Tugela River, a few days earlier. There were only Boers beyond Estcourt. Concern that they would move south in an attempt to capture the rest of Natal was justified; there were only two British battalions to resist the Boer advance. Anxious to reach the front line and report on what he saw, Churchill rode with the armoured train sent as reconnaissance up to Frere carrying rails to keep the track repaired, although only military personnel were authorised to go. A company of Dublin Fusiliers travelled with it as protection. The train was able to proceed north of Chieveley and reach Colenso, which appeared deserted. It returned to Estcourt without encountering any Boers.

On November 14 mounted infantry patrols reported Boers in small parties approaching Estcourt. The advance that had been expected seemed imminent. The armoured train was ordered north again to reconnoitre. It was equipped with a 7-pounder muzzle-loading gun, an armoured car fitted with loopholes, and men from the Dublin Fusiliers and Royal Royal Durban Light Infantry numbering 120 in total. The train reached Frere without incident, and proceed north towards the Tugela River. A considerable number of Boers on horses were spotted about a mile away. The train was ordered to return to Frere and remain there in observation. When the train started its return journey it found the way back blocked by 100 Wakkerstroom commandos.

The Boer's military structure was very loose: individual towns and districts recruited their own commandos, or regiments, and operated semi-independently. The Wakkerstroom Commando had a reputation as a committed, courageous and skilled outfit. They had been watching the train for some time, and observed it was only lightly protected. Increasing speed to avoid the incoming fire, the train rounded a bend and was derailed by a huge stone on the tracks. Churchill displayed qualities for which he was later to become famous. He persuaded the driver, cowering in the shelter of the derailed trucks, to unhitch the engine, clear the damaged trucks from the tracks, connect those still undamaged, and make a dash for it. For over an hour they struggled to escape. The engine was able to move the stone from the track and wriggle past, but the coaches could not follow. Churchill, heedless of his personal safety, ran backwards and forwards, trying to save the situation, but to no avail. Although the engine was able to rattle down the tracks to safety, the trucks, and those men not killed, were left to surrender to the Boers.

At Estcourt the British had established a fortified camp guarding the Ladysmith road. The garrison commander, Colonel Long, had prepared for a hasty retreat. Botha made no attempt to confront this force, but moved around Estcourt to the west. He raised the Vierkleur at Weenen a couple of miles north of Estcourt and cleared the countryside between Colenso and Estcourt. On November 19, Boers were spotted south of Estcourt, sealing the town off. Attempts by the British to counter-attack under cover of darkness failed, mainly due to unfamiliarity with the territory and inadequate maps.

The next sizeable town on the main route towards Durban was Mooi River. There a further four thousand British troops were camped. Botha took up a threatening position, hoping to lure the British into a pitched battle, but General Hildyard took evasive action. Skirmishes between Estcourt and Mooi River favoured the Boers, so the British retired behind their fortifications at Estcourt, withdrawing from Mooi River. The way was now open for a quick Boer advance to Durban. The inhabitants of that city were by now thoroughly alarmed, and many took refuge on ships in the harbour.

True to form, however, Joubert was reluctant to press forward with speed, and proceeded with caution. By November 21, eight days after starting out, his invading force was just south of Estcourt. Botha urged Joubert to head for Durban before it was too late. Joubert was a hesitant, worried man. The *Roslin Castle* had docked in Durban on November 13 with the vanguard of a force that was to total 9,700 men with twenty-four field guns. The reinforcements had begun to move inland.

It was estimated there were now 12,000 British troops on the road north of Pietermaritzburg. Botha proposed circumventing them and heading for Pietermaritzburg, but Joubert felt the risks were too great. On November 23 an unfortunate incident occurred: Joubert's horse threw him. He suffered internal injuries from which he never fully recovered. Botha proposed going on without him, but Joubert was concerned that the young man was not weighing the risks he faced. He ordered Botha back. When Botha refused, Joubert threatened to dismiss him, giving him no alternative but to obey. A great opportunity had been missed. By December 1899 47,000 men had arrived from England and the chance to take Natal had gone. The Boers settled down for a long siege at Ladysmith.

Watching him at first hand, Joubert had been most impressed with Botha's military skills. His energy, spirit and dash allied to a natural genius for operations made him a most unusual leader. Joubert, ageing, tired and not in sympathy with the war, withdrew to direct the siege of Ladysmith, leaving the thirty-seven year old Botha to command the Boers in the field.

Churchill was marched away to Pretoria. With him went fifty-six unwounded or slightly wounded men. Churchill later claimed that Botha had captured him personally, and Botha did not deny it, but he does not mention Botha in his written account of the incident. A Boer officer present at the time names a man called Oosthuisen as seizing Churchill. The prisoners walked as far as Volksrust, on the Transvaal border, before being loaded into a train and transported the rest of the way to Pretoria. They were given food and water during the march, and treated with consideration. At night Churchill was able to talk to the Boers manning the camps at which they stopped . These men were as curious as he was. They could not understand why the British should "take this country away from us."[103] They were particularly bitter towards the capitalists, accusing them of provoking the war and being behind plans to dominate South Africa. What also emerged was Boer rejection of African rights:

"We know how to treat Kaffirs in *this* country.....
Educate a Kaffir! Ah, that's you English all over. No,
no, old chappie. We educate 'em with a stick...They
were put here by the God Almighty to work for us.
We'll stand no damned nonsense from them. We'll keep
them in their proper places."[104]

In Pretoria Churchill was kept in the State Model Schools. Prisoners were supplied with new clothes, bedding, towels and toiletries. They were permitted to buy additional clothes, which implies their money was not taken from them. Churchill's name and reputation was well known to the Boer command, and he was visited frequently by its senior members. They all wished to debate the causes of the war with him, and put over the Boer views to him. Churchill demanded that he be released on the grounds that he was a press correspondent and non-combatant, but his heroics when the train was derailed counted against him.

He set about seeking a means of escape. Offering bribes to the guards failed. However the yard, although illuminated by powerful electric lights, was difficult to guard. On December 12 Churchill took the opportunity when a sentry's back was turned to scale the wall and escape. He made his way to the railway and jumped on an empty coal train as it thundered past, "...my toes bumping on the line – and with a struggle seated myself on the couplings of the fifth truck."[105] He discovered that the trucks were full of empty sacks, so he climbed among them and burrowed in. He was forced to change trains more than once, but finally reached Delagoa Bay some two weeks later. There he boarded a steamer for Durban and rejoined the British army in Natal early in the New Year.

The Boers made out that he had been allowed to escape, and a letter from General Joubert was sent to all the Pretoria newspapers explaining the grounds that prompted him generously to restore his liberty. Yet a massive manhunt was mounted, a warrant was issued for his immediate arrest, three thousand photographs were printed and distributed, and every train searched. Churchill wrote: "I find it very difficult [to believe] in the face of the extraordinary efforts which were made to recapture me."[106]

BULLER.

Having come to the conclusion that his first priority must be to save Natal, Buller set sail for Durban on November 22, taking with him the bulk of the Army Corps. His departure created widespread surprise. Boer spies were rife in Cape Town, and secrecy was essential. Even senior members of his staff did not know he was leaving. His greatest critic, Leo Amery of The Times, was to write that not even Milner was told. This does not ring true. Lansdowne was aware well in advance of his plans, and two of his closest associates, Forestier-Walker and Hely-Hutchinson knew. Amery's assertion was given credence by the memoirs of Lady Edward Cecil, the future Lady Milner. She related that she was asked to break the news to Milner, and that he expressed disbelief. Yet neither Milner's private diary nor his references to Buller (of which there were many) in his writings indicate any surprise at his departure. On November 23 his diary mentions: "Buller having left for Natal." It is likely that Milner had been sworn to silence and maintained that stance throughout the event. Milner objected strongly to Buller leaving, believing his place was in Cape Town – another sign of his anxiety for the Cape Province's security.

Buller reached Durban on November 25. With him were three generals who strongly supported his decision to take personal command in Natal: Clery, Lyttleton and Hildyard. There he learned the good news that the Boers had not pressed home their advantage and missed the opportunity to attack Pietermaritzburg and then Durban. The reinforcements now landing at Durban had made the port secure, and the Boers had withdrawn across the Tugela River and contented themselves with besieging Ladysmith. It was therefore apparent that the Boers had settled for a defensive strategy, protecting the independence of the Transvaal Republic.

On November 29 Buller made contact with White by telegram from Pietermaritzburg, signalling his intention to move towards Ladysmith.

> "If you hear me attacking, join in if you can. I do not know which way I shall come. Stop. How much longer can you hold out?"[107]

White answered:

> "I have provisions for seventy days, and believe I can defend Ladysmith while they last."[108]

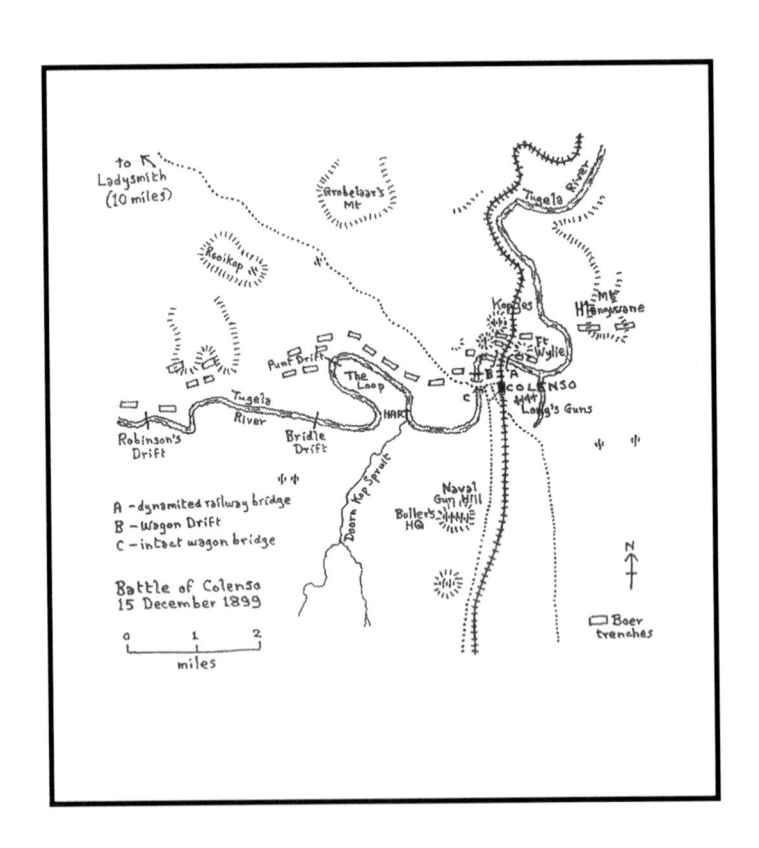

chapter 8.
COLENSO.

BULLER.

BULLER'S INITIAL assessment of the situation facing him at Ladysmith did not make him hopeful. The Tugela River, flowing strongly through steep banks between Ladysmith and Colenso, represented a formidable barrier. There were only five points at which wheeled vehicles could cross it. To the north of the river was a range of hills between the British and Ladysmith, easily defendable by the Boers. Any attempt to outflank the defence would encounter rugged, broken country to which the British infantry were ill-suited. To the south of the river the terrain was open and level; any approach to the river would be extremely hazardous. A good idea of the obstacles in Buller's way can be gained from this despatch by a war correspondent:

> "No map, nor photograph, nor written description can give an idea of the country which lay between Buller and his goal. It was an eruption of high hills, linked together at every point without order or sequence…They stand alone, or shoulder to shoulder, or at right angles, or at a tangent, or join hands across a valley. They never appear the same; some run to a sharp point, some stretch out, forming a table-land, others are gigantic anthills,

others perfect and accurately modelled ramparts. In a ride of half a mile, every hill loses its original aspect and character."[109]

Buller faced a vigorous foe. His task was not helped by White's insistence on retaining the man who had been selected as Buller's Chief of Staff, General Hunter. White considered him indispensable. This was unfortunate, for Hunter was very able and was badly needed by Buller at that time. His time in Ladysmith facing the Boers would have given Buller valuable intelligence at a time when he was woefully short of information, and had totally inadequate maps of the area.

Buller reached the main body of the British Army, camped at Frere, twelve miles south of Colenso and the Tugela River, on December 6. There he found an amazing scene. Frere, named in honour of the previous Governor-General of the Cape, Bartle Frere, normally consisted of a station-master's house, a hotel and three other houses on the main railway line from Durban to Ladysmith. Now a sea of white tents surrounded it. A constant stream of trains had brought nineteen thousand men from Durban. He had at his disposal only 30 field guns. The accepted ratio of guns to men was 5 guns for every thousand men, which meant he should have had 100.

HMS Terrible had followed its sister ship, *Powerful*, to Durban, arriving on November 6. Captain Scott had been appointed Military Commandant there when the Boer threat became apparent. Initially he used his remaining guns to protect Durban. Once the threat to the port was over, the guns, two 4.7-inch naval guns and fourteen twelve-pounders were loaded on trains and taken to the front-line south of Ladysmith. Along the same line came a trainload of sailors with naval searchlights with a range of sixty miles to be used to communicate with Ladysmith by bouncing their beams off the clouds. In addition there were horses, spare parts and supplies, drums of telegraph cable and pontoon bridges.

Buller's arrival was greeted ecstatically. His exploits during the Zulu War were well known to his men, and his reputation as a "soldier's soldier" went before him, like Botha's. His arrival gave them the leadership they craved. One soldier wrote: "Buller's arrival was almost everything. I have never seen troops retempered like this by one man…"[110] The new commander commenced to set up his quarters in typical British officer fashion. His bathroom contained an iron bath and his kitchen was fully equipped. He was said to have confided in one of Queen Victoria's ladies-in-waiting that he always drank a pint of champagne each day, and that the only privation he suffered was an occasional lack of butter. It is said that he ordered his crates of champagne under the disguise of castor oil. When one consignment of 50 cases failed to appear his zealous aides, finding no trace of it, acquired all the castor oil available (20 cases). The general was not pleased!

Maps on the British side were rudimentary. Attempts to reconnoitre the territory were constantly disrupted by the Boers, who sent out scouting parties to chase the surveyors away. The British were forced to rely upon an inch-to-the-mile survey map prepared in Pietermaritzburg. It was based on railway and farm surveys, and on a micro-filmed map sent by carrier pigeon from Ladysmith. The main map contained large areas of blank paper, where little was known of the terrain. More seriously still, the army based at Frere had very little intelligence of Boer positions. Many of the commandos were so well hidden that their location could not be identified.

One of Buller's first acts was to re-establish his beloved Frontier Light Horse as the South African Light Horse. Equipping them with small, tough and mobile horses as opposed to the big British cavalry horses, he appointed one of his best officers, Major J.H.G.Byng, to lead them. They were to distinguish themselves in combat throughout the war, and provide Buller with a mobile force suited to the terrain.

Buller kept in touch with Cape Town over the progress of Methuen's column marching towards Kimberley. The news was not good. The column met stiff resistance, and suffered a bad defeat at the railway junction of Stormberg. The relief effort was checked, and the signs were that Kimberley would remain under siege for some time to come. The relief effort was absorbing valuable manpower, and balking any attempt to march north through the Orange Free State and reach the Transvaal. Rhodes, holed up in Kimberley, did not help matters. He maintained a constant barrage of complaints, demanding that Kimberley be relieved. If not, he threatened, the garrison would yield to the Boers. Such was his status that these threats were taken seriously by the British commanders. In the advance north, priority was given to rescuing Rhodes.

The relief of Ladysmith was now a matter of some urgency. While the British force there remained bottled up, Buller could not release valuable resources to help Methuen. Moreover, he could not advance out of Natal into the Transvaal and distract the Boer defences from resisting the column advancing from the Cape. He had imprecise intelligence of the Boers, but knew them to be in strong positions between Colenso and Ladysmith. The key for him was the crossing of the Tugela. The north bank of the river rises quite steeply, affording positions from which virtually the entire south bank is visible. A range of high hills dotted with trees and boulders make it easy to defend. The south side evens out into a sweep of wide plains, where concealment is difficult.

Buller's first inclination was to attempt to approach Ladysmith via Potgieter's Drift, the most fordable point on the Tugela. This required a forty-five mile march to the west flank, during which his wagon train (which would extend for nine miles) would be exposed. This way he hoped to bypass the main Boer defence on the main road from Colenso. To approach down the main road would be disastrous. Not only would the Boers see the British approach the Tugela over flat ground without cover, but a line of fortified kopjes, or small hills, commanded the north bank. Even if this obstacle could be overcome, there would then be nine miles of fighting over rough ground to reach Ladysmith. Potgieter's Drift represented an easier crossing with fewer kopjies, 2 miles in depth, and then a downhill run to Ladysmith.

Buller's first communications with White were by heliograph. Using powerful mirrors with a small sighting hole in the middle these highly portable instruments could be moved to high ground affording unimpeded lines of sight to the target. In clear, sunny weather a signal could be sent up to 100 miles. The two groups were able to flash Morse code to each other on most days. The exchanges showed White to be a man dispirited and broken. It was highly unlikely that the garrison at Ladysmith would be of assistance in any relief effort; Buller would have to achieve the breakthrough without him.

"Expect to start on 12th December, and take five days," he heliographed, "I think you had better not look forward to helping me before my attack on Lancer Hill [7 miles from Ladysmith] unless you feel certain of where I am."[111]

On December 11 Buller heliographed White informing him that he intended to march to Potgieter's Drift. As he prepared for the attack, however, terrible news came from the Cape. Lieutenant-General Gatacre had lost his way on the march north – lack of appropriate maps again – and had lost 696 men either killed or captured. On the same day he heard that Methuen had been defeated at Magersfontein, with heavy losses, and the advance was stalled. The telegram read: "Our loss is great. Possibility that further advance is questionable, but shall endeavour to hold my own and keep my communications secure." Buller telegraphed back: "Fight or fall back."[112] Methuen seemed to have lost the will to make decisions.

The bad news changed things for Buller. The defeats suffered by Gatacre and Methuen had stopped any progress. If Buller were to suffer a bad defeat in an exposed position he might open up the rest of Natal to the Boers. No assistance could be expected from the Cape columns. The flanking movement through Potgieter's Drift had its risks, and if he did not succeed, his main force, well away from the railway line, with no adequate communications would be as helpless as White's. Buller had to consider the possibility that his force could be surrounded out on the veld if its first thrust was unsuccessful. In a letter to his wife he wrote:

"I had considered that with the enemy dispirited by the failure of their plans in the west the risk was justifiable, but I cannot think that I ought now to take such a risk. From my point of view it will be better to lose Ladysmith altogether than to throw Natal open to the enemy."[113]

He therefore decided, against his better instincts, on a frontal attack up the main road from Colenso, recognising it as "a forlorn hope", but necessary in the circumstances. He later explained: "Colenso was in front of me. I could attack and control the result. But Potgieters [Drift]...I could not pretend I could control that. I might easily have lost my whole force."[114]

BOTHA.

With Joubert too ill to take the field, Botha unofficially commanded the field force. The older Boers resented Botha's rapid rise, and were not prepared to take orders from him. Although both Kruger and Joubert wanted him to assume overall command, he was reluctant to offend the older leaders, Lukas Meyer and Schalk Burgher. The latter was a presidential candidate and a member of the Transvaal Executive Council. Botha mollified them by saying he had not wished for his position, that at thirty-seven he was too young and inexperienced, and depended upon their guidance. Unlike a British commanding officer, surrounded by staff officers and remote from the common soldier, he could not afford to be autocratic, or expect his orders to be obeyed unquestioningly. He obtained agreement by persuasion and cajolment.

He therefore agreed to assist without a formal appointment. The rank and file had no hesitation in responding to his leadership.

Botha lived very humbly. He slept in an ordinary bell tent furnished with a packing case and a chair. He ate the same food as his men. He was accessible to everyone. When an elder Boer entered he would give up his chair and sit on the ground. He had the ability to make individuals feel that they were special, and one by one he induced the elders to speak out, and so participate.

It was not in the Boer nature to take orders willingly. Many had their minds on matters back home. In view of this one of Botha's first acts was to send telegrams to the landrosts [Chief Magistrates] of the eastern districts demanding that they send back any shirkers deserting the commandos. At the same time he created from the many volunteers from Holland, France and Germany a foreign legion divided into separate units according to their nationalities.

For hours Botha discussed tactics with his seniors in the army. He knew that the key point in any conflict was likely to be the hill of Hlangwane, 3616 feet high, on the south side of the Tugela River, dominating the approach to Colenso. Occupying it would be risky, with a river in flood between the mountain and the Boer lines, with no obvious line of retreat. He therefore shrewdly held back until the elders raised the topic. They admitted it was the vital point, and it was agreed that the Boers must hold it in preparation for the British advance. Again, he astutely did not appoint one of the Boer leaders to take the hill, but allowed them to draw lots. The man chosen, Rooi Joshua, gladly took on the task. His men swam the Tugela under cover of darkness and occupied Hlangwane.

BULLER.

Buller, like Botha, had also identified Hlangwane as a key position, and contemplated an attempt to occupy it. Rightly or wrongly, he assumed Botha's men were already there.[115] He wrote:

> "The Hlangwane position was a tempting one to take as a preliminary to crossing the Tugela, but I discarded this idea on the ground that its possession did not in any way assist the crossing…To take Hlangwane would

have been a stiff fight in any case, but, if I took it and then failed at Colenso, I should have had eventually to vacate it."[116]

Buller was right; the Boers had moved up Hlangwane a few hours before the British attack commenced.

The different approaches of the two commanders stood in stark relief: Botha the instinctive, aggressive risk-taker, impatient to advance, to seize fleeting opportunities; Buller, the professional soldier, weighing the risks carefully, reluctant to commit to a move he could not back up.

The naval guns had been brought up to the British lines from Durban, and this heavy artillery commenced pounding the Boer positions at long range. The bombardment came as an unwelcome surprise to the Boers, but much of the fire was wasted as the gunners were guessing at the Boer positions. After two days with few intervals of calm, morale among the Boer irregulars started to drop.

BOTHA.

Botha's identified the pessimism of his men, and his leadership qualities were called upon to hold his force together. Repeatedly he rode along the line, inspecting trenches, encouraging his men to remain firm. He discovered that despite the importance he had placed on holding Hlangwane, the Soutpansberg commando had abandoned it in panic. Botha could not restore the picket without a full meeting of the war committee, which met the following day. They decided to abandon Hlangwane, but Botha refused to accept this decision. He insisted they reconsider. He was helped by a telegram from Kruger that ordered the Boers to hold on to their posts dead or alive. The surrender of vital positions would lead to the surrender of the republic itself. Armed with this order, Botha succeeded in reversing the decision. The Wakkerstroom Commando, a crack outfit loyal to Botha, was ordered to reoccupy it immediately.

The British artillery bombardment was something none of the Boers had experienced before. The intensity and unremitting onslaught came as a great shock to them. Many officers were in favour of abandoning the defence line at the river. Botha had based his defensive strategy on occupying the north bank of the Tugela. He argued that this would deny the British using the north bank to launch an attack on Ladysmith, forcing them to start from further south.

Botha appealed to Paul Kruger for help. Back came the message: "God will fight for you, so give up position under no circumstances."[117] Armed with this telegram, he was able to persuade the Boer elders to hold firm at the Tugela. Due to poor British intelligence, Buller was not aware of the desertion of the occupying force on Hlangwane. Had he been, he could have taken the hill before the Wakkerstroom Commando recovered it. He would have been able to dominate the approach to the Tugela.

That night, December 14, Botha slept on sandbags on the parapet of a gun emplacement. At one o'clock in the morning he was roused by one of the gunners. Across the plain below him the British camp was a blaze of lights. The long-awaited onslaught was about to begin.

4,500 Boers faced 18,000 men commanded by Buller. All Botha's commandos had been pulled back north of the Tugela. Relying upon the British custom of following the railway, he had been sure that the attack would come at Colenso. Throughout the siege it seemed that Botha had an uncanny knack of anticipating Buller's moves. An instinctive tactician, it was almost as though he was reading Buller's mind. Added to this was the fact that from their entrenched positions above the Tugela River the Boers were able to maintain constant watch on British movements to the south. Buller's army was a huge, lumbering host that took time to get moving.

By concentrating his defence at Colenso Botha ran the risk of being outflanked if the British chose to ford the Tugela further to the west, but he was sure Buller would attack head-on. When the British did move he was aware of it. The morning of December 15 dawned bright and clear on an eerily quiet landscape. No movement or sound betrayed the whereabouts of the burghers, ready for action.

Botha wanted to draw Buller across the Tugela before opening fire, as the British would then be trapped with the river at their backs. Two miles back from the river, he watched Buller's advance across the open plain. The railway bridge had been destroyed. Trenches had been dug on the sides and top of the hill overlooking the Tugela where the wagon bridge still remained intact, its approaches guarded. Many of the trenches on the skyline were dummies. He wanted the British to train their guns on unoccupied territory, while he bided his time until the enemy came close. His forces were marshalled very carefully; the success of the Free Staters at Magersfontein and Modder River had been digested and applied. Fifteen-pound French Creusot field guns covered the riverfront from the wagon bridge to an adjacent drift.

Then, to Botha's amazement, believing the Boers to be intimidated by the artillery barrage, the British field artillery under Colonel Long detached itself from the main advance and rushed ahead, positioning twelve field guns a thousand yards from the river. Without waiting for Botha's order, when Long came within rifle range the younger Boers could not hold their fire, and a hail of lead descended upon the British. (Botha, in his journal, strongly refuted that his men had fired prematurely. He maintained that they had obeyed orders to the letter. British observers were adamant; in fact they maintained that had the Boers not opened fire prematurely the British would have been drawn into a trap from which they would have had difficulty escaping). As the Boers used smokeless powder, it was difficult for the watching British commanders to pinpoint the Boer positions. The great Boer Krupp howitzer boomed out from the ridge, and a deadly hail of Mauser fire swept the field.

Time and again Long's men dashed forward in a forlorn attempt to rescue at least some of the guns. The relentless fire from the Boers, whose hunting skills gave them excellent judgment of distance, cut them down. Of the 12 field guns 2 were saved and 10 captured by the Boers.

BULLER.

The British infantry fared little better. Misled by an African guide and lacking reliable maps, Major-General Fitzroy-Hart, commanding the Irish Brigade, advanced into ground where the river described a loop to the north, so that he was bounded on three sides by it. The Dublin Fusiliers attempted to cross the river, but the Boers had dammed it at this point. They expected three feet of water but found there were seven. Instead of attempting to ford the river at the chosen spot - the Bridle Drift, two miles to the west - the Irish were now in range of the Boer guns. Botha gave the order to fire, and the Dubliners and Connaughts felt the full force of the howitzer and Mauser fire. Instead of halting and adopting a defensive position Hart urged his men forward. Four thousand men were crammed into a loop one thousand yards wide.

Discipline disintegrated; no one knew what to do next. Small knots of men would jump up and dash forward, unsupported by their colleagues. The Inniskillings, on the left flank, moved away to the side of the loop and found the Bridle Drift. Although the Boers had dug away part of the drift it was still fordable, and with superiority of numbers it is conceivable the Irish could have stormed the hills. Hart, however, recalled them and abandoned his attempt to cross the river. Buller was left with no option but to call the attack off and retreat to Frere.

BOTHA.

Botha had planned to absorb the assault and then launch a counter-attack from his right flank. Now was the time for that…but nothing happened. Botha's only serious mistake that day was to appoint an elderly Middleburg burgher, Christian Fourie, to command that flank. He refused to budge, and a golden opportunity was missed. Botha wrote later in a telegram to Lukas Meyer:

> "Had the Middleburg and Free State commandos carried out my instruction and crossed the Tugela, we would have taken a thousand prisoners and probably six more guns. Instead they continued to watch the battle, sitting manfully on the mountain."[118]

Botha's despatch to Kruger that evening summed up the day:

> "The God of our fathers has today granted us a brilliant victory. We repulsed the enemy on every side, and from three different points. We allowed them to place twelve of their cannons, amidst a heavy bombardment, right alongside the river, and as soon as their horses were detached, we opened fire upon them with our Mauser musketry, and killed their cannon-service, and shot them so completely out of their position that they only succeeded in rescuing two of their guns. We captured the remaining ten – big, beautiful cannons – together with twelve ammunition wagons, filled to the brim. We

have also made prisoners of war of about 170 of their best men…I think the British losses must have been two thousand men."[119] [The actual number was 1,120: 138 killed, 762 wounded and 220 missing or prisoners].

BULLER.

The loss of the guns was very serious for Buller as he now had only twenty field pieces available. He was shaken to the core. Although he knew that a frontal attack would be difficult, he had not expected the rout that ensued. The British made numerous mistakes as they advanced, and many had paid for them with their lives.

So despondent was he that he decided to call off the attack. It was still only eight o'clock, and only one of the four infantry brigades had entered the fray. To Major-General Hildyard, waiting to lead them into action, Buller said: "I'm afraid Long's guns have got into a terrible mess. I doubt whether we shall be able to attack Colenso today."[120] Critics have judged that he lost his nerve and despaired. His champions aver that he was very angry at Long, and having coolly assessed the risks decided he had to rescue his men at the expense of an advance that day. Unusually for a commanding officer, Buller positioned himself on the battlefield within range of enemy fire. He considered his presence necessary to stiffen the resolve of his soldiers. This action reflected his reputation for not asking his men to do anything he was not prepared to do. There he countermanded an order to supply more ammunition to the guns. Brave attempts to recover Long's abandoned guns were in vain: Botha's sharpshooters were focussed on the plain. Later, critics pointed out that the guns could have been retrieved at dusk with much fewer casualties. Alternatively a fresh supply of ammunition, supported by the naval guns and infantry, could have prolonged the battle.

Further bad news reached Buller: attempts to storm Hlangwane had failed, with heavy losses. The Boers were in position to dominate Colenso. Buller later decided to withdraw his force to Chieveley, near Frere. At no stage had the Ladysmith garrison attempted to help by drawing off some of the Boer fire. Buller feared that the soldiers cooped up in Ladysmith were in worse shape than had previously been reported. He cabled White:

"I tried Colenso yesterday, but failed. The enemy is too strong for my force, except with siege operations, which will take one full month to prepare. Can you last so long? If not, how many days can you give me to take up defensive position, after which I suggest your firing away as much ammunition as you can, and making the best terms you can….Whatever happens recollect to burn your cipher and decipher and code books and any deciphered messages."[121]

At the same time he cabled Lansdowne in London:

"My failure to-day raises a serious question. I do not think I am now strong enough to relieve White. Colenso is a fortress, which I think if not taken in a rush could only be taken by a siege. There is no water within 8 miles of the point of attack, and in this weather that exhausts Infantry. The place is fully entrenched…..My view is that I ought to let Ladysmith go, and occupy good positions for the defence of South Natal, and let time help us…I consider we were in face of 20,000 men to-day. They had the advantage both in arms and in position…I now feel that I cannot say I can relieve Ladymith with my available force, and the best thing I can suggest is that I should occupy defensive positions and fight it out in a country better suited to our tactics."[122]

Much was made at the time, and later, of Buller's apparent decision to abandon the Ladysmith garrison. He argued that he was preparing for all eventualities, and taking from White the responsibility for any surrender should it be necessary. His enemies fastened on the phrase in his cable to Lansdowne: "My view is that I ought to let Ladysmith go." His supporters pointed out that this was a common military term which did not signify abandoning it, but not persisting with attacks, putting the relief to one side for the moment. This interpretation was in keeping with what Buller wrote subsequently. He needed the artillery that had recently arrived in Cape Town. However, it would be a month before the guns could reach him.

In evidence to a the War Commission after the War, Buller was to muse:

"Was it right for me to remain idle during this period? The situation in the Cape Colony was critical: could I do nothing to relieve it? Would it not...be better to attempt Kimberley first and then return to Ladysmith? ...This appeared to me to be the proper military course to adopt. I needed two Divisions: I had but one. I could not employ that Division for the relief of Ladysmith for a month: I could employ it for the relief of Kimberley at once; and at the end of a month another Division would be arriving, if not arrived. There could be little doubt as to the course to be adopted, provided that Ladysmith could hold out for a month. But there was one consideration that made me hesitate. I was personally known to many of the enemy; and I had reason to know that they rated my individual value as a commander more highly perhaps than it deserved. I feared that if I, personally, left Natal, my departure would be more likely than anything else to encourage the Boers to assault Ladysmith in force."[123]

A major problem facing Buller was that he had no idea how many Boers had participated in the battle. They were so well concealed, so cleverly dispersed, that their number could have been 500, 5,000 or 20,000. When the British did get close enough to engage them they simply melted away. Mounted on sturdy horses and ponies, they were extremely mobile. They knew the terrain well, and could disappear quickly. This posed Buller the problem of assessing how large a force he needed to confront them convincingly. Major-General Neville Lyttleton compared the experience at Colenso to action at Omdurman a year earlier, where

"...50,000 fanatics streamed across the open regardless of cover to certain death, while at Colenso I never saw a Boer all day."[124]

In his evidence to the War Commission after the war Buller explained his difficulty in recovering the guns at Colenso, and the nature of the open plain where they were situated. Challenged on the message he had sent back to London, he said that in his opinion it would have been possible for White to break out of Ladysmith. White had provided no support when Buller attacked Colenso. (There is evidence that White thought Buller would move on December 17, and was caught by surprise when the advance commenced on December 15). With the resources at his disposal, and experience of the Boer resistance at Colenso, Buller did not believe he could take Ladysnith for at least a month. He was therefore preparing White for a long siege, and evacuation or surrender if all else failed. He considered that the heliograph to White mentioning surrender might prompt him to attempt a break-out.

To the eyes of the British Government, for a British army to withdraw from the battlefield so precipitously was almost without precedent, and predictably brought a tirade of abuse down on Buller's head. The role of the media, perhaps for the first time in a major war, was important. Dozens of war correspondents had flocked to South Africa, attempting to follow every move. In 1900 the Daily Mail sold nearly a million copies daily. Photographs, and even some cine film, became available to the people in England. Just as today, the correspondents were free with their opinions, looking for an original angle. And just like today, letters from participants were used by the press to show aspects of the conflict from the front.

chapter 9.
WHAT NEXT?

BULLER.

THE DEFEATS in the Cape concerned Buller. He was under pressure from Lansdowne to sack Gatacre and Methuen for their blunders. Yet no suitable alternative commanders were available. His decision to come to Natal now looked questionable. What is not in question is that Buller's cable was to have a disastrous effect upon his reputation and future career. Retribution came swiftly. Within days he was informed that he was to be superseded as Commander-in-Chief in South Africa and relegated to the command in Natal. His successor was not to be Wolseley, whom he would have accepted, but Lord Roberts. As Wolseley's man Buller was not in favour with Roberts. Matters were not helped by the news that Buller had to give Roberts. He cabled: "Your gallant son died today. Condolences. Buller."[125]

When Roberts heard of Buller's advice to White to prepare for surrender he rejected it immediately, and urgently cabled Buller to continue his efforts to relieve Ladysmith. By the time he received it, Buller was feeling less pessimistic about his prospects of taking Ladysmith. He had heard from White, who advised:

> "My suggestion is that you take up strongest position that will enable you to keep touch of enemy and harass

him constantly with artillery fire and in other ways as much as possible. I can make food last for much longer than a month, and will not think of making terms till I am forced to. You may have hit enemy harder than you think. All our native spies report that your artillery fire made a considerable impression on enemy…The losing of 12,000 men here would be a heavy blow to England. We must not yet think of it."[126]

In the month following the disaster at Colenso, Buller's force was raised to 30,000 men as reinforcements poured in. The plain to the south of the Tugela became an amazing tableau. A war correspondent described it thus:

"Before one reaches the firing line he must pass villages of men, camps of men, bivouacs of men, who are feeding, mending, repairing, and burying the men at the 'front.' It is these latter that make the mob of gypsies, which is apparently without head or order or organisation. They stretched across the great basin of the Tugela, like the children of Israel, their camp fires rising to the sky at night like the reflection of great searchlights; by day they swarmed across the plain, like hundreds of moving circus-vans in every direction, with as little obvious intent as herds of buffalo…Hundreds of teams, of sixteen oxen each, crawled like great black water-snakes across the drifts."[127]

Buller had at his disposal ten batteries of artillery, and he was ready to try again to reach Ladysmith. With the reinforcements had come Sir Charles Warren, lately of the Royal Engineers, a sixty year old Lieutenant-Colonel. Warren had spent most of his service on survey work, and never commanded more than a brigade. The War Office told Buller that Warren should take his place should anything happen to him. He was effectively second in command. Buller concurred: "…of the officers here Sir Charles Warren is the best fitted to command in the event of anything happening to me."[128] For this reason Warren was given the task of leading a fresh attack on January 10, 1900.

BOTHA.

On January 6 the Boers, alarmed at the build-up of reinforcements to the south, made a serious attempt to capture Ladysmith. Both sides deployed the maximum forces available to them. The Boers brought back 7,000 men from Colenso and selected a point on the long ridge south of Ladysmith for their attack. Two hills, Wagon Hill and Caesar's Camp, were weakly defended by the British, who had neglected to develop fortifications there. The garrisons consisted of 270 troopers of the Imperial Light Horse and 560 Ist Manchesters with a field battery respectively. Complacent after long days and nights of inaction, these garrisons were taken completely by surprise during the night. The next morning dawned with the Boers in possession of two of the most vital positions in the Ladysmith defences and one of the naval 4.7 inch guns.

Those of the garrisons who escaped being surrounded in the first sally fought back bravely, and a fierce battle commenced, often at very close quarters. Reinforcements were rushed forward from the town, but could not stem the momentum gained by the Boers. Slowly the British were forced back. Artillery on either side could not participate without firing on their own troops. All day the battle raged. The resistance of the British regiments was heroic, but it looked as though the Boers would finally prevail and sweep into Ladysmith.

Then the elements intervened. At 4 p.m. a violent thunderstorm broke. The rain fell in sheets, so that it was impossible to see 100 yards. Huge hailstones fell. The British defenders stood their ground in the deluge, and at last the Boers relinquished the struggle and fell back. The storm lasted nearly twenty-four hours.

When the fury of the storm abated the Devons were pressed forward. Colonel Park gave the order to advance, and with fixed bayonets they charged across a 130-yard wide strip of grass. A hail of deadly Mauser fire met them, but they ran on without faltering. Soon they crested the rise, to find the Boers had retreated. Ladysmith had been saved by the weather, and the bravery of the Devons. British casualties were high: 15 officers and 164 men had been killed, 33 officers and 287 men wounded. On the Boers' side the figures were obscured by their tendency to grossly underestimate their number. The British claimed to have counted 133 Boer dead on Wagon Hill.

Buller needed to consider his next move. By the turn of the year, the

Tugela was in flood, ensuring that no serious attack would be made directly on Colenso. He returned to his original plan of trying to advance to the west of the Boer lines, via Springfield (present-day Winterton) and Potgieter's Drift, which still represented the best crossing place. There he supervised the construction of defences and arranged for reinforcements. He also established a supply base at Springfield, 18 miles north-west of Frere. The Tugela remained fordable despite the raised river level. He did not know it, but at that time a mere 500 to 1,000 Boers faced him. Had he moved swiftly, he could have broken through their lines with ease. But the British army moved cumbersomely, slowly and in the open.

On January 10, a sunny and hot day, the 2nd and 5th Divisions were moved to the heights above Springfield overlooking Potgieter's Drift. The drift was secured, but not without difficulty.

"The passages through the sprites [= spruits; Afrikaans for streams] were nightmares," wrote Atkins. "Carts overturned in the water, wheels off, mules mixed up, fighting and knotting in their harnesses and half drowning, oxen with their heads borne down under water and heaving with all their mighty strength to the opposite bank, a gun or a waggon stuck."[129]

Botha could readily track their movements. He embarked upon a feverish series of visits to all his sectors. It was a ride of three-and-a-half hours to his right flank facing Potgieter's Drift. Botha, now certain of where the next British attack would come, moved to the ridge behind Vaal Krantz and opposite Potgieter's Drift to command the defence. By then he had 4,000 men under his command and four 75mm field guns. An army of 24,000 men with 58 guns opposed him.

Napoleon said that no army carries with it as much baggage as the British. Churchill, observing the advance, seconded this. He wrote:

> "The vast amount of baggage this army takes with it on the march hampers its movements and utterly precludes all possibility of surprising the enemy. I have never before seen even officers accommodated with tents on service....But here today, within striking distance of a mobile enemy whom we wished to circumvent, every private soldier has canvas shelter, and the other arrangements are on an equally elaborate scale. The consequence is that the roads are crowded, drifts are

blocked, marching troops are delayed, and rapidity of movement is out of the question. Meanwhile the enemy completes the fortification of his positions and the cost of capturing them rises. It is poor economy to let a soldier live well for three days at the price of killing him on the fourth."[130]

In contrast the Boers slept in the open, carried strips of dried, salted beef (called biltong), bags of biscuits and two hundred rounds of ammunition. Consequently a Boer could cover in one day the distance it took the British three days to complete. It was hence not surprising that a force of 4,000 Boers could outmanoeuvre the entire British army.

BULLER.

Lord Dundonald led his cavalry, the South African Light Horse (Buller's beloved Frontier Light Horse) forward across the Tugela River in advance of the army. He found empty farms... and not a trace of the enemy. Before him lay Spearman's Hill, dominating Potgier's Drift. With 700 troopers he scaled the hill, reaching the summit as night fell. There he found an elaborate system of trenches dug by the Boers, but still no sign of the enemy. He signalled his success to Buller, asking him for immediate support. He felt very exposed so far in advance with such a small force. Buller moved up to the foot of the hill and positioned his naval guns on the hill. Humour among the soldiers ran:

> "What are we showing ourselves and our guns here for?" Answer: "To give the enemy plenty of time to get ready."[131]

General Warren was given a free hand to proceed as he judged best once he was north of the Tugela. 9,000 men remained at Potgieter's Drift, under the command of General Neville Lyttleton, supported by two 4.7 inch naval guns and six 15-pounders. Warren made extremely slow progress, observed all the while by the Boers. He did not start to cross the Tugela until January 17, and only moved forward towards the range of hills on January 20. Churchill wrote:

> "It was not possible to stand unmoved and watch the

ceaseless living stream – miles of stern-looking men, marching in fours so quickly that they often had to run to keep up, of artillery, ammunition columns, supply columns baggage, slaughter-cattle, thirty great pontoons, white-hooded, red-crossed ambulance waggons, all the accessories of an army hurrying forward under cover of night – and before them a guiding star, the red gleam of war."[132]

Progress was laborious and painfully slow. Warren would not advance without his baggage train and support services. The Tugela River was in full spate, and the crossing was difficult. Nearly 500 ox and mule waggons, ambulances, artillery, and ammunition were sent over. This crossing took the best part of two days.

All this time the Boers sat and watched. They could be clearly seen preparing lines of entrenched defences on the hills ahead. They fired virtually no shots at the British, content to wait and defend. Any thought of a surprise attack vanished as the ponderous army lumbered forward. Attempts to draw the Boers into firing so that their defence lines and gun placements could be pinpointed failed. Cannily Botha instructed them to stay inactive and watchful.

On January 18, 1900, the Mounted Brigade under Lord Dundonald moved along the Acton Homes road. At midday they observed a small force of Boers moving in the same direction. Major Graham of the Natal Carbineers was given permission to ambush them. Taking 350 men in a combined force of the Imperial Light Horse, King's Royal Rifles' Mounted Infantry and the Natal Carbineers he moved forward rapidly, unobserved, and took up a position commanding the road. The Boers received a sustained volley of rifle fire at 300 yards. Within a short time the party was surrounded and forced to surrender. Twenty-four unwounded Boers were made prisoner and eight badly wounded attended to. Between 25 and 30 Boers were killed. The wounded were well tended to with blankets pillows, water and biscuits.

Warren, alarmed at the distance separating his only mounted force from the main body, recalled Dundonald. During the night of the 19th/20th he instructed one force to move to the extreme left and challenge the positions of the Boers to the north-east of Spion Kop. Although Three Tree Hill and Bastion Hill were taken, they could not be held. From the surrounding hills, many higher than the ones they had captured, came a murderous and accurate fire, pouring in on the British from all sides.

Two Generals

Warren recalled the troops. From the time of crossing the Tugela the British had suffered 34 killed and 293 wounded.

Further attempts were made to push the Boers back. General Lyttleton made a direct attack on the Boer trenches that lined the eastern slope of Spion Kop and the southern slope of Brakfontein. He was supported by fire from howitzers and naval guns. They encountered stiff resistance and were slowly forced back. Twenty men were lost. Unlike the Boers and local volunteers, who were well versed in using available cover and camouflage, the British did not conceal themselves and suffered accordingly. It was evident that the laborious build-up of the British had enabled Botha to prepare his defences well. Each row of trenches concealed another row behind it, between 400 and 1,000 yards away, and then another and even a fourth. So any success in breaching the first line of defence would simply encounter others. Frontal assault was not practical; it would lead to heavy losses.

What Buller planned, however, was to attract the Boers' attention to his position and then strike elsewhere. He was learning from past mistakes, and aware that the Boers were observing his every move. Five miles west of Potgieter's Drift were two fords known as Trikardt's Drift and Wagon Drift. Roads to these ran from Springfield, and could not be seen by the Boers due to the height of the south bank of the Tugela. Between Potgieter's Drift and Ladysmith, twelve miles away, lay one ridge of hills, the Tabanyama, barring progress. A picket of only 500 Free Staters and Pretoria burghers were positioned there. Warren's force numbered 15,000 men and 36 guns. If the range could be taken Ladysmith would lie open before them.

On January 18 Lord Dundonald's cavalry took up a strong position on the extreme right of the Boers. However, Warren believed that concealed in the hills were thousands of Boers in well-entrenched positions. He had no intention of advancing until his force was fully assembled on the north bank of the Tugela. This took three days. The Boers, watching these leisurely preparations, were able to dig in on Tabanyama, a three-mile long plateau with a number of spurs projecting southwards. Warren made a series of ineffectual attacks on the hill before turning his attention to alternatives. The Boers deployed their defence accordingly, extending their line to the right and occupying strong, entrenched positions between the two highest hills in the range, Vaal Krantz and Spion Kop. Buller could see that a direct advance from Potgieter's Drift was not tenable, as the route would take his force between the heights of Vaal Krantz and Doorn Kop in the east and Spion Kop in the west, where they would be vulnerable to the Boer guns and snipers.

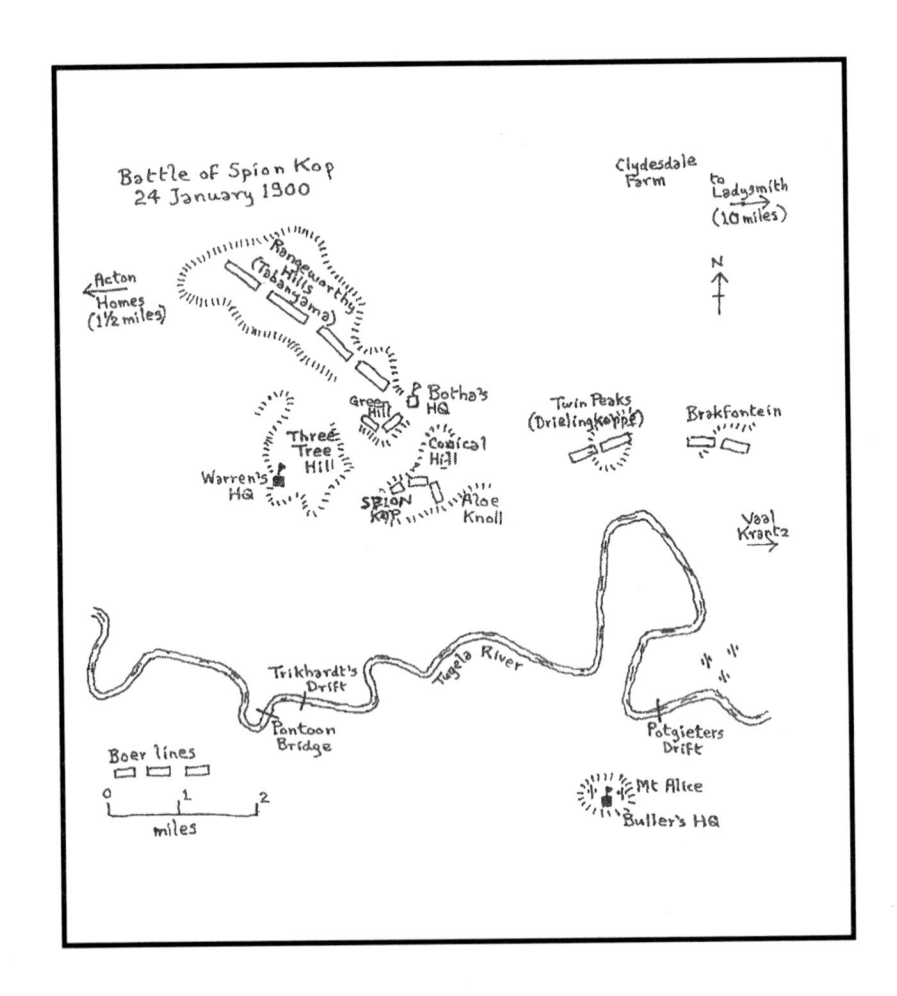

chapter 10.
SPION KOP.

BULLER.

WARREN TURNED his attention to the south-west of Tabanyama. Spion Kop was the highest peak in the range, a flat-topped hill 1,470 feet above the Tugela River. Although the hill formed part of the Boer defensive line Botha was reluctant to place too many men on the summit as it was subjected to constant bombardment from Buller's naval guns on Mount Alice to the south. A token sentry guard was posted.

Buller watched Warren's movements from his headquarters on Mount Alice with some impatience. It had taken five days from the initial crossing of the river to prepare for the assault on Spion Kop. Still Buller did not interfere. Leo Amery in The Times described him as being like an impartial umpire at manoeuvres. Fatally, he stood aside and let Warren direct operations. This was a most unusual step to take, given that the distance between Buller's field headquarters and Warren was no more than eight miles.

Warren, in a valley two miles west of Spion Kop could not see the top of the hill, and had very sketchy communications with his front line. Buller on the other hand was able to watch most of what was happening from his observation post. Why did he not retain command? Warren had been imposed upon him. He came with a high reputation for operations in South Africa. Perhaps Buller's confidence had been shattered by the defeat at Colenso. Nevertheless the tardiness with which Warren went about his manoeuvres gave Buller ample opportunities to intervene and take direction.

Buller rode over to consult with Warren on January 22nd. Warren informed him that he proposed to demoralize the Boers with three or four days' continuous shelling. Buller's patience finally gave out. He pointed out the amount of time that had elapsed during which Warren had achieved nothing. Either he attacked now or he would withdraw the force back behind the Tugela River. Buller recommended a flanking movement around Spion Kop, but left the decision to Warren.

Buller wanted his force to skirt Spion Kop to the west and attempt to break through to Ladysmith via the Rangeworthy Hills. Warren countered that he could not establish an artillery position, as he was under constant threat from the Boers. Buller would not impose a decision on Warren. Instead of attempting to outflank the Boers, which he considered too risky, Warren decided to take Spion Kop and then use his artillery to rout the Boers gathered on the plain before Ladysmith. The sides of Spion Kop were so precipitous that he reckoned the Boers would not expect him to attack.

By then the number of Boers preparing to defend the western approaches to Ladysmith had been increased from some 600 to reportedly 7,000. This was an exaggeration, but the Boer force close to Spion Kop certainly numbered several thousand, although there were a mere 50 burghers, part of the commando from Vryheid, and German volunteers on the summit.

On January 23, on a pitch-black night the British general Woodgate led the Lancashire Brigade up the loose scree on the side of Spion Kop. Lieutenant-Colonel Thorneycroft commanding the Mounted Infantry, some "Uitlanders" and half a company of engineers accompanied them. Progress was slow, due to concern that they would lose their way, but by daybreak the summit had been reached without challenge from the Boers. Thick mist blanketed the top, and the leaders ran into a Boer picket, which was quickly despatched. One of the sappers began to tape out a curved, three hundred yard line of trenches on what seemed the forward crest of the summit. It seemed that they had secured Spion Kop. However, inadequate maps gave the British no inkling of what was to follow.

BOTHA.

The Boer picket had fled back to Botha's tent, a mile and a quarter to the north. Their initial reaction was to panic, believing this to be part of a widespread breakthrough. Botha took the news calmly. The Boers would have to take the hill back. He knew it was the key to unlocking the door to Ladysmith. By the force of his personality he rallied his men. He insisted the hill must be held at all costs. Although Spion Kop stood out as the highest of the hills, other hills in the vicinity were of comparable height.

Botha's artillery was well positioned on several of these hills, and now five field guns and two pom-poms started to pour a deadly fire onto the force occupying a plateau no more than four hundred yards wide. As the mist cleared the British could see that they were occupying only one of three positions at the summit, which seemed to stretch interminably back to the north-east. Due to the steepness of the northern slope, any Boer advance would not be seen from where they were entrenched. The plateau could only be controlled from the northern summit. Instead of pushing on to occupy the rest of the summit, the British halted. Perhaps the climb had exhausted them. The trenches they had dug in the stony ground were too shallow to provide adequate protection.

Under cover of the artillery bombardment, the Boers' Carolina Commando, ninety strong, started to climb Spion Kop from the Boer side. The Pretoria Commando soon joined them there. Once the sun broke out of the mist, a Boer heliographer stationed below the summit was able to signal back to Botha a situation report. Armed with the whereabouts of the British on the summit, Botha's artillery was able to mount a deadly fire on their lines. Two 75mm Creusot field guns, a 75mm Krupp field gun and a pom-pom were located on Tabanyama, while a 75mm Krupp gun was situated close to Botha's position on a small hill close to Spion Kop. Two further guns on the ridges to the east of Spion Kop meant that a raking cross-fire on the British could be maintained. Churchill counted shells falling on the summit at the rate of seven per minute. The British on the crest were driven back to their trenches. Much of the fighting was hand-to-hand, and both sides sustained heavy losses.

Throughout the day Botha sent up regular reinforcements: Krugersdorpers, German volunteers and Johannesburgers. The fight lasted most of the day, with the opponents often no more than a couple of hundred yards apart. The top commanders on the British side, unlike Botha, did not venture onto the hill, and only had a very hazy idea of what was occurring there. No attempt was made to send artillery or reinforcements up the steep slope, and supplies of ammunition and water were sparse. Some time before 10 a.m. General Woodgate received a mortal shot in his eye.

As ever John Atkins, correspondent for the Manchester Guardian, recorded the assault graphically. Watching from below, he wrote:

> "I saw three shells strike a certain trench within a minute. Each struck it full in the face, and the brown dust rose and drifted away with the white smoke. The trench was toothed against the sky like a saw – made, I supposed, of sharp rocks built into a rampart. Another shell struck it, and then – heavens! – the trench rose up and moved forward. The trench was men; the teeth against the sky were men. They ran forward bending their bodies into a curve, as men do when they run under a heavy fire; they looked like a cornfield with a heavy wind sweeping over it from behind….They flickered up, fleeted rapidly and silently across the sky, and flickered down into the rocks without the appearance of either a substantial beginning or end to the movement."[133]

BULLER.

The news of Woodgate's death caused Warren to order up General Coke with fresh troops from the 2nd Middlesex, 2nd Dorsetshires and Imperial Light Infantry. Coke was the most senior officer in the field, but was lame due to an old wound. Buller, hearing of the order, was uneasy. He said to Warren:

> "Unless you put some really good, hard-fighting man in command on the top, you will lose the hill. I suggest Thorneycroft."[134]

Thorneycroft was already there, and had distinguished himself in the confrontation. Warren accepted the suggestion, and appointed

Thorneycroft to command. He neglected to inform Coke of the change however, so there were now two commanders on the hill.

Throughout the day the battle ebbed and flowed. Heavy artillery fire from the Boers rained down on the British trenches, and the Boer infantry closed to less than one hundred yards under its cover. Repeatedly they were forced back by desperate bayonet charges. The anxious observers below in the valley received no news of the battle until late in the afternoon, when General Coke reported that unless the British artillery could silence the Boer guns it would be impossible to endure another day on the summit. Churchill, having made his way to the top, verified this:

> "Streams of wounded met us and obstructed our path. ....There was, moreover, a small but steady leakage of unwounded men of all corps. Some of these cursed and swore. Others were utterly exhausted, and fell on the hill-side in stupor. Others again, seemed drunk, though they had had no liquor....We were so profoundly impressed by the spectacle and the situation that we resolved to go and tell Sir Charles Warren what we had seen....One thing was quite clear – unless good and efficient cover could be made during the night, and unless guns could be dragged to the summit of the hill to match the Boer artillery, the infantry could not, perhaps would not, endure another day. The human machine will not stand certain strains for long."[135]

Accordingly Warren instructed Coke to withdraw all but two battalions to the shelter of the southern slope and come down to confer with him. Coke left his second in command, Colonel Hill, in charge, thus further confusing the command structure at the top.

BOTHA.

Both sides had taken such heavy losses, and were so exhausted that at nightfall unbeknown to each other, they both withdrew from the hill. General Schalk Burgher sent Botha advice that further resistance was futile as the Boers could no longer hold the line. Botha pleaded with him: "Let us fight and die together, but, brother, please do not us yield an inch to the English."[136]

Colonel Thorneycroft assessed that his men could not hold the hill. Their losses were considerable; they were now exhausted. Although instructed to hold on to the last, he made the decision to withdraw. No staff officer had visited the summit during the day. They were only dimly aware of the situation there. Thus as reinforcements were preparing to climb the hill the bloodied and exhausted warriors streamed back down.

Deneys Reitz, present on the hill, described what happened next:

> "When we reached the bottom most of the horses were gone, the men who had retired having taken their mounts and ridden away....When we reached the laager we found everything in a state of chaos. The wagons were being hurriedly packed, and the entire Carolina commando was making ready to retire...Fortunately.... there came the sound of galloping hoofs, and a man rode into our midst who shouted for them to halt. I could not see his face in the dark, but word went round that it was Louis Botha...He addressed the men from the saddle, telling them of the shame that would be theirs if they deserted their posts in this hour of danger; and so eloquent was his appeal that in a few minutes the men were filing off into the dark to reoccupy their positions...I believe that he spent the rest of the night riding from commando to commando exhorting and threatening, until he persuaded the men to return to the line, thus averting a great disaster."[137]

The Carolina men had borne the brunt of the morning action, yet responded well to Botha. Not so everyone. Schalk Burgher and his Lydenberg commando had had enough, and galloped away across the plain. With them went their Krupp field gun and pom-pom. Watchers at Ladysmith could see the Boers streaming back from the hill and riding away. Yet inexplicably White failed to inform Buller and Warren, who remained ignorant of the opportunity presented to them to occupy the hill.

Fortunately, Botha could call upon the Utrecht burghers, stationed on an adjoining hill, to take the central position previously occupied by Burgher. He sent a message to Kruger:

> "The bravery and courage of our burghers I cannot praise too highly…The artillery has worked beautifully and if the enemy does not retreat during the night, the fight will be continued tomorrow."[138]

Botha spent the night watching Spion Kop, waiting for the British to appear over the crest and breach his thin line of defenders. The garrison at Ladysmith could have seized this moment to harry the Boers from the rear. The men there, weakened by hunger and dispirited, could only watch at a distance. Botha's secretary, Sandberg, said in his memoirs that he and Botha were so tired that they dozed off at their desks.

BULLER.

The tardiness that had marked Warren's advance previously now proved disastrous. Confusion and muddle, with nobody quite knowing who was in command, led to inaction. Soon after dawn on the following morning, Jan Kemp, commanding the Krugersdorpers on the slope of the hill, looked up and could see no one on the summit. Reacting more quickly than the British, the Krugersdorpers scrambled up the steep slope and reoccupied the summit. They held their rifles above their heads and waved their hats to their comrades below. Soon hundreds of burghers were scaling the hill. The Boers had won the epic battle of Spion Kop. The British had lost 1,500 men killed, wounded or captured, to 335 by the Boers.

When Buller heard the news of the withdrawal from Spion Kop he immediately decided to take direct command. He had already considered replacing Warren as a result of his unsatisfactory direction of the attack prior to Spion Kop, but had decided against it:

> "Had he been sent out to me on the same footing as any other officer I should not have hesitated – or, rather, I should never have entrusted him with this command at all. But he had been sent out to me as my appointed second in command.…General Warren was evidently not carrying out the orders which he had received from

> me....I saw, for my own part, that the advantages for which I had hoped from his crossing had been let slip, and that my own plan of operation had been hopelessly wrecked. It was open to me to take over his command myself, but in that case I should not be able to direct the most important part and the most critical part of the whole movement, namely the flank attack from Potgieter's."[139]

In later reports Buller maintained that if he had assumed command and subsequently been shot Warren, as second in command would have been discredited and with diminished authority.

Buller had no alternative but to pull his force back over the Tugela.

Winston Churchill, reporting as a journalist from the battlefield, captured the moment, portraying Buller in a very positive light:

> "He arrived on the field calm, cheerful, inscrutable as ever, rode hither and thither with a weary Staff and a huge notebook, gripped the whole business in his strong hands, and so shook it into shape that we crossed the river in safety, comfort, and good order, with most remarkable mechanical precision, and without the loss of a single man or a pound of stores...this withdrawal showed that this force possesses both a leader and machinery of organization, and it is this, and this alone, that has preserved our confidence."[140]

He also commented on the significance of the retreat and on Buller's leadership:

> "A successful retreat is a poor thing for a relieving army to boast of when their gallant friends are hard pressed and worn out...... We believe that Buller gauged the capacity of one subordinate at Colenso, of another at Spion Kop, and that now he will do things himself, as he was meant to do. I know not why he has waited so long...But the army believes that this is all over now, and that for the future Buller will trust no one but himself in great matters; and it is because they believe this that the soldiers are looking forward with confidence and

eagerness to the third and last attempt – for the sands of Ladysmith have run down very low – to shatter the Boer lines."[141]

Clearly Churchill's opinion of Buller had risen after observing him in the field. In his book, "My Early Years" he wrote of Buller:
"He was a characteristic British personality. He looked stolid. He said little and what he said was obscure."

General Roberts, hearing of the defeat, sent a despatch to London full of recriminations. He approved of Buller's original plan to outflank the Boers and believed it would have succeeded if properly executed. He did though blame Buller for his "disinclination to assert his authority;" Warren for his "errors of judgment" and "want of administrative capacity" and for not visiting the summit; and Thorneycroft for his "unwarrantable and needless assumption of responsibility." He thus ignored Warren's directive appointing Thorneycroft to command the summit force.

Roberts counselled Buller against a further advance. His confidence in the British effort to relieve Ladysmith was at rock bottom. He advised Buller to abandon the idea of relieving Ladysmith for the time being and adopt a defensive stance. Wolseley and the War Office, appalled at the reverses suffered by Buller, went further. They actually suggested that Buller should permanently abandon Ladysmith. (This advice was later withdrawn). White and any able-bodied men left in Ladysmith should be ordered to cut their way out. Stores should be blown up and those left behind should surrender.

Roberts advised Buller that by February 28 he expected to be in Bloemfontein, thus relieving pressure on Natal. Buller rejected the advice to go onto the defensive or to abandon Ladysmith. He did not believe any success Roberts had would lessen the resistance he was facing: these were Transvalers, intent on defending their homeland to the death, while Roberts was fighting Free Staters. The Transvalers had shown that they were not prepared to move into the Orange Free State in support of their compatriots. Buller would continue to face the full might of the Transvaal burghers. Moreover, the news from White in Ladysmith was concerning. A fifth of his force were ill or injured and they were in desperate straits. Buller wrote:

> "On the 27th [January], Sir George White informed me that if I tried again and failed, Ladysmith was

doomed. He could feed the men for another month, but not the horses, and without guns his force could do nothing."[142]

Consequently Buller decided on a new attack, this time along another track leading to Ladysmith past Vaal Krantz. He had received 2,400 new drafts from England, more than replacing the losses at Colenso and Spion Kop. In addition two 5-inch siege guns and a 6-inch naval gun were sent up from Durban. He now had 78 guns available, ready for the fresh assault. Vaal Krantz was part of a range of kopjes on the north bank of the Tugela, a few miles east of Spion Kop. The mountain barrier here was narrower than elsewhere. They were on a more direct route to Ladysmith, and if they could be taken, the way would be open to relieve the garrison.

Buller was aware that Boer defences would be strong for that reason, but what he did not know was that the conflict at Spion Kop affected his adversary almost as much as his army. Three of the Boer commanders – Schalk Burgher, Joubert and A.P. Cronje – were ill and had left the front. Many of the burghers, conscious that they were neglecting their farms, had drifted off home. Botha was exhausted; he needed a rest. He also went home. At most there were 4,000 Boers between Buller and Ladysmith.

Botha did not rest for long. At the end of January he visited Pretoria for discussions on strategy. General Joubert soon recalled him urgently, as the British prepared for a new offensive. He reached the Boer defences the day after the British advance commenced.

Certain history books dismiss the battle for Vaal Krantz as a minor skirmish. There is a case to be made for arguing that it was of huge significance. Unaware that a frontal attack in numbers might succeed, Buller had formed a subtle plan. Whilst the 4th Brigade advanced on Vaal Krantz another brigade would make a move north-west towards a kopje called Brakfontein in order to distract the Boers. Two further brigades would stand in readiness to back up the 4th. On February 5, 1900, a brigade of infantry backed by artillery made a move towards Brakfontein, manoeuvring smartly but taking care not to engage the enemy. Some shots were fired on both sides and one soldier killed. This was merely a diversion. Soon British field guns opened up on Vaal Krantz and a pontoon bridge was thrown across the Tugela. The Durham Light

Infantry swarmed across and, led by General Lyttleton, stormed the hill. The British occupied Vaal Krantz by four in the afternoon.

Once again failure by the British to provide an effective intelligence service, or prepare for the campaign with appropriate maps of the area proved their undoing. Instead of an isolated summit, Vaal Krantz turned out to be linked to a spur surrounded by other hills unseen from Colenso. Thus the British infantry were subjected to withering artillery fire, and were unable to establish a position in which the guns they hoped to bring to the top could be located. Attempts by the British artillery to silence the Boer barrage failed. The Boers were able to conceal their heavy guns. Firing smokeless shells, they could not be accurately located.

General Lyttleton, having led his men to the summit of Vaal Krantz, looked for reinforcements that were supposed to follow. Instead he received an order from Buller to withdraw. As the commander in the field he ignored the order, arguing that Buller was unaware of the extent of his success. Buller did not insist upon him retreating, but he did not urge him forward either. Lyttleton and his men were left sitting on the crest of the ridge for a day and a half while the Boers shelled them with 100 pound shells from a large Creusot gun on top of a neighbouring hill, Doornkloof.

Buller contacted Roberts, asking for instructions.

> "After fighting all day yesterday, though with but small loss, I have pierced the enemy's line, and hold a hill which divides their position, and will, if I can advance, give me access to the Ladysmith plain, when I should be ten miles from White, with but one place for the enemy to stand between us. But to get my artillery and supplies on to the plain, I must drive back the enemy either to my right or on my left. It is an operation which will cost from 2,000 to 3,000 men; and I am not confident, though hopeful, I can do it. The question is how would such a loss affect your plans, and do you think the chance of the relief of Ladysmith worth the risk? It is the only possible way to relieve White; if I give up this chance I know no other."[143]

Roberts replied:

> "Ladysmith must be relieved, even at the cost you

anticipate. I would certainly persevere, and my hope is that the enemy will be so severely punished as to enable White's garrison to be withdrawn without great difficulty."[144]

Buller, still unable to make up his mind, held a council of war with his senior offices, who agreed with him that it would be futile to press on. One officer – Hart – disagreed, and later criticised Buller publicly for calling the advance on Vaal Krantz back. This was to provoke controversy about Buller's tactics and stomach for the fight, and led to his nickname "Sir Reverse Buller." Whether this was justified depends on one's assessment of the very difficult task facing him over broken terrain, and the performance of some of his support staff.

Buller telegraphed Roberts informing him of the decision, saying that the Boer positions in front of Vaal Krantz were too strong (although he only had a hazy idea of the topography and even less idea of how many of the enemy there were). A golden opportunity to break through to Ladysmith was thus missed. The troops duly fell back to Chieveley. By February 11 Buller's entire army was congregated around Chieveley, with only a small force guarding the Tugela crossings. Springfield bridge was destroyed to protect the British flank.

A Boer summed up the enemy view of the British:

"We admit that the British soldiers are the best in the world, and your regimental officers the bravest, but – we rely on your Generals."[145]

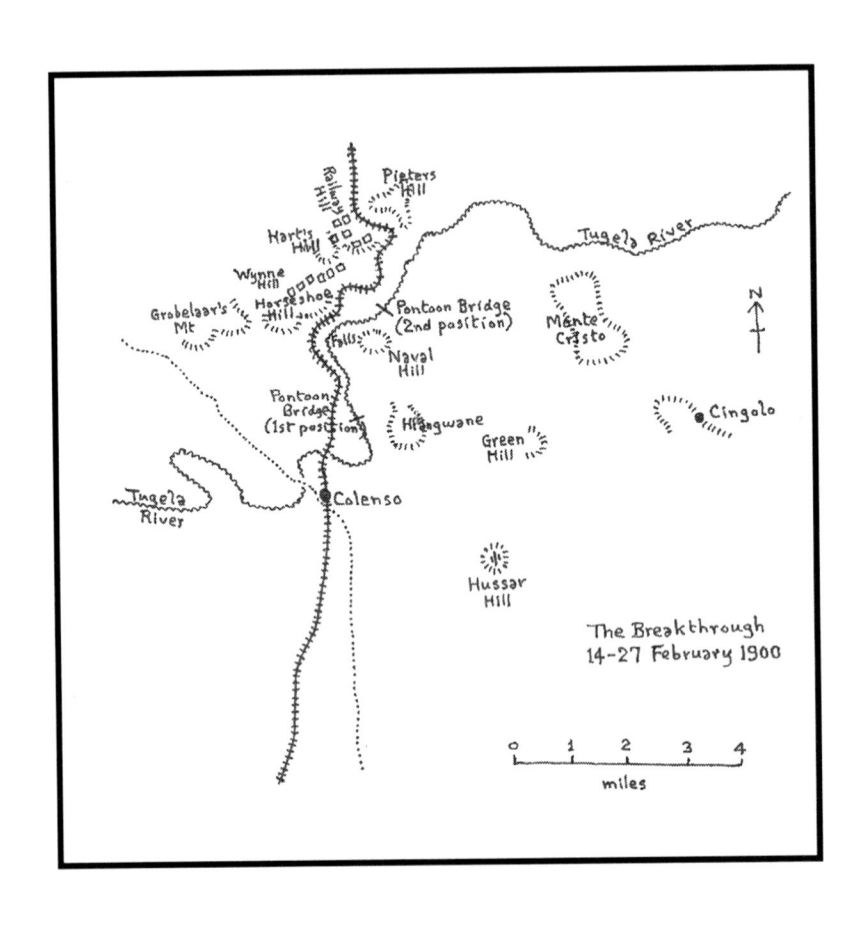

chapter 11.
LADYSMITH IS RELIEVED.

BULLER.

ANOTHER APPROACH to Ladysmith needed to be found. But where? Hlangwane, Warren felt, was the obvious alternative. They had tried a frontal attack on Colenso, then an approach along the western flank. Both had failed. The east was the only course left to them. Infighting broke out among the generals. One, Lyttleton, who had been close to Buller, wrote to his wife:

> "I have lost all confidence in Buller as a General and am sure he has himself."[146]

His men had not lost confidence. Many of the officers remained loyal. Major Henry Wilson, Lyttleton's brigade major, supported Buller's decision. He believed that to have pressed on from Vaal Krantz would have ended in disaster. He conceded it might have been possible to punch a hole in the Boer defences, but he estimated that they were facing between 8,000 and 12,000 well-entrenched defenders in natural fortresses, and ultimate success was far from guaranteed. Failure to reach Ladysmith would have resulted in major casualties. In future years, when the relief of Ladysmith was debated and Buller's performance assessed, what happened at Vaal Krantz was to feature prominently.

There followed an intense exchange between Buller and Roberts.

Buller made a strong plea for reinforcements. He argued that the relief of Ladysmith was now urgent, as White could not hold out for much longer. This could only be achieved with a much larger force than he had at his disposal. He explained to Roberts that he had expected some of the men pouring into Cape Town from overseas to augment his army, but they had been diverted to the Free State. Roberts expected to be in Bloemfontein by February 28, and reasoned that some of the Boers in Natal would be redirected to the Free State's defence. He wrote to Buller on February 10:

> "To send you large reinforcements now would entail abandonment of plan of operations. I must therefore request that, while maintaining bold front, you will act strictly on the defensive until I have time to see whether operations I am undertaking will produce effect I hope for. The repeated loss of men on Tugela River without satisfactory results is that which our small army cannot afford."[147]

Buller's reply was spirited:

> "...do not tell me to remain on the defensive. To do that means to leave the whole Boer force free to attack Ladysmith."[148]

Roberts responded with an insult. Knowing Buller had taken direct command from Warren, he cabled:

> "I should like to have the view of your second in command on this question, which is one of such urgent importance to our position in South Africa that it is very necessary I should know whether Sir Charles Warren shares your views."[149]

Warren signalled that he did indeed concur with Buller.

Buller turned his attention to Hlangwane. As we have seen, at the outset of the confrontation Botha had identified the hill as crucial to the defence of Ladysmith, and had positioned one of his crack commandos on the top. The Tugela River cut a six mile gorge through the hills to the east of Colenso, making it difficult for the Boers to move reinforcements rapidly to support the Hlangwane defenders. Buller could see that control of Hlangwane would give him an excellent protected route to Ladysmith. Hlangwane was only five hundred feet high, overlooked by ridges to the east. It was pitted with ravines and covered in thorn bushes. This had deterred the British from attacking it previously.

Now Buller took a different tack. Instead of approaching the stronghold head-on, he adapted his tactics to those applied by the Boers. To the south-east of Hlangwane lay a series of ridges, each higher than Hlangwane, occupied by the Boers. He would attack the positions held by the enemy on the ridges with sharp, concentrated forays supported by artillery fire. His aim was to erode the Boer defences bit by bit before attempting the major prize. He had 25,000 men at his disposal and 70 guns. He also had 22 machine guns. The Boers had a mere 8 guns.

Buller began his advance by moving his guns forward in tandem with the infantry as each target was attacked. The guns fired closely in front of the infantry, clearing the way for them. With temperatures exceeding 100 degrees fahrenheit in the shade, progress was slow. Ever mindful of his troops' welfare, Buller refused to push them too hard. Water had to be brought forward from Frere by ox-wagon in 200-gallon tanks, each just enough to fill a single battalion's water bottles. On February 14, having defended Hussar Hill, four miles north of Chieveley during the day, the Boers fell back in the evening. They remained defensively minded, unwilling to take risks by extending their lines.

A group of Dundonald's irregulars, mainly colonial volunteers but including the South African Light Horse rushed forward up the hill. With them went Winston Churchill, now a regular cavalry officer. There followed a race to the summit as the Boers, too late, realised their error. The colonials won the race and occupied Hussar Hill. Once entrenchments were built, powerful artillery was positioned on the hill. The naval 12-pounders were protected by sandbags; the howitzers and field guns stood in the open. From Hussar Hill the troops looked out across the Gomba valley to Cingolo.

On February 15 Dundonald moved on to Cingolo. The summer heat was stifling. A fierce artillery duel developed, the smokeless shells used by the Boers again making it difficult for the British to locate their guns. Some ground was won as the British infantry inched forward under the protection of the field guns.

On the 17th the push forward began in earnest. Dundonald's men started a sweep ten miles to the east using the trees and boulders as cover. They scaled the steep side of Cingolo and reached the summit at the southern end by 11 a.m. There they encountered 100 Boers who were forced back along the ridge. This encouraged other British brigades to close on the hill from other directions. By mid-afternoon there remained no Boers on Cingolo. From the summit Ladysmith could clearly be seen in the distance.

The next major prize for the British was the mountain Monte Cristo, connected to Cingolo by a narrow neck of land. At 2,500 feet Monte Cristo was the highest point in the area, and possession would make the defence of nearby Hlangwane untenable. Botha had been ill, and in his absence Lukas Meyer had found command of the widespread Boer defence difficult. Botha returned to Colenso on February 17 and set about rescuing what he could of the situation. On February 18 Hildyard led his 2nd Brigade, the West Yorks, the East Surrey and the Queen's up a steep slope to the summit. Churchill reported:

> "The musketry swelled into a constant crackle like the noise of a good fire roaring up the chimney, but in spite of more than 100 casualties, the advance never checked for an instant. And by half-past ten o'clock the bayonets of the attacking infantry began to glitter among the trees of the summit...I have never seen an enemy leave the field in such a hurry as did these valiant Boers."[150]

Churchill described the moment:

> "From the captured ridge we could look right down into Ladysmith....Only eight miles away stood the poor little persecuted town, with whose fate is wrapped up the honour of the Empire, and for whose sake so many hundred good soldiers have given life or limb – a twenty-acre patch of tin houses and blue gum trees, but famous to the uttermost ends of the earth."[151]

The Boers still held Hlangwane, and Botha based his defence on a line from the mountain to the river crossing at Colenso, defending the north bank of the Tugela. Unfortunately he was informed that the rearguard on Hlangwane had decided to withdraw across the river.

The next day the British captured Hlangwane, exposed on the flank by the occupation of Monte Cristo. The Boers deserted their positions, leaving all their equipment on the hill. The garrison in Ladysmith watched the steady advance. With rising expectations they saw British soldiers standing on the summit of Monte Cristo, then Hlangwane. The installation by the British of heavy guns on the summit opened the way to Colenso. On Monday, February 19, two infantry companies marched into Colenso unopposed, and within hours the railway link south had been restored.

Surgeon Blake-Knox described what he found on the hills captured:

> "The Boer trenches...were a marvellous example of the ingenuity, cunning and patience of the enemy with which we had to deal. Looking at the entrenchments from the British side, even with a powerful telescope, one would have been deceived, so artfully were they concealed by a facing of bushes or sods, so well put together and matching the surrounding ground that it was almost impossible to detect any irregularity of surface."[152]

Originally Buller had planned a wide easterly sweep towards Ladysmith. He reasoned that to attack from Colenso would involve tough, head-on fighting again. The main road to Ladysmith was flanked by high hills offering natural defence lines which the Boers were bound to occupy. White informed Buller that the main Boer position was at Pieters Hill, five miles north of Colenso, the last defensive position on the downhill run into Ladysmith. Buller's intelligence officer reported that although on paper the easterly sweep looked the easier approach, the veld was in fact broken country with deep gorges through which it would be nearly impossible to drag the guns.

Good news came that Roberts, with an overwhelming force, had relieved Kimberley and marched on to Bloemfontein. The Boer commander, Cronje, had been soundly defeated, and had suffered major casualties. As a consequence, many of the Free Staters were leaving the Ladysmith area to rally to the aid of their compatriots around Bloemfontein. Buller considered that he may be facing a much smaller rearguard than he had envisaged.

Ladysmith had been under siege for over one hundred days. Buller was conscious that a combination of illness and lack of rations was taking its toll on the garrison. He was not sure White could hold out much longer. There was cause to make haste with the final assault.

On February 22 the British again crossed the Tugela two miles north of Colenso by pontoon bridge. Although the Free Staters had departed, fresh Transvalers were arriving to take their place, and the British faced strong opposition. Some 4,000 to 5,000 Boers were now deployed on a 6-mile front from the heights of Colenso to Pieter's Hill. Botha commanded the right flank and Lukas Meyer the left.

Churchill wrote:

> "Sir Redvers Buller, however, still believing he had only a rearguard in front of him, was determined to persevere. It is, perhaps, his strongest characteristic obstinately to pursue his plan in spite of all advice, in spite, too, of his horror of bloodshed, until himself convinced that it is impracticable. The moment he is satisfied that this is the case no considerations of sentiment or effect prevent him from coming back and starting afresh. No modern General ever cared less for what the world might say.... Nor would the General consent to imperil the ultimate success by asking his soldiers to make the supreme effort to redress a false tactical move. It was a principle which led us to much blood and bitter disappointment, but in the end to victory."[153]

For five days the British struggled forward along the railway line from hillock to hillock, pounding enemy positions with their guns. The fierce fighting took a heavy toll on both sides, with British casualties amounting to 2,000 men, mostly infantry. Experience of facing the Boers had not caused the infantry to change their tactics. Buller adhered to standard British strategy. The infantry still marched in Aldershot order – columns of four – instead of spacing out across the veld. This afforded the Boer marksmen easy targets. The British leaders still depended upon overwhelming numbers to succeed, at considerable cost.

BOTHA.

When the British captured Cingolo, and then Monte Cristo, hundreds of Boers left the defensive line and went home. It seemed that there was now no chance of resisting a British advance on Ladysmith. Botha asked for Kruger's permission to withdraw beyond Ladysmith. Kruger called on the Bible for justifying continued resistance. He refused to allow Botha to retreat.

Botha later made formal complaints to Buller about the use of the Red Cross. He claimed that the British infantry had sheltered behind Red Cross tents and advanced behind Red Cross attendants when they came out onto the battlefield to see to the wounded. As the Boers ceased fire when the Red Cross appeared, he claimed this was in contravention of the Geneva Convention. Buller strongly denied the charge. He stated that both sides had flown the Red Cross flag in order to tend to the wounded, and firing had stopped. The Boers, first onto the field, saw to their own men and then gave the British wounded some water and took away their rifles. They then proceeded to strip the dead and wounded of clothing and personal possessions. The watching British soldiers, infuriated, opened fire.

Paradoxically, the broken nature of the terrain worked to the advantage of the British. As they gained ground, they were able to move reinforcements up the deep gorges without exposing them to the Boers on the hills. Botha was caught unawares. From his position on Pieter's Hill he considered the country too rugged for Buller to cross the Tugela, but now he saw that the British attack was being covered by converging fire from long-range artillery which was clearing the ground a couple of hundred yards ahead of them. The hillside ahead of the advancing troops boiled with disintegrating rocks and flying shrapnel. Buller had developed this tactic since Colenso – a new approach to attacks that worked brilliantly.

War correspondent Davis described what he saw:

> "Up at the front, brown and yellow regiments are lying crouched behind brown and yellow rocks and stones. Are far as you can see, the hills are sown with them.... Sometimes the men rise and fire, and there is a feverish flutter of musketry, sometimes they lie motionless for hours while the guns make the way straight."[154]

Botha realised that he had been outmanoeuvred for once. His flanks were exposed and there was a danger of the British getting in behind him. He summoned up all his reserves. Soon it was hand-to-hand fighting on the ground between Railway Hill and Hart's Hill. The Boers were well entrenched, and put up strong resistance, but a flood of infantry coming from several directions overwhelmed them. Pieters

Hill would represent the point of last resistance. Now the 4.7 inch naval guns removed that resistance. A continual barrage of shells descended upon the Boer trenches. Morale was sapped. A Boer officer could be seen bringing back men who had deserted the trenches. As one British officer later wrote: "No one could live under such a fire."[155]

British cheers rose across the full line of the attacking force as the Boers finally deserted their positions and retreated. Buller's staff removed their helmets and cheered as well, shaking hands. Observers in Ladysmith watched a five-mile snake of Boer wagons accompanied by a large body of mounted men leaving the battlefield northwards. To the men watching through binoculars it was a dream come true. There was no doubt about it. The siege was about to be lifted. Now was the opportunity to pursue and hunt down the defeated enemy, but White's infantry were too weak and his cavalry bereft of horses, most of which had been eaten.

BULLER.

Buller felt that his men, too, were exhausted, and would be better used relieving Ladysmith. Late on the afternoon of February 28, two squadrons of mounted infantry totalling 120 men were seen winding over the low ridge to the east of Bulwana, so recently the site of the Boers' most fearsome weapon, Long Tom, a long range Creusot field gun. (Long Tom had been hastily dismantled under fire from the naval guns). Led by Lieutenant-Colonel Hubert Gough, at 6pm the weary column rode into Ladysmith between lines of emaciated but jubilant townsfolk. Churchill rode with him:

> "Never shall I forget that ride. The evening was deliciously cool....we turned the shoulder of a hill, and there before us lay the tin houses and dark trees we had come so far to see and save...Suddenly there was a challenge. 'Halt, who goes there?' 'The Ladysmith Relief Column.'...a score of men came running, cheering feebly, and some were crying. In the half-light they looked ghastly pale and thin. A poor, white-faced officer waved his helmet to and fro, and laughed foolishly...with Gough, the youngest regimental commander in the army, and one

of the best, at the head of the column we forded Klip River and rode into the town."[156]

White was there to meet them, on horseback, in his best uniform, but looking old and broken. The advance column was followed the next day by 75 wagons of food and medical stores. The work needed to restore the troops and the infrastructure was considerable. White's men were in a pitiful state. 3,500 sick and wounded would need to be evacuated. Those still standing were in urgent need of nourishment.

Buller asked one of the officers, Colonel Stoneman, how much longer they could have held out. He replied:

> "The garrison, sir, could have lived for three weeks longer, but the natives and sick in hospital would have been starved to death a fortnight earlier."[157]

Buller estimated it would take six weeks to three months to restore the garrison to fighting shape. Every railway bridge and culvert north of the Tugela needed rebuilding. His own troops needed rekitting.

Tensions still existed in Ladysmith. Many of the garrison did not hide their feelings at the slowness of the relief. There was a degree of reserve displayed by these men towards their rescuers. According to Thomas Pakenham, one of White's officers, Colonel Henry Rawlinson, remarked: "…it is astounding that they did not get through before."[158] Others mocked White, criticising him for his passivity and indecision. It was decided to stage a march-past to revive spirits, so three days later Buller led his two divisions through the town. Rawlinson recorded the occasion:

> "I never heard the troops cheer like they did when they passed Sir George White today – they waved their helmets in the air and simply yelled, such magnificent men, too, full of reservists of course, making our poor garrison look mere boys – their clothes are tattered and torn of course, for it is now 18 days since they changed them – their khaki is split and torn to pieces, some of them hardly decent."[159]

White put on a small banquet for Buller, using his last reserves of food kept for such an occasion. Unfortunately Buller appears to have made a tactless remark about the abundance of food, causing an angry reaction among White's staff. One of White's staff reported a few days later:

> "Buller himself arrived and made himself as unpleasant as he could. We had saved up a few stores…and used up everything giving him a good lunch. The ungrateful ruffian now goes about saying that the Ladysmith garrison lived like fighting cocks and that stories of hardship are all nonsense."[160]

White felt resentful of Buller's criticism, and his confidant, Ian Hamilton, part of Roberts "ring," was furious with Buller. A number of anti-Buller stories from his own staff were spread. The setbacks suffered earlier in the campaign had led to a growing disillusion among Buller's staff. Many officers were critical of Buller's command, highlighting the errors that had been made. Many had felt the rough edge of his tongue and were licking their wounds. Buller, a shy man, was not a good communicator, and in not explaining himself to his officers he had opened a dangerous rift with them. This feeling was not shared by the rank-and-file. Appreciative of his evident concern for their welfare, the soldiers idolised him. Corporal Hurley of the 3rd battalion 60th regiment, wrote home to his sister:

> "General Buller has had a hard task, the hardest of any, and if people at home find any fault with him it is because they are ignorant of the country, the enemy and their positions. All the men under Buller's command… would go through fire and water for him."[161]

Later, when Colonel Rawlinson, a keen supporter of Roberts, took the train down to Durban past the battlefields where so many men had died, he was astonished. Looking at the thorn-covered mountainsides, the gorges and precipices offering Botha's men natural defensive positions, he realised for the first time the challenges that had faced Buller. He wrote in his diary: "Most interesting – it was marvellous they got through at all."[162]

The relief of Ladysmith had resulted in losses to the British of 300 officers and more than 5,000 men, more than 20 per cent of his army.

chapter 12.
AFTER LADYSMITH.

BULLER.

BULLER RECOGNISED the pressing need to follow up the relief of Ladysmith with an offensive, but it would take time to prepare an advance. He lost no time in reconnoitering the land to the north of Ladysmith. White reported that there was a large Boer force dug in along the Biggarsberg range, sixty miles to the north between Dundee and Ladysmith. Scouts found few signs of Boers on the roads.

On March 2 Buller climbed Bulwana Hill. It was a very good day for observing, and he could see as far as the passes in the Drakensberg, the natural barrier between Natal, the Transvaal and Orange Free State. With the exception of some wagons on the top of a pass he could find no Boers. He assessed that there was no chance of the Boers making a stand south of Laing's Nek, on the Natal/Transvaal border. On March 7 he cabled Roberts. He believed he could outflank the Biggarsberg line in the west by attacking the Drakensberg passes on the Free State frontier.

A key point in the Drakensberg close to the Biggarsberg was Van Reenen Pass, which commanded the eastern Orange Free State. Behind the Boers lay Laing's Nek and Majuba. Roberts was concerned that the Boers defending the passes could threaten his progress north from Bloemfontein. Buller argued that possession of the passes would clear the way to advance to the Wakkerstroom–Vryheid district just inside the Transvaal. The force now stationed at Ladysmith would be ready in three weeks. Roberts had been informed that the Boer force in Natal numbered 13,000. He ordered Buller to remain on the defensive, in spite of Buller's strong objections.

Roberts was pursuing his own agenda. On March 13 he entered Bloemfontein without resistance: the Boers had melted away. He telegraphed Buller with instructions:

> "I do not think it would be wise now to embark on extensive operations in Natal, which is evidently extremely suitable for the enemy's tactics and very difficult for our troops. To force the passes of the Drakensberg would undoubtedly be a very hazardous operation, and would probably enable the Boers, with a small force, to hold up a very much larger number of men for some considerable time."[163]

Roberts ordered Buller to send a division across to him by way of East London. He made it clear that his first priority was the defeat of the Transvaal and the capture of Pretoria. To that end he was pressing northward with all his might, heedless of what he was leaving behind. He needed maximum resources, and did not wish Buller's actions to detract from that. Critics have suggested that there was an element of rivalry in this: the friction that existed between Roberts' and Wolseley's rings had become a matter of pride. Roberts did not want Buller to reach the Transvaal before him. Certainly Roberts was intent on reaching Pretoria quickly. He believed the psychological effect of capturing the Transvalers' capital would be immense.

On March 15, Roberts wrote to Queen Victoria:

> "The Orange Free State….is rapidly settling down…. men are laying down their arms and retiring to their usual occupations. It seems unlikely that this State will give much more trouble. The Transvalers will probably hold out, but their numbers must be greatly reduced, and I trust it will not be very long before the war will have been brought to a satisfactory conclusion."[164]

Buller had fought alongside the Boers in the Zulu War. He understood their mentality. He urged Roberts to rethink his strategy. He presciently predicted that the set-piece war would fragment into a series of guerrilla skirmishes. Any Boer successes would encourage the population to support them again. If Roberts did not sweep the country thoroughly as he advanced, he would leave behind him pockets of resistance that could cause him problems in the future. Buller knew from experience how adept the Boers were at moving quickly in small groups to avoid trouble.

BOTHA.

The Pretoria Executive under Kruger now contemplated the possible fall of Johannesburg. Should the gold mines be destroyed? Kruger was in favour, as he thought the mere threat would force Continental shareholders to put pressure on their governments to assist the Transvaal Republic. Francis Reitz, State Secretary of the Transvaal, secretly told the state mine engineer to drill holes in the shafts for dynamite placement. This move was soon widely known. Botha hurried back to Pretoria and confronted Kruger. Unless the order was countermanded, he and his commandos would cease fighting and return to Johannesburg to protect the mines. He argued strongly that after the war, whatever happened, the mines would be the economic lifeblood of the Transvaal, and must be sustained. Kruger reluctantly agreed, and ordered the dynamiting to be suspended. Reitz still went ahead and primed some mines, although whether Kruger knew of this is questionable. Kruger harboured resentment against Botha for this confrontation, which was to influence his attitude towards Botha later.

In late March 1900 the Commander-in-Chief of the Boers, General Piet Joubert summoned his senior officers to Glencoe. He explained that he felt too ill and weak to continue in command, and formally appointed Botha as Assistant Commandant-General "...and I trust you will be as loyal to him as you have been to me."[165] This announcement was met with stony silence. The natural successor to Joubert was a much older and more experienced man, General Jacobus De la Rey, a renowned warrior, but Joubert sensed that Botha was a better strategist. His instinctive approach on the battlefield was soundly thought out and usually right. Besides, he had youth on his side. Although the older officers looked on him with some doubt, he had already proved his leadership in the field, and now he had matured into a natural leader. He was, like Buller, a man who would inspire his men.

A French newspaper interviewed Botha in April. He described his leadership style as follows:

> "I am not a tactician in the European sense of the word. I should not perhaps be worth much on a European war. Here I am useful because of the experience I have acquired by practice. And the best practice is war. I do not belong to any school."[166]

The official account of events record that Joubert then retired to his farm and died peacefully on March 27. However, there is an alternative version of what happened. Joubert's reluctance to press home attacks, particularly during the advance towards Durban, and his pacific attitude towards warfare had attracted harsh criticism. On March 20 a Council of War at Kroonstad found him guilty of dereliction of duty, and it is said, though not substantiated, that he was sentenced to death. Botha, De Wet and Pretorius were present at this Council of War. Pretorius wrote that Botha placed a Mauser bullet and a glass of poison in front of Joubert, and told him to choose. He chose the poison, and died immediately. Other historians are doubtful of this version of events, although stories persisted long after the meeting of plots and skulduggery that led to the elimination of Joubert.

Botha was Joubert's natural successor, but complications arose. Both De la Rey and Meyer were senior to Botha in age and experience. However De la Rey knew nothing of Natal, while Meyer was considered a poor military commander. Kruger judged Botha to be a bit headstrong (his advance towards Pietermaritzburg) and insubordinate. He was still resentful of Botha's opposition to him over the proposed dynamiting of the mines. Kruger was a tyrant; he wanted to control every aspect of his regime. Botha complained that he could not even shift a commando of 100 men from one position to another without submitting the proposition to Pretoria. On one occasion he only received authorisation after the proposed movement had been nullified.[167] Kruger also felt that Botha, born and resident in Natal, was not a Transvaler, and therefore a "foreigner."[168]

Smuts, at that time serving Kruger, wrote to Botha:

> "The Government at first intended to appoint you Acting

Commandant-General for the whole Republic and the President went as far as to indicate this publicly....As, however, there were other candidates and we wished to avoid all envy, we have thought it better to leave matters in status quo for the time being, namely, you as chief general in Natal and De la Rey in the Orange Free State."[169]

In May Kruger said: "It was the late General Joubert's wish that Mr Botha should assume this important position after him,"[170] He went on to say that the Transvaal Constitution stipulated that the Commandant-General had to be elected by the people. Of course Kruger had the power to appoint Botha. It was generally recognised that the days of elections by the burghers were no more. So Botha was never formally elected, and his title remained Acting Commandant-General, Natal.

Botha's first action was to reorganise his forces, shedding incompetent officers, pushing younger, more vigorous men into prominent positions. Unlike Buller, bound by the conventions and traditions of the British Army, he possessed the freedom to make these changes on his own authority. He tightened discipline and improved transport. In the face of the massive force of British reinforcements pouring into Natal through Durban, he was going to need every resource at his command to withstand them. He visited the Free State, where morale had sagged disastrously in the face of the seemingly unstoppable advance by Roberts. The Boer Army was always a loosely knit grouping of commandos with more concern for their homesteads and farms than the great cause of Afrikanerdom. Individuals were inclined to leave the battlefield when it suited them, and particularly when the conflict became hot. The Free Staters acted independently of the Transvalers, and now they looked as if they had had enough. Botha, privately, expressed dismay at what he found.

The retreat from Ladysmith, and the defeats suffered in the Orange Free State, had caused the Boers to become demoralised. Many of the commandos, never willing to submit to strict discipline, yearned for home and their farms. Botha visited as many of his men as he could, impressing upon them the consequences of withdrawal. Their very livelihood and freedom was at stake. His powers of persuasion now drew new recruits to the ranks, and by May the shattered remnants of the army which had besieged Ladysmith had been forged into a fresh fighting force, ready to defend the Transvaal. Had Buller pressed home his advance after Ladysmith had been relieved, it is possible the war would have been swiftly concluded. The Boers were in full retreat. Had they been defeated, with Roberts threatening Pretoria, it is difficult to see that the Boers could have continued the struggle.

Whilst Botha was facing the British in Natal, the Boer resistance in the Orange Free State was led by General Christiaan Rudolph De Wet. De Wet had a reputation as a wily and courageous leader. He had taken part in the Battle of Majuba. He became a member of the Volksraad in 1897 but remained fiercely loyal to the Orange Free State Republic, on whose Volksraad he also sat. In the 1895 Free State presidential election he supported the successful candidate, Marthinus Steyn, and remained close to him through the Boer War. At the beginning of the war De Wet fought in Natal, but then returned to the Free State to serve under Piet Cronje as a general. Now he could again show his mettle.

With the British occupying Bloemfontein, De Wet moved on the waterworks for that city at Sannah's Post, twenty-three miles to the east. His intelligence reports informed him that it was only defended by a couple of a hundred men. Mindful of the huge British army at Bloemfontein, he needed to strike fast and then escape.

A column of 1,700 men from the British 2nd Cavalry Brigade joined the garrison at Sannah's Post where on March 31 a Boer commando confronted them at Thabanchu. The British commander was Brigadier-General Robert Broadwood, a favourite of Roberts and Kitchener. Failing to send out scouts, Broadwood found himself in a trap set by De Wet. His retreat to Bloemfontein was cut off and the post surrounded by 1,500 Boers. In the fire fight that ensued the Boers captured seven field guns, 117 wagons and took 428 prisoners.

More was to follow. With a force of only eight hundred, some of whom were not properly armed, De Wet carried out a series of daring raids. He attacked a garrison of six hundred Royal Irish Rifles near Reddersburg on April 3. After twenty-four hours of intensive fighting the entire garrison surrendered. This victory enhanced his reputation as a leader and soldier. He came to be seen as the Free State's most effective leader.

Later that month Botha visited De Wet on his farm in the Free State. The British were steadily advancing towards Pretoria through the Free State, and in early May Roberts entered the Western Transvaal with 40,000 men. De Wet told Botha that his commando consisted of eight men and a heliograph operator. Botha advised him to yield ground to the British until help could be sent.

chapter 13.
DEFENCE OF THE TRANSVAAL.

BOTHA.

BOTHA MET the Free State leaders a few days later in an attempt to persuade them to intervene in the British advance, which had reached Kroonstad. They were unwilling to leave the Free State, and it was agreed that the armies of the two republics should defend their own territory. There had never been a supreme command, and, as in the past, the two forces had jealously guarded their independence. Lord Kitchener, who had come out to assume the position of Roberts' chief of staff, did not believe the Free Staters were prepared to continue the struggle for much longer.

Botha, with 3,000 burghers, moved to Virginia siding, south of Kroonstad, to resist Roberts' advance but on May 10 General French outflanked the Boers on the right and forced him to retreat. With the fall of Kroonstad went the Free Staters' last stronghold. They were unwilling to leave their republic and fight for the Transvalers' cause. Botha crossed back into the Transvaal to defend Pretoria.

On May 24 Roberts annexed the Free State by proclamation and the irresistible British tide swept on towards Johannesburg. Botha planned to defend Johannesburg by drawing up a defence line south of the city. Roberts was marching up the railway while General French commanded the main road from Bloemfontein. Botha found that of the 6,000 men he expected to have in the defence line, 3,000 had ridden off to the north, pausing only to loot Johannesburg. The remaining 3,000 would be no match for the huge British army.

Commandant Krause, the Boer officer in charge of Johannesburg, sent a message to Roberts assuring him that the mines would be left intact and that he would surrender if Roberts gave him twenty-four hours to withdraw his force from the town. Roberts, anxious to preserve the town and its precious gold mines, agreed, halting his two divisions on the outskirts at Germiston. It was to prove a blunder of catastrophic proportions. He had the means to destroy a large army and potentially finish the war there and then. Instead, the Boer army remained intact, able to fight on.

On May 31 the British army entered Johannesburg. Botha's army retreated northwards to Pretoria carrying with them all their heavy guns, boxes of gold from the mines, gold and coin from the Mint and the Standard Bank, and supplies. A huge crowd gathered in the streets of Johannesburg to watch Roberts' entry into the city. Most were friendly, sporting red, white and blue badges, but there was also a sprinkling of people lamenting the occasion. The most vociferous celebrations came from the Africans. There were 14,000 of them working on the mines. Chamberlain had promised in 1899 "most favoured nation status for coloured British subjects in the Transvaal." The mineworkers believed that vow was about to be realised. Their hopes were immediately dashed. The two principal civil commissioners Roberts appointed to administer the Rand under the military governor were employees of the mining firms, and Uitlanders. Their interests lay solely in the efficient operation of the mines. The workers were quickly herded back to work. There was no discussion of political rights.

BULLER.

The Boers were surprised and puzzled to find that Buller had not followed up his success at Ladysmith. Their interpretation was that rivalry between Roberts and Buller had resulted in Buller being artificially delayed so that Roberts could reach the Transvaal first. Buller himself showed intense frustration in his letters to his wife:

"I am very vexed with Roberts; he has me condemned

to inactivity here, when I could have done a great deal to help him."[171]

This is borne out by the exchange of messages between them. On March 31 Buller wrote to Roberts:

> "I ought to have enough mounted men to be able to move about the 6th [April]. As far as Natal is concerned, the best thing I can do is to attack the enemy at Biggarsberg and drive them back north of Newcastle and restore the railway….as far as I can make out the best Transvalers are leaving here….expect them to go in front of you… If I can force the enemy north of Newcastle, I ought to be able to get over the Drakensberg with two Divisions. Subject to your approval the foregoing is what I propose to do."[172]

Roberts replied on April 4:

> "…the situation has very considerably altered, and I have come to the conclusion that the war will be ended more speedily by bringing one of your Divisions to the Orange Free State instead of its being used to force the Drakensberg passes."[173]

Buller wrote to Wolseley on April 9 from Ladysmith:

> "My view was that directly I got to Ladysmith I should have cleared Natal as soon as possible and also seized Harrismith, and I thought I was strong enough to do both if left alone, but he [Lord Roberts] would not hear of my doing anything…It makes me quite wild to think I have 12,000 Boers in front of me whom I would have dispersed if allowed with the greatest ease, but who now tie me and prevent my giving him the aid he wants. It seems to me though, that he is more wrong than ever to take troops from me. He ought to tell me now, ought to have told me ten days ago, to fight for all I am worth." [174]

Later, in a letter to the War Office in London, Roberts wrote:

> "...when [in March] Sir Redvers Buller suggested that he should take offensive action,.....I approved of his proposals. But owing to information which subsequently reached Sir Redvers Buller regarding the strength and disposition of the enemy, owing also to the continued unfitness of the Ladysmith garrison to take the field, he considered himself unable to carry his plans into effect."[175]

Not what Buller was saying! Later Roberts was to suggest to Lansdowne that only carefully selected correspondence between Buller and himself should be made available for others to read, but Lansdowne, the politician replied on August 15, 1902:

> "I do not understand principle on which you have selected telegram[s], ...if the correspondence is to be given up at all it had better be complete, omissions may give rise to complaints."[176]

Buller suggested he should at least attempt to reoccupy Dundee and take Newcastle. Botha had 8,000 mounted men and thirty guns in the Biggarsberg mountain range, north of Ladysmith. On May 2, Roberts instructed Buller to engage the enemy's attention at Biggarsberg. This was a straw Buller grasped with alacrity. There were two openings in the Biggarsberg range that he felt he could exploit. One carried the road and railway north to Glencoe and Newcastle, the other the road to Dundee down which the Dundee garrison had retreated after the battle of Talana. Both were heavily fortified. Leaving the original Ladysmith garrison in situ, he directed the 5th Division along the Glencoe railway line whilst he led the 2nd Division towards Dundee on May 7.

Buller approached the Biggarsberg range in a wide turning movement. He was learning the lessons of warfare in South Africa: travelling light, using cavalry and mobile guns. He surprised the Boers by the speed of his movement. By May 13 he was in the mountains and threatening the Boer's rear. They abandoned their positions along the length of the defensive line. By May 16 Dundonald was in Glencoe. Buller was exuberant. He wrote home:

> "I have surprised and outmanoeuvred the Boers and

have got a considerable force out of an enormously strong position, with very small, and indeed infinitesimally small loss."[177]

Buoyed by this success, Buller pushed on to Newcastle. At Laing's Nek he found the Boers, four or five thousand strong, had dug themselves in to what he considered to be an unassailable position with rows of entrenchments and hidden gun emplacements. Scouts reported back that the defensive line of the Boers stretched from Mount Pogwana, east of the Buffalo River along a ridge that included Majuba and Laing's Nek, to the Drakensberg at Quagga's Nek in the south-west, a distance of twenty miles. Mountains to the west and broken country to the east made it difficult to carry out a flanking movement. On Pogwana the Boers had mounted a big Creusot field gun.

Buller paused for supplies to be replenished, reinforcements to be brought forward and the railway repaired. He used this time to make contact with the Boer commander facing him, Louis' brother, Christiaan Botha. Buller estimated that there were 10,000 men under Botha's command in Natal. The Wakkerstroom Commando, which Christiaan Botha commanded, was well known to Buller. Twenty years earlier all the officers, or their fathers, had served under Buller in the Zulu War. He pointed out that Roberts was advancing behind him, and suggested that Botha should discuss surrender terms to avoid further loss of life and send his men back to their farms. If they surrendered the field guns they could take their rifles home with them, although Lord Roberts would probably order their disarmament later

A three-day armistice followed while Botha consulted with his superiors, but it became evident that he was merely playing for time, and had been instructed to carry on the struggle. Roberts was appalled when he heard of Buller's offer. He insisted upon unconditional surrender. The soldiers were to be sent home without their weapons and the officers imprisoned.

Roberts' column occupied Johannesburg, and with the Rand gold mines now in his possession, Roberts did not feel he needed to make concessions. In his opinion the war was nearly over. Buller did not feel he had lost anything by the approach, as it allowed him to complete his preparations. He also pointed out that if the Boers continued to resist it would cost him 500 men killed and wounded to "get out of Natal."[178] Roberts ordered him not to attack Laing's Nek – he had already exceeded his instructions – but Buller had no intention of doing so by a direct attack.

On June 6 a brigade of Hildyard's division moved on Botha's Pass, west of Laing's Nek and rising 1,500 feet above the plain. This pass to the south of Quagga's Nek was less well defended and was more easily accessible, with a zigzag road to the summit. While one division engaged the Boers posted in the pass, another seized two outlying hills east of the pass and established artillery there to shell the pass. One of them, Van Wyk's Hill, had been left unguarded by the Boers. Its possession by the South African Light Horse gave the British command of Botha's Pass. Two days later, on the 8th, the pass was taken, infantry climbing the steep slopes to the summit, 6,000 feet above sea level, under cover of the artillery. British casualties totalled 16 killed or wounded. That night Buller slept on Botha's Pass without food or blankets, so that he could resume the chase as soon as possible. The position was consolidated on the 9th by moving guns to the summit.

On the 10th Buller turned north-east to strike at the railway behind Laing's Nek in order to cut off the Boers' supply line and retreat route. He encountered another Boer stronghold at Alleman's Nek, fifteen miles on. He surprised his enemy by appearing in front of them, as the Boers were concentrating on consolidating their position at Quagga's Nek. Again Buller showed that he had learnt from past mistakes. Using the artillery in coordination with the infantry to advance by clearing the way in front of them with an intense barrage, he drove the Boers, with a strong force, back from ridge to ridge until they broke and fled. British casualties numbered 150 killed or wounded. Buller considered that in the light of the strong force they were facing in an entrenched position, these casualties were relatively light.

On June 12 the railway, 11 miles further on, was reached, but the delay in removing the Boers from Alleman's Nek had enabled their main force to get away from Laing's Nek. Buller was content, however. Natal had been cleared.

Rather ironically, four hours after learning that the Boers had abandoned Laing's Nek he received a telegram from Roberts advising him not to try to oust them as "the Boers were at least 4,500 strong …and it was too great a risk of heavy loss."[179] For once, Buller had outmanoeuvred the Boers at every point. On June 15 he led his troops into Volksrust unopposed, and received a warm welcome from the British residents there.

On June 18 Roberts telegraphed Buller impressing upon him the importance of occupying Standerton. General Clary's division immediately advanced from Laing's Nek and together with the 11th Brigade entered Standerton unopposed on June 22. As the Boers retreated they disrupted the railway. Repairs to the railway as they advanced now permitted the British to bring up their reinforcements and supplies.

In 1909 a French military critic, General Langlois, expressed the opinion that Buller, and not Roberts, had the toughest job of the war, and that he adapted his tactics to meet the challenge:

> "...the proper use of cover, of infantry advancing in rushes, co-ordinated in turn with creeping barrages of artillery: these were the tactics of truly modern war, first evolved by Buller in Natal."

The press was generally favourable. One paper commented:

> "With the enemy in full flight, and Natal at last cleared of their presence, Sir Redvers Buller has, after many months, reaped the reward of his unwearied patience and dogged persistency.....the troops realised what splendid results had been achieved by the flanking movement at the least possible expenditure of life."[180]

BOTHA.

Botha and Smuts were shocked at the collapse of Boer morale. It seemed that the Boers had lost the will to fight. They poured into Pretoria as a disorganised rabble, scattering across the city. Botha and Smuts met their senior officers at the telegraph office in central Pretoria. A telegram was drafted to Kruger suggesting immediate surrender. Kruger contacted President Steyn of the Free State. Were the Free Staters prepared to lay down their arms? Steyn's reply was short and to the point: *"We* shall never surrender."[181] He virtually accused the Transvalers of cowardice. Kruger, and the officers gathered in Pretoria, felt their honour and courage was being questioned.

Kruger was in despair. Against his will, the old firebrand saw that the only way the Boer cause could be kept alive was if he could avoid capture. On May 29 he said a brief farewell to his invalid wife, the last time he would see her, and with his advisers he was smuggled out of Pretoria. He took the train going north-east along the Delagoa Railway towards Machadodorp. The last guns were removed from the four forts built after the Jameson Raid. Pretoria, their capital, the symbol of Boer nationhood, was defenceless. This caused any remaining resistance to collapse, and the burghers started streaming home.

President Steyn's resolve to continue the war changed the Transvalers' stance. Talk of surrender was abandoned. Botha and Smuts decided that they would fight to the death. The honour of their race was at stake. Boer gloom lifted as quickly as it had descended. Botha realised that the Boer army had escaped to the east more or less intact, ready to fight again if asked. Roberts may have captured the key Transvaal towns, but he had failed to corral the Boers.

Botha made a rousing speech in front of the Pretoria Raadsaal (town hall), vowing to fight on. He reminded the huge crowd that had gathered there that George Washington had surrendered his capital to the British several times and still won the American War of Independence. He announced measures to maintain order in Pretoria, and urged everyone capable of doing so to help in the defence of the town. The women presented him with a beautiful silken Vierkleur into which had been stitched the words: "Strijdt met Gods Hulp" [Fight with God's Aid]. Botha told General De Wet that he would fight on even if Pretoria fell.[182]

Sir Ian Hamilton had joined Roberts with a large force of mounted troops. The odds facing the Boers in Pretoria were overwhelming. Yet the end was curiously anti-climactic. Lieutenant W.W.R. Watson was sent with a white flag into Pretoria, asking for directions to Botha's house. There he demanded unconditional surrender. Botha was given the impression that Roberts' entire army had entered the town. To avoid annihilation he felt he had no choice but to surrender the town to the British. When the British reached the city two days later, on June 5, Botha had no alternative but to follow the retreat. Jan Smuts, who had transferred his loyalty to Botha and was to be a crucial influence in what ensued, took half a million pounds in money and gold out of Pretoria when he left.

Roberts believed that with the capture of Pretoria the war was over. Botha needed time to rally his troops. He sent word to Roberts via his secretary that he wished to negotiate peace. Roberts asked Botha's wife Annie, who had remained in Pretoria, to act as go-between, and a meeting was arranged outside the city. The Boer command was split. Many, most notably the Free Staters, insisted they should fight to the bitter end. It was decided to break off negotiations with Roberts and fight on. It has been said that De Wet's success against the British in the northern Free State, with victories at Sannaspos and along the railway line north of Kroonstad, inside the Transvaal encouraged resistance. In fact the news of his victory only reached Botha after the decision was taken to fight on.

Botha had decided to make a stand on a ridge 15 miles east of Pretoria. With the pick of his burghers, and many guns, this was a strong position. He planned to hold the centre firm while the two "wings" moved forward and cut off the British from their base at Pretoria.

BULLER.

The British strategy was very similar: engage the Boers attention with a frontal attack while the two arms turned the Boer flanks. General French, on the left, collided with De la Rey also moving forward. Stalemate ensued. On the British right Broadwood found the Boers arranged in a semi-circle round his flank. The key point in the terrain here was a ridge known as Diamond Hill. Roberts, confident he had already won the war, had reduced his front-line force to 16,000 men. Botha, on the other hand, by the strength of his personality, had managed to scrape together 5,000 Transvaal burghers. The battle ranged for two days, June 11 and 12, over thirty miles of open veld, with the British outnumbering the Boers by three to one. The outcome was inconclusive. The British lost 14 men killed and 144 wounded. The Boer casualties were greater; perhaps 300 to 400 and they were forced to retreat. Nevertheless Botha had shown that he was a master at preparing his troops and leading on such a huge stage.

Meanwhile the Free Staters were having great success in disrupting supply lines to the south. Botha had written to their high command: "What I desire…now that the great force of the enemy is here, is to get behind him and break or interrupt his communications."[183] In the Orange Free State the De Wet brothers, using guerrilla tactics, attacked the vital railway line and cut telegraph wires. They came across a convoy carrying supplies from the railway and captured it: fifty-six food wagons and 160 Highlanders.

The marauding De Wets followed this up with an even greater triumph. Between Kroonstad and the Vaal, the northern border of the Free State, lay Roodewal. At the station there was a huge amount of ammunition, mailbags and other supplies, awaiting the restoration of a destroyed railway bridge. De Wet's farm lay only four miles from the station. He had been told that the station was lightly guarded. This was not entirely accurate. A British infantry battalion, the 4th Derbyshires, had been sent up the railway line on June 5. They were raw militia, however, set down near the railway bridge at dusk, and in no position to defend themselves against experienced Boer guerrillas.

On June 6 800 Boers fell on Roodewal. After several hours fighting from behind the embankment, but lacking field guns, the Derbyshires surrendered. British casualties numbered 38, with 104 wounded, 486 officers and men captured. Boer casualties were negligible. News of this success once again lifted morale in the Transvaal, and strengthened the Transvalers' resolve.

Roberts responded to the disruption of supply lines by taking the war to the civilian population. One of his problems was in identifying the small Boer commando groups as they roamed the country. These bands were helped and supported by the farming community, who gave them shelter and food as they moved. Roberts ordered that the farmers should be punished. On June 16, 1900 he proclaimed that damage to railways, bridges and telegraph wires could not be done "without the knowledge and connivance of the neighbouring inhabitants."[184] To set examples that would act as a deterrent, he ordered selected farms to be burnt. Women and children were turned out onto the open veld, homesteads demolished and stock either taken or destroyed.

This policy was a very controversial one, which would bring recriminations, dissent among the British and a legacy of bitterness with the Boers that lingers to this day. It assisted in creating a fervent form of Afrikaner nationalism, which was to blossom after the war into implacable opposition to the British.

Roberts was concerned that his attenuated supply line through the Free State was at constant risk from marauding bands of Boers. He saw that the railway from Durban northwards represented a much better route, and he urged Buller to press on towards Pretoria, in order to augment his column there.

Buller, impatient at being held back, needed no further encouragement. With three divisions he crossed into the Transvaal and reached Standerton, 50 miles up the railway line towards Johannesburg, on June 22. There he halted for six days to repair the railway line. Harassed by snipers, General Clery led the advance to Heidelberg. Greylingstad was reached on July 2 and Vlakfontein on the 4th. Shortly thereafter the advancing British column made contact with Roberts.

Buller took the reopened railway to meet Roberts on July 7 in Pretoria. Despite their differences, the two men avoided displaying disagreement publicly. Both thought the war would soon be over, and that the Boers would be driven out of the eastern Transvaal and "into the sea" at Delagoa Bay.[185]

Communications remained a problem, however. Roberts was still being supplied from Cape Town, and the railway was subjected to repeated sabotage by the bands of roaming Boers. Buller was now over 300 miles from Durban, and although Durban was secure he was still subject to delays in receiving adequate supplies. Kitchener, who at Lord Salisbury's insistence had come to South Africa as Roberts' Chief of Staff, was present at the meeting between Roberts and Buller. He asked Buller when he thought the war would be over. He replied: "Nine weeks from the 1st of July." Kitchener responded: "I hope to do it in less than that."[186] Both Roberts and Kitchener believed that by taking Pretoria they had all but brought an end to the war.

Doubtless a major British success at Brandwater Basin in the northern Free State, where a large Boer force without its main leaders was cornered and forced to surrender, added to this confidence. De Wet had proved a thorn in the flesh of the British in the Free State, and a concerted effort was made to corner him. Five columns under the overall command of Lieutenant-General Archibald Hunter converged on De Wet's commando in the green valley of the Brandwater River against the backdrop of high mountains separating the Free State from Basutoland.

The Basuto ruler had been forbidden by the British Resident from giving the Boers safe passage through his country. It looked as though the Boers were cornered. However, the number of passes through the mountains made it impossible for the British to cover all routes. About a third of the Boer commando, 1,800 men, slipped through the central pass of Slabbert's Nek. Unaware that the British could not cover every escape route, the remainder barricaded themselves inside the basin. The

British converged on them through six wagon roads. Sporadic resistance gave way to a sense of hopelessness when the Boers realised the size of the enemy force. They had little stomach for a fight: they wanted to go home. 4,314 men, including three generals and 6 commandants, were taken prisoner. Hunter was disappointed to find that De Wet had slipped away with the first escapees. The surrender opened the route north through Bethlehem, and removed a serious irritant in the Free State.

With communications vastly improved by the Brandwater Basin victory, Roberts was prepared to move against Botha. He set out to sweep the Boers and their government east to the Mocambique border, and into exile. Equally, Buller was keen to push on. Kruger and his government had taken refuge in Machadodorp on the railway line to Delagoa Bay, and what was left of Botha's troops were collected at Middelburg, further west. On July 25 General French's cavalry seized Middelburg, forcing Botha out. The major British supply base was subsequently established there.

Roberts wanted Buller to take an infantry division and two brigades of horsemen to finish off the Boer resistance. This required a hundred-mile march across the high veld by way of Carolina. Buller started out on August 7 with 12,000 men, 3,000 horses and 42 guns. There was no railway to speed his progress, and the 761 ox-wagons slowed his advance. Small bands of Boers attempted to hinder his progress, but they were swatted away. On August 11 he occupied Ermelo without opposition. On August 14 he reached Carolina and made contact with French. He was near enough to strike at Machadodorp, but was stopped by Roberts. He complained to his wife:

> "I have twelve thousand men here, and I doubt his [Botha] having five thousand, and certainly half of those do not want to fight. It is an unfortunate delay, at an unfortunate moment, but the end of the war must come soon; we are now practically holding the high veldt, they will die if kept there beyond the middle of September….a pity as during this week Kruger with us so near will certainly move back from Machadodorp, while if I had forced right forward from Carolina or Machadodorp I should have caught some of his staff, and I was strong enough to do so."[187]

chapter 14.
THE LAST PITCHED BATTLE.

BOTHA.

BOTHA NOW made a last stand in an attempt to prevent the British from reaching Machadodorp and sweeping the eastern Transvaal clear. He commanded the entire Boer defence and, for the first time in the war the four Creusot Long Toms were present. Lack of sufficient ammunition posed a serious problem, and was to be key in the ensuing battle.

Botha was concerned to protect the railway line east to the border with Mocambique, the Boers' lifeline. East of Belfast he spread his 5,000 men thinly over a 50-mile front. He had 20 guns including 4 Long Toms. Roberts' and Bullers' combined British force totalled 18,700 men with 82 guns and 25 machine-guns. Botha chose for his last, concerted stand an escarpment that was a natural fortress. Although heavily outnumbered, he had the advantage of the high ground. Between him and the British was a level plain that could be swept by rifle fire. Behind him the ground fell sharply away to the lowlands that stretched to the Portuguese border.

BULLER.

Roberts arrived at Belfast on August 25. Together with Buller, French and Pole-Carew he drafted a strategy. Initially he wanted Buller to move in an easterly direction towards the Carolina-Machadodorp road in order to cut off the Boer retreat. Buller did not agree. He pointed out that the ground was very boggy and that he would need to cross a river, the Leeuspruit, by a single drift. He proposed that he go northward, a much more passable route. Roberts finally conceded. French and Pole-Carew would concentrate their attack north of the railway and Buller's Natal field army of 11,000 men would advance directly on Machadodorp. The combined British force of 20,000 was brought into position along a 20km front against Botha's 5,000 spread over a much more extended line.

On August 27 the watching Boers saw a vast dust cloud in the distance, and shortly thereafter a huge mass of British infantry appeared on the skyline. Within an hour a heavy bombardment opened up from the British batteries. As in previous encounters the Boers had concealed their positions so skilfully that there were few casualties. Night fell without an infantry attack.

The shelling recommenced early on August 28. This time it was so intense that Deneys Reitz was to write:

> "We were shelled to such an extent that one dared scarcely look over the edge of the breast works for the whirring of metal and the whizzing of bullets."[188]

Later that day a small earthquake – a rare occurrence in that part of the highveld – shook the Boer position. In the afternoon Reitz, at the centre of the defence, spotted a detachment of infantry coming down a defile to his left. He and his colleagues were able to drive them back, killing and wounding about fifteen men. This was to be the Boers' last success of the clash.

Buller's choice of route was vindicated. A key point was the junction of the Carolina and Dalmanutha roads, where the farm Bergendal was situated. Information was received that this was where the extreme left of Botha's line was. It was defended by a commando of the Johannesburg police (known as ZARPS = Zuid-Afrikaansche Rijdende Politie), with instructions to defend it to the bitter end.

Employing the lessons learned at Ladysmith, Buller co-ordinated his artillery and troop movements. Accurate bombarding of the Boer positions continued non-stop for three hours with a combination of howitzers in the field supported by 4.7 inch naval guns in Belfast. The heavy shells from the naval guns blew to pieces some heavy blocks of rock on the hill behind which the ZARP had taken their positions. Two infantry battalions advanced 1,500 yards over open ground. The ZARP remained in position, maintaining steady and accurate fire. Heavily outnumbered, and with limited ammunition the ZARP finally capitulated and the kopje was captured. This success, combined with General French threat to the right flank led to the collapse of the entire Boer line. At times the fighting was fierce, and three VC's were awarded.

The Boer defence had been smashed and the burghers abandoned Machadodorp and surrounding defences. Buller believed he had come close to catching Kruger. His frustration with Roberts boiled over in his next letter to his wife:

> "I am as happy as a pig. We had a very pretty little fight, with the Field Marshal and the whole Guards Brigade looking on. Certainly it went off very well and exactly as I could have wished.......Tomorrow I am off to Lydenberg.....The end cannot be far off now, I believe, but between you and me I do wish the Field Marshal would move a bit quicker. He lets so many chances slip....it was not the least pleasure that I defeated the army and opened the road to Machadodorp, while Lord Roberts' army, which had got there before me, had missed the chance and had to sit looking on."[189]

Roberts in correspondence blamed Buller for delays, and his sympathisers repeated these accusations publicly. An official history of the war did, however, contain the criticism that Roberts waited for seven months before calling for Buller's co-operation.[190]

chapter 15.
GUERRILLA WARFARE.

BOTHA.

BERGENDAL WAS to be the last major confrontation of the war. From that point the Boers resorted to guerrilla tactics. They broke up into separate columns. One fled south-east towards Barberton and was pursued by French's cavalry. One group followed the railway eastwards, chased by Pole-Carew. The third went north, Buller's responsibility. Lydenberg lay forty miles away from the main railway. The terrain between Machadodorp and Lydenberg was very rugged. Accurate artillery fire from the Boers delayed his progress. A frontal attack was out of the question. Hamilton was sent with 3,000 infantry to augment Buller's six battalions, and by arriving on a converging course towards the rear while Buller's guns distracted the Boers from the front, he forced them to retreat beyond Lydenberg.

On the morning of September 5 Buller led his column into Lydenberg. A pretty little town with some fine shops, it had hitherto remained out of the fighting. Among the population was a sizeable number of English-speaking residents, who welcomed Buller and his men. Now the Boers used their remaining Long Tom to fire long-range shells into the town. The troops took this as routine, but the inhabitants, unused to warfare, were considerably alarmed. One English mother rushed to the British headquarters to complain that, as she lived near the camp, shells were bursting close to her house. As her baby was asleep inside and she did not want it disturbed, she requested that the Boers be told to stop aiming shells so close to her![191]

English papers identified what they saw as an act of Boer treachery. The Courier reported that Botha had requested that ambulances be sent to recover British casualties in his care. When Buller responded, the ambulances were commandeered and 40 men taken prisoner.[192]

Botha had formed a healthy respect for his opponent. The enemy admired Buller's doggedness and his willingness to take on difficult tasks as much as his own men. In fact, Botha and Buller were never to meet face to face.

A weekly paper in England reported:

> "While chasing the Boer forces [Buller in the Lydenberg Valley] reached a certain store five minutes after Botha had left it. The storekeeper said he had asked Botha whether he was going to fight. 'No,' said the Boer general, 'I am not, because four times have I chosen apparently impregnable positions, and each time those confounded soldiers of Buller's, carrying loads on their backs have walked over it as if it had been level country.'"[193]

The Boers found a strong defensive position at the 1,800-foot high Paardeplaats mountain. Its sheer sides made an attack by infantry extremely difficult and hazardous. Employing the lessons learnt in Natal, however, Hamilton and Lyttleton's divisions, moving swiftly, and supported by excellent artillery fire, swept the Boers from the summit on September 8 at the cost of 31 men. From then on there were no pitched battles in the hills, but a series of skirmishes with small bands of Boers. The terrain favoured the guerrillas, but Buller was successful in forcing the Boers out of their strongholds and back to the north with less than a hundred casualties.

Pressed by Buller, Botha fell back from Pilgrimsrest. At Hectorspruit he contracted malaria, but managed to evade Buller and reach Nylstroom, where he held a council of war attended by, among others, Presidents Steyn and Kruger. It was agreed that Botha would fight over the plains of the High Veld while the Free Staters would mount a raid on the Cape Colony. The Boers thought that there were many people in the Cape whose sympathies lay with them.

Even before Roberts had crossed the Vaal Kruger was having doubts about continuing the war. He could see no long-term future in a struggle against an overwhelming force. He was in constant touch with President Steyn of the Orange Free State who, as we have seen, took a different view. For Steyn, it was a fight to the finish. Without gold or diamonds in the Free State, his was an ideological struggle to preserve independence and the purity of Afrikaner nationalism. If his people believed God was with them when the war started, what had changed?

Kruger had no answer to Steyn's obduracy. On September 3, he responded from Nelspruit by declaring the annexation null and void. With the British moving on his position, however, he had no alternative but to leave the country. Moving to Mocambique on September 11, he received help from the young Queen Wilhelmina of the Netherlands who found him refuge in Europe.

Botha was present in Nelspruit when Kruger made the decision to leave. He now had a free hand to reorganise the Boer military system. The British, who rightly saw him as the key to the Boer resistance, were pressing him.

Schalk Burgher as Acting President replaced Kruger, but Burgher was weak and indecisive. The real leader of the Boers was now Louis Botha.

Harassed all the way, Botha led his troops through Barberton and into rugged, mountainous territory. Close to the Portuguese border were 5,000 horsemen awaiting his orders. By riding hard, often all night, they shook off the British "by fifty or sixty miles"[194] A new phase in the war was about to start. Surplus guns were destroyed or thrown into the Crocodile River, the sick and wounded were sent over the Portuguese border and stores were either distributed among the men or burnt. Botha led the way into the bush to begin a guerrilla offensive.

On finally clearing the main Boer army from the east, Roberts proclaimed the Transvaal once more annexed to the British. Critics pointed out that he actually held only one tenth of the republic, but Roberts received strong support from Milner, for whom the annexation was a dream come true. He wrote: "The ultimate end is a self-governing white Community, supported by well-treated and justly governed black labour from Cape Town to Zambesi."[195]

BULLER.

A week after Paardeplaats, Buller asked Roberts to relieve him. He was disillusioned with Roberts' leadership, and was near exhaustion after nearly a year of unremitting warfare. Roberts, equally, felt he had had enough, and that now the war had degenerated into a number of guerrilla engagements he was no longer needed. He suggested Buller take his place. The British Government had not forgotten the disasters Buller had presided over before Ladysmith was relieved. Lansdowne replied that the government did not have sufficient confidence in Buller to allow him to succeed Roberts.

At the end of October, Buller took the train to Durban and sailed for Southampton. A banquet and sword of honour was presented to him in Durban, and huge crowds turned out to hail him when the ship docked in Cape Town. At Southampton he was greeted by cheering crowds as a national hero and Queen Victoria received him at Windsor Castle.

His future, however, was bleak. The government conferred no honours whatsoever on him. He was returned to his pre-war job, training the Army Corps at Aldershot. In contrast, when Roberts returned in December he was given an earldom and £100,000. The British Government saw him as the general who saved the situation in South Africa, and had all but won the war. He succeeded Wolseley as Commander-in-Chief of the British Army.

Perhaps one of the greatest accolades granted to Buller came from a Boer officer. Questioned by the Ceylon Times on May 30, 1901, as to the Boers' opinion of the British generals against whom they had fought, the officers present were unanimous in according Buller the palm. A Landrost said:

> "He fought me and did what was set for him to do. When Sir Redvers Buller met us, we were an unbeaten army, flushed with success, and he had the hardest of all possible tasks before him. But he did what we never thought he would do, what we never believed he could do. Lord Roberts is the British hero, and all I say is that he drove a beaten and disorganized army before him like a lot of sheep, following up the work Buller had done."[196]

BOTHA.

Botha had not been idle during the long retreat. The Boers were demoralised, and many wished for nothing but to return to their farms. Botha, however, would not rest. He crisscrossed the countryside, chivvying backsliders, visiting farms and small bands of commandos, convincing them the fight was still worth the effort. Instead of facing the British army in pitched battle, where the odds were now firmly in favour of the British, he organised his force into small, mobile bands of guerrillas. This played to the Boers' strengths. At home in the saddle, used to a life on the veld where they travelled great distances, they were able to attack specific targets and then move swiftly away.

As we have seen, Botha was not a conventional leader. He followed no set pattern or routine. Many of his decisions were instinctive. His men, farmers mainly, were at home in the bush. Lord Kitchener was finding him difficult to pin down. Kitchener's biographer wrote:

> "[Botha] with a fine contempt for formulae, deliberately inaugurated operations which were regularly adapted to their arena and organization."[197]

Railways, regarded by the British as their life-blood for supplies and the movement of troops, were constantly attacked. The local rural populace, almost unanimously on the side of the Boers, ensured these bands were fed and supplied with fresh horses and ammunition. Frustrated by the resistance, and the Boer ability to sustain their operations from the farms, Roberts threatened to destroy the farms in the neighbourhood of railways that the Boers sabotaged. The question arose: what to do with the displaced families?

Roberts wrote to Botha requesting that he accommodate the women from the farms. Botha was astounded. Until then the war had been fought along conventional lines; he could not believe the British would take the fight to women and children. He wrote to Roberts in protest, to no effect.

Horatio Herbert Kitchener had assumed command of the British effort as successor to Roberts. He was not happy to be in South Africa, and wished to be rid of it as soon as possible. What he really wanted was command of the British forces in India. The guerrilla activities made him very frustrated. A ruthless and ambitious man, he had little sympathy for the Boers. He therefore pursued the scorched earth policy with renewed vigour. By the end of the war about 30,000 farms had been razed to the ground.

Roberts was keen to rid Pretoria of the remaining wives of Boer leaders. He was suspicious that they were using their position to spy on the British, and communicate his intentions to their menfolk. Old Mrs Kruger still lived there, as did Annie Botha. Botha took this very badly. He wrote to Roberts:

> "The pretext mentioned by you, viz. that by such action you wish to protect yourself against any information being brought over to us, is doubtless a delusion, since such precaution was not deemed necessary by you when our troops were in the immediate vicinity of Pretoria."[198]

Reluctantly Roberts allowed the leaders' wives to remain in Pretoria, and Mrs Kruger died shortly thereafter.

Harried from town to town, Botha evaded capture narrowly on several occasions. He and his closest followers suffered hunger and thirst. They were deprived of regular sleep, and lacked the clothing to protect them from the cold highveld winter. For months they existed on what they could scavenge from the countryside, mainly mealies and biltong. The British policy of destroying farms deprived the Boers of the support they had previously received from local farmers. Those farms that were still standing were afraid of reprisals should they help the roving bands of Boers.

Botha's men marvelled at his judgement. Without maps and without formal training, he was able to calculate the size of the pursuing British columns, their rate of progress and where they would camp. Time and again he slipped out of a deadly encounter when it seemed inevitable he would be cornered. An observer wrote: "Louis Botha would always find a way round. I don't know how he did it; perhaps he did not know himself. His judgement was perfect."[199]

Most important, however, was the personal impact Botha made on his followers. Despite the privations he managed to turn himself out in neat clothes, looking handsome and assured. His kindness towards others was legendary and he made his men feel he really cared for their well-being. To any man who wanted to see him, he was immediately accessible. If anyone had a problem, he knew he would receive a sympathetic hearing and sound advice. He was a good listener.[200] In this sense he was very like

Buller. The burghers adored him. Many would have done anything for him. He visited several of the small laagers camped in the veld, carefully selecting young men whom he judged had the right commitment to the cause, and possessed the courage to resist the British. This way he assembled a body of soldiers around him who were skilled and able.

In an attempt to bring the guerrilla warfare to an end, Roberts offered Botha and General De la Rey annuities of £10,000 if they surrendered, but Botha had no intention of giving up. He issued a proclamation on October 6 denying rumours that he had surrendered, and warning his men of lying rumours and British overtures. He met his war council at Nylstroom and organised his highveld campaign.

Roberts told an audience in Durban at the start of December that the war was practically over. This was a prelude to him relinquishing command and returning to Britain. Kitchener, taking his place, assessed the Boers' fighting force to be around 20,000 men, while he had ten times that number. He reasoned that he needed to do two things to finish the war. First, he needed a plan that would allow his army to control increasing parts of the country without penetration by the guerrillas. Second, he had to somehow cut off their lines of supply and sustenance, and persuade them that the war was not worth continuing.

In order to gain control Kitchener aimed to divide up the country into "paddocks" by establishing blockhouses with fortifications, barriers and traps that would be systematically laid out along an advancing line. He hoped this would herd the Boers into enclosures that would eventually lead to their surrender. The second goal he did achieve quickly: he forced Boer families out of farmhouses into concentration camps. The farms were set on fire and the livestock confiscated. Buller's South African Light Horse, highly mobile, were in their element during this phase of the war. Using commando tactics and moving swiftly, they scoured the land, driving the resisting Boers towards the blockhouses, taking prisoners and sweeping up resistance.

Stubbornly the Boers fought on. To relieve the mounting pressure in the Free State and Transvaal, Smuts took a commando into the Cape and Botha turned his attention once more to Natal. In September 1901 he assembled 1,000 men and mounted a raid into Natal. He did not have high hopes of success, but looked for a rally to re-inspire his jaded and dejected troops, who were scattered in small bands across the eastern Transvaal. Initial forays brought success. On September 17, for instance, at Blood River Poort, near Piet Retief, he confronted a strong British force and prevailed. Six British officers and 38 men were either killed or wounded. A further 200 men were taken prisoner. Botha reported:

"I was really sorry that the Government could not see how beautifully the burghers stormed over the bare plain up to the guns, and it is a wonder that not more on our side were harmed."[201]

Botha's aim was to capture Dundee, but there he encountered very poor weather. Eleven days of continuous rain weakened the horses. The British attacked a patrol, and the fracas alerted the main British force of 16,000 men with 40 guns. Although the Boers advanced to Babanango in Zululand they were harassed by the British every step of the way. Botha wrote:

> "The enemy seems to be ready for us and to know our plans."[202]

However, he would not relinquish the notion of taking the fight to the enemy.

On October 6, after a night march, he attacked the British on his own farm at Vryheid. The fighting lasted all day, but the British force was 3,000 strong with 4 guns and 3 pom-poms, opposition the Boers could not overcome. They were not helped by desertions:

> "The burghers had fairly good positions....Unfortunately Ermelo [commando] left their position without necessity after the enemy had been beaten back time after time by the other commandos and we could see the enemy retire. This caused the enemy to come back and take possession of the Ermelo positions without opposition, through which the other commandos were obliged to retire. This was one of the best fights we have had for months....The loss of the enemy must have been considerable."[203]

On October 30 Botha was more successful. Some of Colonel Benson's experienced units had been replaced by untried ones. When some of his wagons became bogged down Botha struck. Marching 70 miles in quick time with 500 reinforcements for the local commando he attacked the British at Bakenlaagte. His 1200 mounted men drove the British back and pinned them down on a ridge known as Gun Hill. Here Benson fought to the last, being among 66 British killed. This engagement was hailed as one of the most remarkable of the war. The Boers, shouting and firing from the saddle, dashed a mile and a half, overwhelming the infantry and decimating their ranks. They confronted the British at close quarters, capturing their guns.

Kitchener responded with a message to London:

> "If a column like Benson's, operating twenty miles outside our lines, is not fairly safe, it is a very serious matter, and will require a large addition to our forces to carry on the war."[204]

chapter 16.
PEACE.

BOTHA.

BOTHA KNEW the war was lost. In his mind the only question was how good a peace he could negotiate. The more successful his guerrilla activities were, the better chance he had of striking a good compromise. His wife Annie still lived in a small house that she rented in Pretoria. She was left in peace and well treated by the British. Relations between the English and Afrikaans were cordial, and Annie attended English parties, where she sang.

Kitchener asked her to find out whether Botha was prepared to meet him for peace talks. She reached her husband by rail and road, and a meeting was duly arranged. At Middelburg on February 28, 1901, Botha and Kitchener met. Rather surprisingly, according to Kitchener, the two men took to each other almost immediately. Kitchener wrote:

> "Botha has a nice unassuming manner and seems desirous of finishing the war, but somewhat doubtful of being able to induce his men to accept peace without independence in some form."[205]

Indeed, the Free State leaders, Steyn, De Wet and Hertzog were outraged at the idea of Botha negotiating with the British. President Steyn was furious that he had not been consulted, and was suspicious that Botha was prepared to compromise their ideals for the sake of a settled peace. De Wet stated flatly: "...the only object for which we are fighting is the independence of our Republics and our national existence."[206] However, unity among the Afrikaners was disintegrating. By March 1902 nearly 2,000 prisoners had been persuaded to fight for the British in the Transvaal and the Free State. They had great value as guides and scouts, due to their intimate knowledge of the countryside and familiarity with Boer tactics.

Kitchener swiftly and firmly told Botha that independence was out of the question. He argued that independence would in any event be dangerous, given the mixed population and the legacy of the war.

Botha was prepared to concede this point, but came armed with a list of demands. This included amnesty for acts of war, payment of the Transvaal Republic's debts and exclusion of the black races from any voting rights. He also wanted restitution of the farms and equality for the English and Dutch languages. Kitchener asked whether Botha could assure him that all commandos would lay down their arms. Botha could not give this undertaking. The Boer command was a very loose structure, and Botha was dependent upon the co-operation of the Free Staters. However it was apparent that both men were giving thought to the time when Boer and British could live side by side in peace.

Kitchener noted:

> "Botha is a quiet, capable man, and I have no doubt carries considerable weight with his burghers; he will be, I should think, of valuable assistance to the future government of the country in an official capacity."[207]

Kitchener at once contacted his government in London. A grant of one million pounds to rebuild and restock farms was the equivalent of one month's expenditure on the war effort. If that was what it would take to agree peace terms, Kitchener was all for it.

The written proposal arising from the Middelburg meeting, which Kitchener sent to Botha, incorporated all the issues they had agreed upon. However it is often overlooked that the British and Boers agreed upon the status of the Africans. A clause in the letter by Kitchener reads:

> "As regards the extension of franchise to Kaffirs in the Transvaal and Orange River Colony, it is not the

intention of His Majesty's Government to give such franchise before representative Government is granted to those Colonies, and if then given it will be so limited as to secure the just predominance of the white race."[208]

As at the beginning of hostilities, the obstacle to any peace agreement was Lord Milner. Representing the British Government politically as Governor of the Cape Colony, he had considerable authority at his elbow. He was unprepared to give amnesty to the inhabitants of the Natal and Cape Colonies who had supported the Boer cause. He believed the British were close to total victory. He wanted the Boers to be crushed, and a united South Africa ruled by the British. Kitchener was troubled:

"Milner's views may be strictly just, but they are to my mind vindictive, and I do not know of a case in history when, under similar circumstances, an amnesty has not been granted…We are now carrying this war on to put two or three hundred Dutchmen in prison at the end of it. It seems to me absurd and wrong."[209]

Botha had come to the same conclusion as Kitchener. To prolong a war which was now bound to be won by the British would simply be a waste of lives. On account of Milner's intransigence the war was to drag on for another year with many lives lost as a consequence.

Milner's policy of unconditional surrender was unpopular in London. Joseph Chamberlain, Secretary of State for the Colonies, warned him that "if some progress is not made before long I think public dissatisfaction may become serious and threaten the existence of the Government in spite of its enormous majority."[210]

A curious sidelight of the negotiations was an encounter between Kitchener and Botha that occurred the evening the talks ended. It was related that before the delegations returned to their lines, Kitchener invited Botha to a game of bridge. Botha said he only knew whist, and Kitchener assured him this would enable him to learn bridge. They played for some hours, Botha losing £15. He showed every sign of having enjoyed himself, and from then on sought any opportunity he could to play. As the Boers had no cards of their own, he asked Kitchener for some, and the next day Kitchener sent him fifty packs.

The meeting with Kitchener fundamentally affected Botha's thinking.

Not only could he see a way and time when Britons and Boers could co-exist, but he realised the commitment of the colonial power. A War Commission after the war recorded that 448,435 British troops had been sent to South Africa, augmented by 52,414 local men. The total cost of the war to Britain was estimated at £222 million, a fortune in those days. Botha by now had realised that there was no possibility of South Africa being built on independent Boer states.

The Free State leaders did not share this feeling. They felt they had been dragged into the war by the Transvalers, and would have preferred to maintain their independence. They hankered for a return to the pre-war state, and were not prepared to compromise. Botha could see that whilst the Free State would remain predominantly Afrikaans, the inflow of Uitlanders combined with those Boers who had abandoned the struggle would soon form a majority in the Transvaal. Unless he could strike a deal with the British – and soon – he risked seeing the leaders of the "Volk" banished and his land left to the mercy of the British without check. Botha was faced with no alternative but to agree a settlement with the British.

In the second half of 1901 Botha's homestead at Waterval was dynamited. There was no military reason for the act; it looked vindictive. Botha's reaction, curiously, was one of relief. His house had suffered the same fate as hundreds of his staunch supporters, though in fact it had been spared for a long time. The fact that it had not been destroyed previously caused resentment among some of the Boers who felt he was receiving favoured treatment and wondered why. Harried by the British, who saw his capture as crucial to the end of the war, he disappeared into the hills around Vryheid.

Through many skirmishes, some successful, others not so, Botha continued to work towards peace. He was increasingly anguished by the loss of life, which he saw as senseless. On March 4, 1902, Kitchener wrote to the Transvaal executive proposing a peace settlement. When Botha saw the letter, delivered to him in the field, he said: "The war is over."[211] He sensed that the commandos would be prepared to lay down their arms. Under a guarantee of safe conduct he travelled to Vryheid, but the sight of armed Zulus there caused him to refuse to lay down his arms, and he returned to the veld. The animosity between the Boers and the Zulus remained long-standing. He was worried that should the Boers lay down their arms the Zulus would take the opportunity to seek reprisals. In fact a few nights later these Zulus attacked a small Boer laager at Holkrantz, near Vryheid, killing everyone they found. (The Transvaal had annexed Holkrantz, part of Zululand, after the Zulu War). Recognising that peace talks now were inevitable, he was able to persuade the Free Staters to join him in a meeting with Kitchener.

On April 9 six Transvaal leaders and five from the Orange Free State met at Klerksdorp to agree their negotiating position. They agreed that neither was to negotiate separately. However, the Free Staters, led by President Steyn, quickly asserted that "independence was an essential condition for any peace."[212] They argued that if it was not possible to fight on "unconditional submission was preferable to making terms with the British."[213] Steyn was concerned about what would follow a peace pact. Submission would keep his future options open.

Botha, supported by De la Rey and De Wet, argued that it was better to bind the British to the grant of self-government and economic reconstruction. He was looking far ahead. Steyn feared Milner's vow to "break the back of Afrikanerdom," but hoped that war-weariness and shifting attitudes in Britain would lead to the republics being restored. The Transvalers adopted a pragmatic stance. They recognised that independence was now not possible. The best they could do was to negotiate peace terms that would give them an element of self-government under British rule and protection of their most important interests: property and their language.

On April 12 the two sides met in Pretoria at Melrose House, where Kitchener was living. The arrival of the Boers was kept as quiet as possible. The Transvalers and Free Staters were housed in separate quarters: it was evident that their differences had not been resolved. Kitchener pointed out that a British victory was inevitable, and pleaded with the Free Staters to recognise this. He promised a grant of self-rule "in the near future." After referring the proposals to London he confirmed that independence was unacceptable, and would not be granted.

At a second meeting Lord Milner, anxious to ensure his strong views prevailed, joined the discussions. The Boers were well aware of his implacable opposition, and eyed him with cold hatred. Milner proposed a period for reflection on their respective positions. The Boers stated that the proposals were so fundamental that they had no constitutional authority to negotiate them. The will of the people was paramount. Direct popular representatives, elected by the people would decide their position. It was agreed that thirty Tranvaal representatives and the same number of Free Staters would meet at Vereeniging in May to agree the Boer position. Both Kitchener and Botha were jubilant. Kitchener wrote home that he expected there to be peace by May 20.

When the delegations met in Vereeniging on May 15, the talks commenced in a huge and opulent marquee. On May 16, Botha made a key speech which, in retrospect, won the day for him. He outlined the hopelessness of the Boer position in the field, he warned them of the growing threat from armed Africans, he pointed out that to wait for European intervention was futile and he emphasised the misery of Boer families caught in the conflict. He argued:

"You are confronted with the necessity of taking a highly important resolution.... We cannot procrastinate until we have dwindled to a few thousand, and then hope to be able to negotiate. It will be too late then. If we are to negotiate at all, now is the time.....if... we do make terms, we shall obtain responsible government, and our language rights will be maintained....Are we to fight until we are absolutely overwhelmed, so that thirty years will have to elapse before we can raise our heads again?"[214]

Jan Smuts, though not part of the delegation, had been invited to participate, and supported Botha's stand. Botha's impassioned arguments were listened to carefully. Then came the crucial moment. That great warrior, De la Rey, rose to his feet slowly:

> "So far as I myself am concerned, I cannot think of laying down my arms. Yet it appears to me that some parts of the country will be compelled by starvation to give up the struggle." He dismissed as unrealistic the hope that sympathetic European powers would intervene. "There has been talk of fighting to the bitter end...but has not the bitter end come? I believe that the time has come to negotiate. England will never again give us the chance of doing so, should we allow this opportunity to slip by."[215]

The extremists were shattered; nobody could deny De la Rey's right to speak for the resistance. The peace discussions, it seemed, were bound to proceed to a conclusion.

However, Kitchener and Milner were still at odds. Milner continued to take an unyielding line, while Kitchener was all for compromise. Backwards and forwards the arguments swung, until finally on May 31 agreement was reached. The Boers were to be granted £3 million to assist economic reconstruction. The Dutch language would still be taught, and those who had fought honourably in the war would be pardoned, and allowed to keep their arms. There would be no independence, but limited self-government supervised by the British, and a defence alliance would be entered into. The Free Staters had fought a bitter last-ditch stand. The breakthrough had come when a frustrated Kitchener, balked by Milner from making concessions, took Smuts aside and pointed out that within two years there would be a Liberal government in Britain which would lead to the granting of independence to South Africa.

Botha's speech at this meeting was significant:

> "We came here with the earnest desire to make peace. I fancy that, if our scheme is carried out, Boer and Briton will be able to live side by side. I assume that neither party wishes to oppress the other race."[216]

Although both Milner and the Boer leaders were incensed that Smuts and Kitchener should agree a deal between them without recourse, the pact sealed the peace. Milner's new proposal stipulated that the Boers would at once lay down their arms and no longer oppose the authority of King Edward VII. Prisoners of war on both sides would be repatriated without recrimination. The Dutch language would be taught in schools and the possession of rifles for self-protection would be permitted. Africans would not be given the vote. The Transvalers, led by Botha and Smuts, strongly supported by General De la Rey, who was held in great esteem, wanted to accept the terms there and then.

Botha stressed the shortages of maize and cattle being suffered, the plight of the Boer families and the general exhaustion of troops and horses. In the past year he had lost over 6,000 burghers killed and captured. Of the 10,800 men remaining nearly 3,300 were without horses. He pointed out that their weakness was likely to be exploited by belligerent African tribes.

The Free Staters, led by President Steyn, De Wet and Herzog were still against accepting terms. They still hankered after an independent republic. Steyn became seriously ill. When the Free Staters needed him most he was unable to respond and was forced to abandon the talks. Without him De Wet and Herzog could not persuade others to oppose the agreement, and it was carried by 54 votes to 6 on May 31. A young British newspaper reporter overheard the final discussion between the

Boer leaders and two British officers summoned to Botha's tent, and the Daily Mail in London had the scoop of the decade. The reporter's name was Edgar Wallace, later to become a famous writer of thriller novels.

Botha's reputation was enhanced by the peace discussions. Even his enemies agreed that his speeches had come straight from the heart, that his intentions were honourable, that he had remained resolute. Of the troops sent to South Africa by the British, 22,000 had died. The Boer losses were about 24,000 of whom 20,000 were women and children in concentration camps. 31,600 Boers had been taken prisoner.

chapter 17.
AFTER THE WAR.

BULLER.

ON THE face of it, Buller's return to England in early November 1900 was a triumph. His arrival at Aldershot surpassed all previous ceremonial occasions. A series of excursion trains carried thousands of Londoners to the small military town. His train, festooned with flags, drew into the station to the sound of school children singing "Home Sweet Home." Dignitaries greeted him from specially erected grandstands. Wounded soldiers in wagonettes cheered him. Members of the Aldershot Fire Brigade drew his carriage through the streets lined with troops and the densely-packed public. Masts along the way, covered with flags, capped by gilded crowns, carried banners proclaiming "He obeyed the Empire's Call," and "The Nation Thanks You." Letters flooded into his country home, Downes, congratulating him. Poems and patriotic songs were dedicated to him. Postcards of Buller even appeared on the streets of Paris. Buttons with his picture on were widely worn. Numerous baby boys were named after him.

His return to Aldershot, where the work was not onerous, gave Buller time to recuperate. Reunited with his family, he looked forward to the year 1901 with happy anticipation. His superiors did not temper the adulation afforded him by the public at first. Indeed, Wolseley had given him to believe that he had a good chance of succeeding him as

Commander-in-Chief of the British Army. It was only on Roberts' return, and the announcement that Wolseley was to give way to Roberts, that Buller began to realise that all might not be as right as he assumed. Wolseley and Roberts had, for years, been bitter rivals, with their own followings and supporters within the government. Now it seemed that Roberts had won, and Buller's relationship with Roberts was sufficiently uneasy for him to fear the worst. It was not long coming.

A general election in October 1900, timed by the government to coincide with what they thought would be an end to the Boer War, had returned Lord Salisbury and the Conservatives to power with an increased majority. The new Secretary-of-State for War, St John Brodrick, an admirer of Roberts, shared Lansdowne's dislike and criticism of Buller. Brodrick was already on record as deploring Buller's leadership in South Africa. As Under-Secretary to Lansdowne, two weeks after the battle of Colenso he had written a venomous and indiscreet letter to a social friend deploring just about everything Buller was doing. Now he commented: "Sir Redvers Buller had little opinion of Indian soldiers and none of Sir George White; hence the Ladysmith imbroglio."[217]

More publicly, sections of the press were very critical of him. In particular, the instruction to White to surrender sat very badly. Leo Amery, a journalist with The Times who was one of the few British reporters to have remained close to the battle front in Natal (and was nearly captured with his colleague, Winston Churchill), maintained that Buller had simply told White to surrender forthwith. Amery was to write one of the definitive histories of the Boer War, "The Times History of the South African War" in seven volumes, which was to influence many observers' opinions. The message Buller sent to Lansdowne is misquoted in the book as "…[that] the relief of Ladysmith was impossible, that Sir G. White would be compelled to lay down his arms, and that he proposed to entrench himself in a defensive position near Chieveley."[218]

Amery and Buller had clashed before. Amery, a contemporary of Churchill at Harrow was a great admirer of Joseph Chamberlain. He was to enter politics in 1911 and hold the seat of Birmingham South until 1945 as a Liberal Unionist, a party which merged with the Conservatives in 1912. Buller did not like the Press in general, and Amery received less than sympathetic treatment from Buller. The Times had supported the aims of the Jameson Raid, and was very friendly with some of the participants. Buller had refused to allow any of these men to take part in the campaign, which The Times resented. Buller sought, but was refused, an injunction to prevent publication of the History.

Although Amery claimed that he wished to produce "a really accurate and impartial work,"[219] he had a hidden agenda. Critical of the British High Command, he was campaigning for army reform. Unfortunately for Buller, Amery's focus fell on him. A reviewer in the American Historical Review wrote in 1907 that Amery could not resist "scourging his victims with whips steeped in acid brine." Amery was close to General Roberts.

The original texts of the message to White and the telegrams to Lansdowne, which would have fleshed out his instructions and put them in the context of what was happening at the time, were suppressed by the government. Lansdowne sent a message to Buller that

> "…in the interests of the public, [what I] cannot permit is that you should publish, as you appear to desire to do, the heliogram to Sir George White, apart from his reply."[220]

Buller replied:

> "All I have ever asked for and all I have pressed you to do, though I observe that you are reported to have denied the fact in the House of Commons, is to permit the publication of the telegram which I sent to Sir George White on 16th December 1899, a completely inaccurate report of which has been published."[221]

Lansdowne believed that the ignominy of defeat at Colenso was such that to make public the heliogram to White, and reveal Buller's dispute with the Government, would add fuel to the fire. Buller was all for making a personal statement to refute his critics, but Campbell-Bannerman, to whom he turned for advice, urged him to hold back and thereby occupy the higher moral ground. Buller accepted this advice.

A war correspondent present at Ladysmith supported Buller with a letter to The Sunday Times. He wrote:

> "I happen to know more about Ladysmith than I have permission to write, but I can assert that the famous message to Sir George White was a portion of the relieving General's very necessary precautionary

arrangements made in advance, as is always done, for the worst as for the best. No 'telegram' really exists, as the messages were heliographed in cipher....duly received by Sir George White who openly discussed their receipt, and so clear an understanding was there that the defender of Ladysmith has never ceased to praise Sir Redvers for the part played throughout the whole siege. I am aware that some of the orders covered possible capitulation, very necessary orders too, were noted by certain signallers for whose imperfect knowledge this smattering of light assumed the garb of dictatorial orders for surrender. If a 'telegram' exists anywhere it is merely one of these uncertified copies made from the flashes, and General Buller, knowing that his own and Sir George White's copies are intact, is on safe ground in challenging the production of 'evidence' which a non-strategical mind has bluntly assumed to be something which it is not."[222]

The full exchange between Buller and White are set out in an appendix at the end of the book.

The public debate came to a head in September 1901. On September 28 Leo Amery, returned from South Africa, writing under the pseudonym "Reformer," had a letter published in The Times which read:

"The utter fatuity of Colenso, the unnecessary abandonment of the guns, the message to Sir G. White suggesting the surrender of Ladysmith, the want of decision at Spion Kop, the half-hearted attempt at Vaal Krantz, the costly blundering back into the Colenso death-trap after the capture of Monte Cristo might have shown the way to the blindest, the inexcusable failure to pursue a demoralised enemy – is this the record for which the Government and Lord Roberts, who know all, have chosen the Commander on whom the first shock of the next war may fall?"[223]

On October 10, at a lunch given by the Queen's Westminster

Volunteers, Buller defended his actions. For the first time he made public the circumstances in which the message to White was sent. He pointed out that he was thereby taking responsibility if White was forced to surrender, but he also made public the wording:

> "I tried Colenso yesterday, but failed. The enemy is too strong for my force, except with siege operations, which will take one full month to prepare. Can you last so long?...If not, how many days can you give me to take up defensive position, after which I suggest your firing away as much ammunition as you can, and making the best terms you can." [224]

This text was somewhat different in tone from the press report that stated he had categorically ordered White to surrender. Given the importance attached to his telegram, it is worth quoting in his defence from that speech:

> "...I thought... I had official information in writing that the garrison could not be fed beyond the end of the year. I was wrong, I have found out since. At the time I thought that and believed it. It was then the 15th of December; the end of the year was fifteen days off. The message I had to send to Sir George White was that I had made the attack and that I had failed, and that I could not possibly make another attempt for a month, and then I was certain I could only do it by slow fighting and not by rushing...I looked at it [the message] two or three times, and said 'It is a mean thing to send a telegram like that. He is a gallant fellow; he will sit still to the end.' I was in command; whatever responsibility there was was mine, and I thought, 'Ought I not to give him some help, some assistance, and some lead, and something which, if it came to the last absolute moment, it would have enabled him to say, "Well, after all, I have Sir Redvers Buller's, as my commander, opinion in favour of this."' Therefore I spatch-cocked into the middle of the telegram a sentence in which I suggested that [if] it would be necessary to abandon, to surrender the garrison, what he should do when he

surrendered, and how he should do it.....I stuck that into the thing simply because, if he ever had to give up, it might be some sort of a cover to a man who I thought in much greater difficulty than I was myself."[225]

Unfortunately, Buller was not a polished speaker, and the anger that he felt at the attacks upon him showed in the emphatic language he used. His explanations were ignored; the tone of the speech merely made matters worse. Roberts seized the chance to be rid of Buller. He announced that either Buller must be dismissed or he should resign. Immediately the Secretary of State wrote to Roberts, telling him that he would submit Buller's removal from his command to the King forthwith.[226] Roberts wrote at the same time to Brodrick:

"Buller's speech yesterday is really an extraordinary help to us, and I am strongly of the opinion that we should take advantage of his indiscretion and remove him from his command....Buller has brought this on himself."[227]

The War Office demanded an explanation for the criticism and comments contained in his speech, which Buller gave, defending his conduct.[228] A separate, private letter to Brodrick was so outspoken that one can only assume he considered the Secretary of State to be on his side. He had, he complained, "been goaded past endurance by the constant stream of misrepresentation and falsehood."[229]

Brodrick interviewed Buller on October 17 and demanded his immediate resignation. Unable to justify his dismissal on the grounds of his outspoken criticism, Brodrick fell back on the charge of making public state secrets. Buller refused. On October 22 he received a letter informing him that he was relieved of his Aldershot command and reduced to half-pay. Buller had his defenders, and sought a court-martial, which he should have been entitled to in the light of the charge, but this was refused by Brodrick. An appeal to the king failed. Edward had succeeded Queen Victoria on her death, and Buller had neglected to curry favour with the new monarch. Buller's position was not helped by the antipathy of the Prime Minister, Lord Salisbury. As early as March 1886 Salisbury had shown a dislike of Buller. He was said to distrust him. He certainly found his outspoken and often bluntly-expressed views objectionable, particularly when they were critical of Government.

Queen Victoria had responded to Salisbury's admission that he distrusted Buller by writing to him on August 22, 1895:

> "I do not share your distrust of Sir R. Buller, who is most honest and straightforward; I believe him to be a thorough gentleman....and [he] had held aloof from the press, which perhaps others have not."[230]

On November 20 1901 Buller wrote to the Adjutant General:

> "It appears to be the intention of the War Office to avoid an impartial enquiry and I must repeat that....I have committed no offence of any sort or kind against the King's Regulations."[231]

In 1902 a weak and ineffective Conservative government sought to find a scapegoat for the errors which had cost the country so much in men and money during the Boer War, and had so nearly led to disaster. That scapegoat was Buller.

There followed an acrimonious exchange of correspondence between Buller and the Government. Much of this was publicised in the daily newspapers, causing the public to take up strong positions on either side of the argument. Buller's defence of his actions at Ladysmith can be observed in the following letter written to Arthur Balfour, at that time in charge of the Foreign Office and soon to succeed Lord Salisbury as Prime Minister. Balfour had been quoted in The Times as deploring Buller's criticism of General Warren's leadership at Spion Kop. Balfour believed that the correct procedure should have been for Buller to forward "a simple narrative unencumbered by controversy....in accordance with the Queen's Regulations."[232] This was taken by Buller to assume that the government wished him to temper the despatch by rewriting it in accordance with the Government's wishes, removing any serious criticisms. Buller replied on February 21, 1902:

> "I was not in command at Spion Kop and was not therefore the person to whom either the Government or the public would naturally look for an account of the battle...it is not in accordance with the Queen's Regulations....for an officer who is not present to attempt to write a despatch purporting to contain a simple narrative of an action which he has neither directed

nor witnessed. It is, I believe, the almost invariable custom for him to forward the narrative of the officer in command, with his own comments. This is what I did, and what Lord Roberts did also, and what would be right for him would be right for me."[233]

By March the row had escalated. Balfour would not yield his position. Buller wrote on March 24:

"I hold the view that if a Cabinet Minister goes out of his way to accuse an officer publicly of having caused public inconvenience by a deliberate breach of regulations, he ought either to prove that statement or to withdraw it.....I...express a pious hope that if any further publication is intended, my words may be published as written and without manipulation, and that the opportunity will be taken to correct in this respect previous publications."[234]

Balfour edited Buller's letter of February 21 to him by removing the reference to Roberts in support of the custom of forwarding the report from the officer on the spot without comment. Henry Norman, who accused the Government of something close to dishonesty, took up Buller's cause in Parliament.

A huge gap developed between the disfavour in which the Government held Buller and the public mood. The Birmingham Pictorial noted on August 7, 1903:

"The usual tendency is to kick a man when he is down, but somehow General Buller's fight with the powers that be at the War Office seems to have made him an even greater hero than he was before the War in South Africa commenced. This, at any rate, seems to be the opinion of the average man. And the average man is no fool in these matters… the War Office would find that, much as men like Lord Roberts, Lord Wolseley, General French and General Baden Powell are admired, they would be left a long way in the rear by the butt of the official critics. Birmingham showed what it thought of Buller on Tuesday, and it is many a year since a visitor to the city, who came in an official manner, had anything like such a reception as had General Buller."[235]

In October 1906 Buller retired to his estates in Devon, uninterrupted by the military demands of his country. He figured prominently in local affairs, fostering education in particular. His popularity with the people of Britain was not diminished by his removal. When he appeared in public he was frequently cheered and engulfed by enthusiastic crowds, partly in reaction to an unpopular government, partly as they felt he was a good man who had served his country well. In 1905 a thirteen-foot-high equestrian statue of him was unveiled in Queen's Street, Exeter.

Buller's health remained good until six months before his death on June 2, 1908, of cancer of the gall bladder and liver. He was 68 years old. Among the many letters of condolence received by his wife was one from Louis Botha.

BOTHA.

Botha now set himself the task of creating "a South African nation within a united South Africa."[236] In an open letter to his people, he wrote:

> "Let us now take each other by the hand for the other great battle which lies ahead of us, the well-being of our people, and set aside all feelings of bitterness, and let us learn to forget and to forgive so that the deep scars made by this war may eventually be healed."[237]

This was not just rhetoric. In a speech in Durban in early June, he openly stated his faith in South Africa's future as part of the British Empire. Many Afrikaners found this difficult to accept.

The wisdom of Botha's opposition to the destruction of the gold mines during the war now came to be seen. Between 1903 and 1907 gold production increased from £12.6 million, already a healthy sum in those days, to £27.5 million. The bedrock of South Africa's economy, this gave everyone confidence about the future.

Milner was now resident in Pretoria, where he assumed the Governorship of the Transvaal. He remained a thorn in Botha's flesh, being difficult to deal with and unsympathetic towards the plight of the many homeless Boer families.

Botha, De Wet and De la Rey set out for Europe to raise funds for the reconstruction. The three famous generals were given a rousing send-off from Cape Town by cheering crowds, seeing them for the first time. The reception when they landed at Southampton was equally enthusiastic. This was noted in Europe. The British Empire was not popular on the Continent, and the feeling there was that British rule in South Africa would not last. Botha confessed that he remained bitter about the past and saw considerable irony in his present position. He was uncomfortable coming to terms with the British establishment.

The coronation of Edward VII was due to take place in August, and the Boer delegation was invited to a naval review at Spithead on their arrival to celebrate it. Botha was advised that this would not be a good idea, as the parade of ships was likely to be somewhat triumphalist. On arriving in England he had received notice that Lukas Meyer, his old mentor and fellow commander, had died; he used this as an excuse to miss the review. So the three generals took a train to London. The Boers' spirited resistance had captured the imagination of the British people. Botha's support for a South Africa in co-operation with the British was seen as noble. Thus on their arrival in London huge, cheering crowds met them, and accompanied them in a slow procession to Horrex's Hotel in Norfolk Street, which was to become a favourite Boer rendezvous.

A secret meeting with King Edward VII was arranged on the royal yacht, the Victoria and Albert, moored at Cowes. A special train took the trio to Southampton, from whence Lord Kitchener took them in his carriage to HMS Wildfire. There they met Roberts, and sailed across the Solent to Cowes. Edward gave them a warm welcome, introducing them to his family, and wished them the very best for the future. He showed sensitivity and sympathy towards the Boer leaders, making it clear he understood their position. This "took a load off my mind" said Botha, and the visit went well thereafter.

They travelled on to Holland in pouring rain. There, if anything, the crowds were even larger and more vociferous. At the Hague Botha said: "We have not come here to rejoice. We are the delegates of a most unhappy people; and we are unhappy because we have done our duty, we have defended our liberty and our independence."[238] Annie Botha and her children had been moved to Holland in the latter stages of the war by her husband, concerned for her safety. In Holland Botha was reunited with his wife, and they moved on together to Brussels where their children were living. The meeting was joyful; his nurse put the baby Botha had not yet seen in his arms.

Botha was acutely aware that many of the European countries, especially Holland, were strongly opposed to the expansion of the British Empire. Anxious to raise funds to repair the war damage, he had a delicate balancing act to manage between the British and Continental countries. In particular, he assessed that the £3 million granted the Boers by the British for war reparations would be hopelessly inadequate, and he sought additional funds. He met Joseph Chamberlain, in London on September 5. Chamberlain's close association with Milner made him a figure detested by the Boers. The warmth with which the Boer generals had been received by the people of London irritated Chamberlain. He refused to discuss the promised £3 million, which was duly paid over.

The generals returned to the Continent, where anti-British feelings were manifest in the demonstrations that accompanied their tour. Very little money was forthcoming, however. By the end of their trip they had managed to raise £103,819, of which £10,000 came from the Carnegie Steel Trust. Botha had to be careful not to offend the British, and managed to remain popular with the British people by his careful and reasonable attitude. At his final meeting with King Edward, he and the other generals were offered knighthoods, which they politely refused. However, Botha professed that he was impressed by what he saw in England. The population had greeted the Boer leaders with enthusiasm, and they had been shown courtesy and friendship wherever they went.

On his return Botha found time to attend to his financial affairs. In 1902 the district of Vryheid had been removed from the Transvaal and added to Natal. Botha wished to remain aligned with the Transvaal, so his ruined farm, Waterval, remained unoccupied. The family went to live in the Transvaal, in Standerton at his farm there, Varkenspruit, which he rechristened "Rusthof." There he set about restoring his fortunes. Between 1903 and 1906 he acquired 4,350 acres, adding another 3,900 acres in 1911/12. Using barbed wire left by the British army, he fenced his farms and divided them into paddocks, stocking them with the very best livestock.

Botha dared to start thinking about a united South Africa, with the Crown Colonies and Boer republics coming together in amity. He did not see a place in that for the black people, who remained a problem for the leaders on both sides. Conscious of the fact that they were in the majority in South Africa, neither the British nor the Boers were prepared to award the blacks or coloureds any electoral franchise whatsoever. But first he had to deal with Milner. The Governor-General provoked hatred among the Boers for his intransigence and aggressive stance, and the Uitlanders – mainly British or other Europeans – did not like him either. His arrogance, aloofness and taste for over-regulation jarred with people anxious to resume their lives and progress in a new, free community.

Kruger remained in permanent exile, still opposed to the involvement of Britain in South Africa. His strong views and recalcitrance made it impossible for him to return and participate in the new South Africa. Moreover, he was in poor health. As Commander-in-Chief of the military, in the absence of Kruger, Botha was the most senior man. Increasingly the Boers looked to him for guidance. His association with Smuts had blossomed into a close friendship based on mutual admiration. He relied upon Smuts to cope with Milner, while he opened his doors to anyone who wished to consult him. And consult him they did, men and women travelling great distances to meet him and tell him of their troubles, seeking advice and help. Botha was barely forty-one, but was increasingly seen as the father of his people. The help he gave was tangible, helping to rebuild and restock farms and meeting claims.

Milner's agenda was very different. His dream was of a South Africa united under the Union Jack, speaking only English, educated in British ways, of great economical value to Britain. When the British Colonial Secretary, Joseph Chamberlain, visited South Africa in December 1902, Botha was ready for him. With an Afrikaner deputation of one hundred he met Chamberlain in Pretoria and attempted to negotiate additional financial help and improve on other aspects, such as amnesty for rebels, but Chamberlain was inflexible. The Treaty of Vereeniging was the charter of the Boer nation, he declared, inviolable. Smuts was infuriated by him, describing him as haughty and insulting. The Boers did manage to agree a loan of £35 million, to be raised by the Transvaal and Orange Free State under Imperial guarantee, mainly to be spent on improving the public services such as railways, water, forestry and local municipalities.

Milner informed Chamberlain that the supply of African labour for the mines was inadequate. He asked for support to introduce Chinese labour. The mine owners were ready to underwrite a loan of £30 million for this importation. Botha and Smuts were vehemently opposed. They argued that South Africa already had enough race problems; importing another race would simply add to the difficulties. They were overridden. The Chinese came in their thousands - to the dismay of most South Africans.

Increasingly Botha saw that his mission was to unite the Afrikaners and English-speaking South Africans into one nation. He was to commit the remainder of his career to achieving this aim. It was evident Milner was not intending to do so, and there were still many Boers who wanted nothing to do with the British, and yearned for their Afrikaner Republic. Botha's first task was to persuade his Afrikaner followers to forgive and forget. He argued that unless both Afrikaans and English were willing to let bygones be bygones, the future of South Africa would be fraught with difficulty, both sides harbouring grudges, suspicion and bitterness. His first proposal was that the English-speaking South Africans be offered the hand of friendship. Then he proposed that the "National Scouts" – a group of Boers who had changed allegiances and worked for the British during the war – be forgiven. Not all his fellow Boers were persuaded. The wounds of the war were still fresh and raw, the injustices too grave to be forgotten.

A ground swell of demand for self-government emerged in 1904. Rumours of conflict in Europe, with the British possibly being drawn in, led some South Africans to believe that the Transvaal would be given back to them or "they would have no trouble in taking it."[239] The trades unions passed resolutions in favour of self-government. Botha declared his intention of calling a Boer conference to discuss the issue.

The unpopularity of Chinese labour in the mines acted as a catalyst to rally the Boers. Their leaders refused to serve under Milner on the Transvaal council. A new party, Het Volk [the people] was formed on May 23, 1904, in the Transvaal to represent the Boers. Botha presided at a congress held in the Volkstem building in Pretoria, at which nearly two hundred delegates attended. Het Volk was to play a leading political role during the next seven years. In the Orange Free State a similar Congress held in December formed a local party called the Orangia Unie which demanded recognition of Dutch as a language on equal terms with English, further grants for farmers and complete self-rule as soon as possible. This party adopted a much harder line than Het Volk, largely due to the attitude of their leader. James Barry Munnik Hertzog. He had been educated at Stellenbosch University, the "home" of Afrikanerdom, before studying law in Holland and Germany. He was a fierce and uncompromising defender of the Afrikaners, and hated Botha for his policy of appeasement towards the British. He called Botha an imperialist, misinterpreting his attempts to bring English-speakers and Afrikaners together into a unified country.

From the start Botha had his eyes set on self-rule, which he recognised could only be achieved if he could persuade the British to identify with a united South Africa. Hertzog also wished for a united South Africa, but one in which Afrikaner and English retained their separate identity, language, culture and way of life. Purity of race was important to him. Throughout this debate the huge majority - the black peoples of South Africa - was ignored. Nobody involved in shaping the future of South Africa saw the indigenous tribes playing a significant role; they were merely a labour source.

The campaigning of General Beyers did not help Botha's cause. The old soldier still enjoyed a sizeable following in the Transvaal. Violent speeches in the northern Transvaal criticised Milner, the "kaffirs" (Africans), English schoolteachers, Johannesburg capitalists and veterinary surgeons. Beyers complained that the Boers were being sidelined. "It will lead to another war in South Africa if the government does not treat us more fairly," he claimed.[240]

Smuts referred to the Milner Administration of 1902 to 1905 as "the darkest period in the history of the Transvaal."[241] With his imperialist agenda, Milner steadfastly blocked any attempts at rapprochement which could dilute British dominance. Before he left for England on April 2, 1905, he said:

> "The Dutch can never own a perfect allegiance merely to Great Britain. The British can never, without moral injury, accept allegiance to any body politic which excludes their motherland. But British and Dutch alike could, without loss of integrity, without any loss of their several traditions, unite in loyal devotion to the Empire-State, in which Great Britain and South Africa would be partners, and could work cordially together for the good of South Africa as a member of that greater whole. And so you see the true Imperialist is also the best South African."[242]

Thus at his departure Milner was no closer to understanding the aspirations of the residents of South Africa, or modifying his imperialist dreams, than he had been when he set about provoking the Boer War.

Milner's departure coincided with the dissolution of the British Parliament, the fall of the Conservative Government and the election of the Liberals under Sir Henry Campbell-Bannerman. The new Prime Minister had been very critical of the Conservative handling of South Africa, and had publicly committed to an immediate grant of self-government. As early as 1901 he had predicted that the British Empire could not be retained by force:

> "If we are to maintain the political supremacy of the British power in South Africa it can only be by conciliation and friendship; it will never be by domination and ascendancy, because the British power cannot, there or elsewhere, rest securely unless it rests upon the willing consent of a sympathetic and contented people."[243]

Smuts was sent to sound out the new government, and met Campbell-Bannerman early in 1906. He listened attentively to what Smuts had to say, which was essentially: do you want friends or enemies? With Botha's prior agreement Smuts assured the Prime Minister of the loyalty of himself and his colleagues if their demands were met. Botha pledged:

> "Speaking with full knowledge and with profound conviction I say that, if the British Government will fully and unreservedly trust my people, they will not be disappointed; they will find their confidence repaid in a thousand ways and will have in the Boer people a source of strength for the British Empire."[244]

Smuts brought with him a Memorandum of Points in Reference to the Transvaal Constitution that summed up Het Volk's position effectively and briefly. When Smuts left Campbell-Bannerman he believed he had persuaded the Prime Minister of their case. On February 8, 1906, Campbell-Bannerman called a Cabinet meeting and spoke forcefully of the need to move forward and recognise Boer aspirations. Within minutes the Cabinet decided to give the Boers responsible government in the Transvaal.

Botha was overjoyed, believing this decision would inspire the people of South Africa with a new feeling of hopefulness and co-operation. He saw this as laying the foundation of a united South Africa and set about his new political mission with zeal.

With polling day set for February 20, 1907, four parties contested the first election: Het Volk, the Responsibles [the English-speakers], the Progressives and Labour. Botha and Smuts toured the country intensively, making speeches, arguing for conciliation and goodwill. With Botha went General De la Rey, that quintessential Boer who trusted Botha implicitly, and consequently supported his views. He was a great asset; many Boers who were concerned at the direction Botha was taking were reassured – if Oom [Uncle] De la Rey was a Botha man, things must be all right. Botha stood for Standerton against an English farmer, Hugh Wyndham. Every night he visited a different town, for the first time driving a motor car. His message of conciliation appealed to a number of English-speaking voters, as a result of which his victory was decisive: 675 votes to 354.

At the election Het Volk gained an absolute majority, winning 37 seats out of 69. The status of Full Responsible Government had been granted to the Transvaal in December 1906, and to the Orange Free State, now known as the Orange River Colony, a few months later. There was talk of Smuts being appointed Premier in the Transvaal, but such was the popularity and prominence of Botha that there was only one option in reality. On March 4, 1907 the Botha Cabinet was sworn in. The Governor-General who had succeeded Milner, Lord Selbourne, wrote to King Edward:

> "[Botha] is a born leader of men, with plenty of moral courage, a man of natural dignity of manner and reserve, who does not wear his heart on his sleeve, and will not go enthusing with English Radicals."[245]

In his inaugural speech Botha pledged that British interests would be absolutely safe in his hands. His first move was to offer the leader of the opposition Responsible Party a place in his Cabinet, and soon the two parties were to merge. Shortly after his election he was invited to attend an Imperial Conference in London, where he met the Premiers of other countries within the British Empire. This gave him status and gravitas. He had become very popular in London, the British people seeing him as a romantic, swashbuckling character. His good looks and natural charm reinforced this image, and he was mobbed wherever he went.

King Edward made a great fuss of him, and he and Annie were invited to numerous receptions and banquets. After his visit he presented the King with the Cullinan diamond, originally of 3,025 carats valued at £250,000, but unsaleable in its original state and size.

President Steyn of the Orange Free State was most disapproving of Botha's new international popularity. Perhaps influenced by Hertzog, he was suspicious of Botha's motives, and on April 16 wrote to John X. Merriman, ex-leader in the Cape:

> "No good will come out of it for us. He told me he is only going to listen, and will not bind us to anything. Still, I am sorry he went…the main object ….is to get money for a land bank. Will [he] get it? I wonder."[246]

On Botha's departure from London Lord Balfour, leader of the parliamentary opposition and Prime Minister prior to Campbell-Bannerman, who admired Botha greatly, said to him: "Well, Botha, you have done it; you have got your Constitution. What will come of it?"

Botha replied that he believed

> "…..that in five years I shall return to this country to ask for the Confederation of South Africa."[247]

Whilst in London Botha formed a most unlikely alliance. At the South African elections Dr Leander Starr Jameson, infamous for the failed Jameson Raid, had been elected Prime Minister of the Cape, ousting Merriman. He was in London for the same conference that Botha was attending, and Botha found to his surprise that he took to the man. Ten years older than Botha, Jameson was a small, sensitive man, not the roistering brigand that his raid had made him out to be. Botha realised that friendly relations with the Cape Province could prove to be extremely useful in fostering his long-term aim of a confederated South Africa. The Jameson Raid was past history; now he offered Jameson the hand of friendship. Politically astute though the move was, it was to appal the Transvaal Boer population, whose picture of Jameson was of the devil incarnate.

Honours continued to accumulate for Botha. He was made a Privy Councillor along with Jameson and the premiers of New Zealand and Natal. He was afforded an honorary doctorate degree by Dublin University and the freedom of the cities of Manchester and Edinburgh.

In stark contrast, he returned home to a frosty reception. The majority of Afrikaners felt they had been betrayed, and that the hospitality and adulation he had received in London had seduced Botha. They could not envisage a South Africa in which the English and Afrikaans co-operated and ruled in harmony. The gift to King Edward of the Cullinan diamond, sixty per cent of which belonged to the Transvaal state, forty per cent to its discoverer in the Premier mine, was abhorrent to a people still struggling economically with the aftermath of the war. These voices were somewhat silenced when the British Parliament voted a guaranteed loan to the Transvaal of £5 million. One of Botha's biographers, Dr F.V.Engelenburg, who was a contemporary of Botha, wryly commented:

> "It is a rather remarkable fact that several ardent 'patriots', who took no pains to hide their disgust at Botha's demonstration of 'English' loyalty, never hesitated for a moment in applying for a Land Bank loan."[248]

One of the first major issues Botha was forced to confront was the question of the Chinese immigrants working on the Witwatersrand mines. They had been brought in to provide a labour pool that the Africans could not, or would not fill, but their presence had led to many problems. Numbering 100,000 they were a noticeable alien presence, with a different culture and different habits. Rightly or wrongly they were blamed for an upsurge in crime in the Johannesburg area, and the government was under pressure to do something.

The Afrikaners were in favour of sending them all home immediately, but Botha could see that this exodus would damage the mines. With the support of the British government, Chinese repatriation was gradual, the pace determined by the ability to replace them with native labour. Strong opposition came from the mine owners, who threatened to close the mines. However one of the gold magnates, J.B.Robinson, broke ranks and offered to help run the mines for the state. The mine owners capitulated. Botha's government undertook actively to recruit African labour to replace the Chinese, and in the three years from March 1907 to August 1910 the number of African mineworkers rose from 81,500 to 185,000 and every Chinaman left the country.

Botha made a point of getting to know Lord Selbourne, Milner's successor as Governor-General of South Africa. The two men became friends with Selbourne coming to realise that the unification of South

Africa under some form of federation was the only practical way forward. The four states had separate governments, different railway systems, legal systems and customs regimes. Botha succeeded in calling the four premiers together to a convention in October 1908 to discuss the prospect of confederation. Initially, it was held in Durban, and moved to Cape Town from mid-November to early February 1909 when the oppressive heat and humidity of Durban became hard to bear. Smuts, so often the brains behind Botha's leadership, prepared assiduously. It was his opinion that union, rather than federation, was the appropriate structure to which they should aspire. Smuts and Botha wanted a South Africa where everyone was equal (as long as their skin was white) and the races were not separated in any way. Confederation could encourage separation of the cultures; union would ensure this was not so.

Thirty-three delegates attended the Convention. Smuts brought nineteen secretaries and advisers, a staff larger by half than the other three territories combined. Sir Henry de Villiers, Chief Justice of the Cape Colony, presided. It was Botha, however, who led the proceedings. His reputation and standing was such that the others listened and followed. He made them feel at ease, comfortable in each other's company. Throughout the convention he emphasized the need for moderation, compromise and willingness to accommodate disparate views. He was greatly aided by President Steyn of the Orange Free State, who backed Botha's dream, and offset the implacable hostility shown by his premier, Hertzog. Jameson, representing the Cape, wrote:

> "Botha is the great factor, and plays a capital game of bridge. He, Steyn, and I are great pals."[249]

Smuts' preparatory work combined with Botha to dominate the Convention. There was significant support for a federal structure similar to that in Australia, but Smuts argued strongly that something closer and tighter was needed in South Africa to bind the white races and separate colonies together. He had worked out every detail of his proposals. He pointed to the union which existed in Britain, "the most successful system the world had ever seen."[250] Despite obvious differences, compromises reached on all major issues enabled the Convention to agree a draft constitution on May 3, 1909, by which time it had moved on to Bloemfontein in the Orange River Colony. A delegation at once set out for England to present their proposals to the British government. Such was the thoroughness with which Smuts, in particular, had prepared the draft, that there was little opposition to it in London. H.H.Asquith, who had succeeded Campbell-Bannerman as Prime Minister, continued with the liberal approach of his predecessor. The Act of Union was passed without difficulty.

The question of who would be the new Union's first Prime Minister posed constitutional problems. As no formal election had been held under the new rules, nobody could claim to have a mandate. As had happened in Australia under similar circumstances, it fell to the Governor-General to identify someone capable of forming a representative government. This government would then call elections to allow the citizens to vote in a new government. Although as encumbent Botha was the obvious choice, his appointment was not inevitable. John X. Merriman, so long dominant in the Cape Colony and a previous premier there, could claim to have the credentials, a good following and substantially more political experience than Botha. Merriman, however, was a prickly man, with an obstinate streak and strong views that were manifested in sudden outbursts.

The election process itself proved to be slightly chaotic. H.J. Lord Gladstone (son of Lord Gladstone who had granted the Transvaal independence after Majuba) who landed in Cape Town on May 17, 1910, succeeded Lord Selbourne as Governor-General. The Act of Union was due to come into force on May 31, and Selbourne sailed for the UK on the 18th. So Gladstone had precisely one day to consult Selbourne, and less than two weeks to make the decision. The consultations he conducted quickly brought the options into focus. Surprisingly, a number of English-speakers favoured Botha. Natal in particular was very hostile towards Merriman. Botha had shown a desire to bring the two races – Afrikaans and English-speakers - together and weld a united South Africa. He proposed a policy of "best men" under which the best qualified man would be appointed to office in the new government regardless of political affiliation. This was anathema to the old political wardog, Merriman. Moreover, Merriman harboured a grudge: the British Governor-General, Bartle Frere had dismissed as the Cape premier in 1878. He was anti-empire, and opposed anything that smacked of British influence. The extremist Afrikaners who wished to be free of the British and form their own republics, and the English-speakers who saw their future outside the British Empire, supported him.

Gladstone could see that Botha would be a unifying influence, that he commanded a strong – possibly majority – following. Moreover, he had been assiduous in cultivating friends and contacts in the British establishment, and confirming his credentials as a loyal supporter of the Empire. Predictably Hertzog was against his appointment, and there was a faction in the Cape which preferred Merriman. The financial power of the mines, within Botha's Transvaal, reinforced the feeling that Botha was the father of his nation. Gladstone formalised both the Union and new Cabinet under Botha on May 31, 1910.

Shortly after the Act of Union, Botha and Smuts founded the South African Party. Predominantly Afrikaans, it comprised the mainstream Afrikaans Bond from the Cape, Het Volk from the Transvaal and the Orangia Unie. A number of English-speakers joined. Botha was careful to include in his Cabinet representatives of all the different white races and opinions in South Africa. Soon, however, the cracks became apparent. Hertzog, pursuing an education policy of bilingualism on equal footing, clashed with the supporters of the British government, known as the Imperialists. The Imperialists, anxious to preserve British customs and maintain British influence in South Africa, infuriated the Afrikaners. Increasingly Botha's desire to weld the white people of South Africa into one homogenous group calling itself South African, was caught between the Boers still hankering for their own republic and the Imperialists.

When the first general election was held in September 1910, a shock awaited Botha. Over-confident, instead of contesting his old seat of Standerton he opted to stand in Pretoria East against Percy Fitzpatrick a well-known and popular figure, leader of the opposition Union Party. When the results were announced it was discovered that Fitzpatrick had won the seat by 1,231 votes to 1,136. Botha felt the humiliation keenly. Undoubtedly it diminished his image of invincibility and authority. He took the seat of Losberg, but foresaw problems ahead.

chapter 18.
FALL FROM GRACE.

BOTHA.

The rift between Botha and the traditional Afrikaners widened perceptibly after the Act of Union. The British treated Botha as they would any Premier from part of the Empire. In 1911 he visited Britain to attend the quadrennial Imperial Conference. He was highly regarded by the British establishment, who offered him a number of honours. Most of these he refused, but he accepted the honorary rank of general in the British Army. His critics among the hardline Afrikaners took this very badly. He participated in conferences in London frequently, was consulted often on a wide range of issues and made many friends in England. Several of his new friends were people who were anathema to Hertzog and his followers, who saw them as bitter enemies who had inflicted terrible wrongs on the Boer nation.

Botha was either blind to this widening rift or did not care. His aim remained to weld South Africa together into a single nation, with enmity between English and Afrikaans speakers relegated to the past. His popularity grew with the English speakers, who trusted him and could agree with his objectives. The more this became evident, the more his old Afrikaans friends were alienated. Hertzog and his followers were increasingly concerned that his people would lose their identity and be subsumed. Botha, at ease in England and comfortable within the Imperial brotherhood, rather tactlessly let his admiration for things British show.

Botha and his family had taken up residence in Groot Schuur, close to Cape Town, during parliamentary sessions. Their time was split between the Cape, Pretoria, and the Botha farm at Rusthof.

Botha was still a farmer at heart. Buxton reported:

> "Botha has a very fine farm. A railway runs through the middle of it, and he has a station not far from the centre, so he is well placed. There are four or five Dutch managers on his farm......Botha believes in well-bred sheep and cattle, the latter mainly Frieslands. He grows a great deal of mealies...At the back of the house is a large enclosure called a 'camp' in which he keeps some wildebeeste, springbok and blesbok."[251]

Groot Schuur was redolent with memories: Rhodes had developed it, and it remained full of mementoes of him. Jameson had lived there as Premier of the Cape Colony. Botha entertained at Groot Schuur often and lavishly. He loved company, and his ability to listen to others and gain their sympathy was well suited to his new lifestyle.

In the new, national cabinet Smuts was given the Finance portfolio. Botha wished to keep Hertzog within the fold if he could, and gave him the portfolios of Justice and Native Affairs. Far from toeing the line, Hertzog used his position to rail against the English speakers. He called them "foreign adventurers" and "bastard sheep," so insulting the inhabitants of English-speaking Natal and the eastern Cape that the clamour grew for his dismissal. Much of Botha's work in bringing the two races together was being undone. He needed to drop Hertzog, yet he hesitated to take such a radical step and alienate the traditional Afrikaners even more.

On December 7, 1912, Hertzog made a speech in which he said that the imperial connections were good only in so far as they served the interests of South Africa. Loyalty and conciliation were empty words. As the row developed, Hertzog's abiding hatred of Botha became evident. Even where they agreed – and Botha also felt that imperialism was only useful where it served South Africa – Hertzog's extreme language, grim demeanour and ability to alienate a large section of the white community made him uncomfortable to have in government.

Botha finally took the plunge. Constitutionally it was questionable whether he could sack Hertzog. Another way of removing him had to be found. In December 1912 he tendered his resignation to the Governor-General, sure of the support of the majority of the Cabinet. Lord Gladstone asked him to reconstitute the government, which he readily did, omitting Hertzog from the Cabinet. He issued a statement in which he explained his actions:

> "General Hertzog has gratuitously and unnecessarily put the question whether the interests of South Africa should take precedence over those of the British Empire. This question should not have been put…..The true interests of South Africa are not, and need not be, in conflict with those of the Empire from which we derive our free Constitution. The only effect of speeches such as that made….will be to cause doubt as to the real policy of the Government, to create misunderstanding and estrangement between the different sections of South Africa's people, and to undo the great work which has been built up in the last four or five years with so much labour and devotion. I wish to emphasize that to me the interest of South Africa is supreme, and I believe this view is almost generally shared by the population of our Union. This, however, does not exclude that I, myself, and the South African Party, fully appreciate the Imperial ideal. Under our free Constitution within the Empire, the South African nation can fully develop its local patriotism and national instincts…. General Hertzog's policy was different from that of the Prime Minister…In these circumstances it was impossible for me to continue at the head of the Government, and, as General Hertzog proved to be not prepared to resign, nothing else remained for me but to dissolve the Government by my own resignation."[252]

Steyn made desperate attempts to keep Hertzog in the cabinet. The Afrikaners, solidly behind Hertzog, were appalled that he had been excluded. General consensus was that Botha was openly showing his preference for English-speaking South Africa and was placing the interests of Britain before his own people. The Afrikaners did not accept his argument that he was guarding the interests of a united, white, South Africa. General De Wet, who had fought shoulder to shoulder with Botha, participated in the peace negotiations as a leader of his people and visited Europe with Botha, harboured a private dislike for his Prime Minister. He hated the British, and had accused Botha and Smuts during the Vereeniging peace conference of negotiating with Milner and Kitchener behind the backs of his colleagues. Now, in support of Hertzog, he said:

> "It is all very well to say we have to live side by side. It is true, but it does not mean we have to get under one blanket."[253]

Matters came to a head at a party congress in the latter half of 1913. Botha addressed the meeting for over an hour, explaining why he felt it was necessary to support the British Empire. Hertzog responded with his well-known objections, and then De Wet rose.

> "Our Court of Appeal is the People. There is deadlock and it must be solved."[254]

He moved that Botha stand down as leader of the party, that Steyn should take over and find a new Prime Minister, under whom both Botha and Hertzog would serve. The party voted by 130 to 90 votes to support Botha. Hertzog, De Wet and the Orange Free State representatives rose and walked out. The split was final.

Despite his strong stand and deep-felt convictions, the split devastated Botha. He was never thereafter quite to come to terms with the gulf formed within the Boer ranks. Hertzog rallied his supporters in Bloemfontein and formed a new, independent political organisation that he named the National Party.

After the Act of Union, South Africa's economy blossomed. A stable and sympathetic government encouraged foreign investment and development of the commercial sector within the country. An important piece of legislation in 1913 was to set the tone for decades to come. Concerned about the rapid expansion of the black people within South Africa, the Union Government's Department of Native Affairs recognised the native population as a separate community, and set aside 22 million acres as scheduled areas for them. The indigenous black Africans and whites were to live separately, and were not allowed by law to buy land from each other. This was the foundation of the notorious apartheid (Afrikaans for "separateness") policy run by National Party governments after the Second World War.

Simmering discontent among miners on the Witwatersrand came to a head in 1913. Since 1907 they had expressed their concern about imported labour – mainly Chinese – and although Botha had addressed this problem and repatriated the immigrants after 1910, the growth of trades unions and unsatisfactory working conditions led to increasing militancy. A dispute between the general manager and miners arose at the New Kleinfontein Gold Mine on July 4. A general strike of all miners on the Rand was called by the Trade Union. The government, who turned out the military and police in Johannesburg to break up mass meetings, resisted it. Twenty miners were killed and forty-seven people injured, many of them innocent bystanders. Bravely Botha and Smuts drove from Pretoria to the centre of Johannesburg in an open car without escort to talk to the strikers. Feelings were running so high that their lives were in danger. They held a conference with four of the strike leaders in the Carlton Hotel. A settlement, the Bain Treaty, was agreed, meeting most of the strikers' demands. Botha and Smuts were in no position to argue.

Smuts stated:

> "We made peace because the Imperial forces informed us that the mob was beyond their control....Anything could happen that night: the town might be sacked and the mines permanently ruined."[255]

It was not long before unrest erupted again. This time it was led by the railwaymen, in protest at workers being laid off in an attempt to make the railways profitable. The trade unions were strong enough to influence the working population as a whole, and in January 1914 a general strike was called, involving 20,000 men. Smuts was prepared this time. Under the authority of the Defence Act he called out the burgher commandos and the Active Citizen Force and proclaimed Martial Law on the Rand. Thirty thousand Afrikaner horsemen maintained order. The strikers submitted and surrendered. Nine of the strike leaders were arrested and deported by Smuts, although he had no legal right so to do.

Botha reaped the whirlwind reaction that followed the deportation. His enemies portrayed him as an enemy of the people. The suspicions and criticism that he was a puppet of the British Empire, and had betrayed the Boers, surfaced again. Botha remained adamant that as the leader of the nation he must assert his authority for the peace of the country.

Amid the turmoil an astute young Indian lawyer seized the opportunity to take up grievances of the large Indian populations in the Transvaal and Natal. Caught between the indigenous Africans and the dominant whites, these communities had few rights and were discriminated against. Whilst many grievances remained, using passive resistance considerable progress was made in improving their lot. The lawyer's name was Mahatma Ghandi.

World affairs were about to intervene and challenge Botha's position in a way that he had not had to face before. On a visit to Germany he became alarmed by the mood there. He warned Churchill:

> "Do not trust these people. I know they are very dangerous. They mean you mischief. I hear things you would not hear. Mind you have all your ships ready. I can feel that there is danger in the air. And what is more, when the day comes I am going to be ready too. When they attack you, I am going to attack German South-West Africa and clear them out once and for all."[256]

In the scramble for Africa among European powers Germany had established a sizeable colony in South-West Africa, now known as Namibia. The South Africans, and the British in particular, had for some time been conscious of a rival power on the doorstep, and the First World War was to bring this to a head. Botha was aware that a number of the Afrikaners were sympathetic to the Germans, and may take advantage of European conflict to break with the British and seize full independence.

The Commander of the Transvaal militia, Christian Beyers, did not help Botha's cause. A deeply religious man of striking appearance, he became a talisman for the Afrikaners alarmed at Botha's pro-British tendencies. It was rumoured that at an interview with the Kaiser he had been promised that if the Afrikaners stood by Germany, South Africa would be proclaimed an Afrikaner Republic after the war.

Beyers had fought with distinction as a general during the Boer War. He was seen by the Afrikaners as one of the Transvaal leaders, and enhanced his reputation as a politician as Speaker of the Lower House once Transvaal was granted responsible government. He was considered tolerant and impartial, and was respected by the English-speaking South Africans. Appointed commander of the Citizen Forces of South Africa, he visited Holland, Germany, Switzerland and Britain in 1912. Kaiser Wilhelm II showed him great attention, and he returned to South Africa impressed by Germany's might and convinced that co-operation with Germany would lead his people to freedom.

Shortly after returning from Germany, Botha and his wife visited Rhodesia. They planned to return on a German ship from Delagoa Bay, but a telegram from Churchill changed that. War was imminent, and Botha risked being taken by the Germans and carried north to German East Africa. He hurried back to Pretoria overland. Concerns about the sentiments of Afrikaners were confirmed at a garden party given by the British Commander-in-Chief at his official residence in Pretoria. Beyers, when asked his opinion, responded passionately: "The German armies will sweep across the world. There is nothing that can stop them."[257]

When war was declared on August 4, 1914, Botha knew that South Africa could not choose neutrality. In 1911, with the possibility of war looming, he said:

> "There is no such thing as optional neutrality. Should the day ever dawn when the common Fatherland is attacked, Dutch and English Africanders would be found defending the Fatherland to the very last."[258]

There were people who asserted that South Africa should remain neutral and on September 28, 1914, Botha further defined his attitude. He was not a lawyer, but simply a farmer who used his common sense, and who desired to lead his people honestly and truly according to his best lights. To him, using his common sense, all this talk of neutrality appeared to be the biggest nonsense he had ever listened to.

> "In the past the people of South Africa had said to the British Government, 'Trust us and we shall prove ourselves worthy of that trust.' Would they now, when for the first time they were faced with great troubles, stand aside? Surely that was not like the people of this country with their great history! To-day they must prove to the British Empire which was watching them, that they were worthy and more than worthy of the trust

which had been reposed in them, and by doing so they would create for themselves a greater future than would otherwise be possible."[259]

Bismarck had annexed South-West Africa, the territory adjoining the Cape, to Germany in 1884. It had three viable ports, Walvis Bay, Swakopmund and Luderitzbucht. Walvis Bay had been occupied by the British before the German annexation, but had been seized by the Germans at the outbreak of war. The other two ports however, though inferior to Walvis Bay, could be used by the German fleet to threaten Atlantic sea traffic and South Africa's attenuated coastline. Strategically and geographically, it would be impossible to stay out of the conflict. A naval war would involve the Cape, and South-West Africa, whose ports offered anchorage for fleets of either the British or Germans.

South-West Africa was a vast territory: 322,000 square miles stretching from Angola in the north to the Orange River in the south. Much of it was arid desert and uninhabitable. Germany had a regular armed force of 2,000 men with 140 officers posted there. In addition, the settlers could provide 7,000 reservists. The posts were well armed with modern weapons, and the army was well led by experienced German officers. The principal town, Windhoek, had a powerful radio station able to communicate to Berlin on the movement of shipping along the west coast of Africa.

Botha affirmed his allegiance to Britain immediately war broke out, and undertook to defend South Africa against the Germans. Predictably, the British asked Botha to seize the harbours of German South-West Africa and occupy the principal town, Windhoek. This would require an expeditionary force acting proactively; a different situation to the defence of one's own country. Botha recognised at once the difficulty he would have in obtaining Afrikaner support. Worse, such action could provoke a violent backlash. It was contrary to Hertzog's doctrine of 'South Africa First' to which Botha professed to adhere. How was he to raise the necessary force to achieve a successful invasion without the cooperation of Hertzog and his followers?

His old friend, De la Rey, did not help his cause. A stalwart of the Afrikaner cause, he had become convinced that Botha's way was the appropriate one for South Africa to follow, and had supported him strongly although his own inclinations were anti-British. His allegiance had helped immeasurably in carrying the white people of South

Africa with Botha, and had acted as a counterbalance to the extreme conservatives and the views of Hertzog. De la Rey now felt the time was right to 'throw off the British yoke' and declare an independent republic. He had always believed that it was towards such a republic that Botha was taking the country. Botha had not explained that he recognised the impracticality of such a move, and in an uncertain, turbulent world he was committed to the British Empire.

Stories had circulated about what Botha had pledged at Vereeniging, when the treaty leading to the Union had been agreed. He was said to have told Afrikaners that the time would come when Britain would face difficulties, and then the Boers would take the country back. He was said to have promised that it was his aim to use unification to create a republic.

Most bizarrely of all, a prophet. Niklaas van Rensburg told De la Rey that he was the instrument chosen by God to lead his people to a great free republic. De la Rey believed him. Many Afrikaners worried that De la Rey was not being rational. Others were inclined to follow him, if only for their own ends.

De la Rey called a meeting of like-minded folk at Treurfontein, near Lichtenburg. He planned to ride to Pretoria with thousands of followers. There a great rally would be held and a new republic declared. Botha would be sent for and carried on the shoulders of the people and named President of the South African Republic. The people of South Africa would be happy and free again.

De la Rey was not normally given to preaching insurrection: there must be some broader support. Perhaps Botha was behind it all? Belatedly, Botha decided it was time to level with De la Rey. He had allowed the general to believe a free republic was feasible; now he needed to explain this was impractical. De la Rey was invited to Pretoria. There he met Botha and Smuts. They talked long into the night. Botha stated firmly that it was never their intention to take advantage of Britain's difficulties to break away.

De la Rey could not grasp this. He kept repeating that it was the call of God to the Boer people that they release themselves from the agreement made at Vereeniging. Botha pleaded with him to cancel the rally at Treurfontein, or at least not attend it. De la Rey simply reiterated that he had a message from God, and he must go. He used texts from the Bible to support his resolve. He also argued that South Africans should not concern themselves with England's war. He warned that if

Botha planned to invade South-West Africa he would oppose it. Botha replied: "I have sworn my loyalty to the British Government," at which De la Rey responded: "And I have sworn my loyalty to the Union of South Africa!"[260]

Worn out, the two great generals parted in peace. De la Rey was steady in his resolve to attend the Treurfontein rally, but agreed to counsel calmness. Botha used all his wiles to smooth the old man's feathers, but the meeting upset him badly. He felt like a traitor to the Afrikaner cause, and it was to affect him for the rest of his life. De la Rey was as good as his word. The Treurfontein meeting was duly held, at which he proposed a motion of confidence in the Government, which was carried. The crisis was temporarily averted.

Wasting no time, Botha met his military commanders to discuss South-West Africa. Many, including Commander-in-Chief Beyers, were strongly against an invasion. Beyers let it be known that he would resign if an expedition was mounted. Botha showed again his persuasive powers and leadership. By the time the meeting broke up most of them supported him. Hearing of this meeting, Hertzog used the first congress of the National Party on August 26 in Pretoria to condemn the plan.

With the exception of sixteen hundred infantry, the last remaining British troops had, with Botha's approval, been withdrawn from South Africa to serve in Europe. This meant that any military campaign Botha mounted would need to be manned by South Africans. When he became more explicit about his intentions in South-West Africa there was a degree of reluctance on the part of his supporters to go along with an invasion. Supporting the British war effort in Europe was one thing: an unprovoked attack on a neighbouring territory was another. Botha needed to identify the Germans more specifically as a threatening enemy. This he did. In a speech near Potchefstroom, the army headquarters, he said:

> "Germany is looking for a place to send its overpopulation, and it sees South Africa as a fat lamb ready for the slaughter. German agents with their seditious talk are already doing much harm in South Africa."[261]

He hinted that he was in possession of secret information that would alarm the public. A small German raiding party had crossed into South Africa from South-West Africa at a place called Nakob. Although it had retired almost immediately, this incursion was used as an example of Germany's intentions.

At the debate in Parliament on whether the invasion should take place, Hertzog argued strongly that Botha's first duty was to South Africa, and not Britain. He asked the question: what if Germany won the war? He proposed that the Union should be ready to defend its borders, but not act aggressively. Smuts, however, carried the day with a strong speech on liberty:

> "South Africa...fought for liberty...I said that liberty had been guaranteed and here we are today as free people, able to develop as we please and able to do what we want; and opposed to us is a military compulsion and autocracy which is threatening to suppress and isolate the smaller nations...the question which has to be decided is whether we are going to do our duty, not only to ourselves, but to the whole world; whether we are to maintain our rights which we have fought for."[262]

The House of Assembly carried the motion to support Britain by ninety-two votes to twelve. When the same motion came before the Senate, De la Rey felt he had reached the end of the road. Although he would not vote against the government, he could not support it either, and walked out, returning to his home. This distressed Botha: they had shared so much travail. He could not persuade the old man to return, and finally saw him off at the station in an emotional scene.

Beyers fulfilled his promise to resign. He set off from Pretoria with De la Rey for an anti-invasion rally in Potchefstroom. As they passed through Johannesburg they encountered police roadblocks, set up to apprehend the Foster gang, criminals responsible for a series of daring armed robberies in the area. De la Rey, believing the roadblocks had been set up by the government, who had got wind of their mission, instructed the driver not to stop. The first two blocks were breached without incident, but at the third a policeman fired a single shot which struck the ground and tore into the back of the car, killing De la Rey instantly. The demonstration at Potchefstroom was immediately cancelled, and the country went into mourning. De la Rey's funeral at Lichtenburg became a tense affair. Attended by Botha and Smuts, it also attracted many of their opponents. There were whispers that the killing had been deliberate; or that Beyers was the target and De la Rey had shielded him. Some talked of assassinating Botha, others of taking Botha and Smuts prisoner. Botha's eulogy on De la Rey, obviously heartfelt and genuine, went a long way to mollify emotions.

In the face of mounting opposition, Botha gathered the Commandants at Pretoria and asked for volunteers to fight in South-West Africa. All those present offered themselves without hesitation. The opportunity to go to war under the legendary Botha was too good to miss. Beyers in the Transvaal and De Wet in the Free State were making speeches accusing the Botha government of having murdered De la Rey because he was opposed to the expedition. De Wet advocated armed resistance against the government. Smuts immediately declared Martial Law. Hertzog, while making public speeches criticising Botha and Smuts, was careful not to align himself with the rebels. Beyers, equally, was careful to make it known publicly that "rebellious war was the farthest thing from his mind."[263]

The dissenters responded promptly. Colonel Salomon Gerhardus Maritz, in charge of training camps in Upington, near the South-West African border, launched an armed rebellion. Although an officer in the Boer War, he loathed Botha and all he stood for. He was pro-German and virulently anti-British, and was in friendly contact with the German authorities across the border. To them he looked for supplies of arms and ammunition, but the Germans were cautious and evasive. Smuts and Botha were afraid that Maritz would mobilise the trainees, in number about 600, against them. They instructed him to move his men up to the border, to see what he would do. His response was defiant. He could not move against the Germans "with these children" and warned them that the people of South Africa would not support an invasion. He went on to say that if he was ordered to invade he would resign.

Botha called on Coen Brits, a trusted friend, to take over at Upington. A huge man with an enormous capacity for alcohol, Brits adored Botha. Botha had saved his life during the Boer War when his horse was shot from under him and he became entangled in barbed wire. Botha noticed he had not joined his commando, and went back alone under heavy fire to save him. This action was in many ways similar to Buller's at Hlobane, which won him the Victoria Cross. Once Botha had mobilised his commando in readiness, Brits cabled Botha: "Mobilization complete. Who must I fight? The English or the Germans?"[264]

On September 13 Botha summoned Maritz to Pretoria. Maritz refused to come. Brits was sent to confront Maritz, who had assembled his men twenty-five miles west of Upington, and asked them to defect to the Germans. There was no evidence that they would be well accepted by the Germans who did not trust Maritz. Although they would have liked to see an uprising in South Africa they were not convinced that there was any Afrikaner support of note for Maritz. A car took Maritz across the border, and he returned on October 7 dressed in a nazi uniform. Attempts by Brits to subdue Maritz were met with insouciance. Major Ben Bouwer, sent from Upington to relieve Maritz of his command was arrested. Maritz raised the old Vierkleur, called himself General, and declared South Africa independent and at war with England.

General De Wet called for Botha to resign, and a General Election to be held. He, Beyers and a firebrand called Kemp aligned themselves with Maritz. By October 19 De Wet and Beyers had assembled their own commandos and the revolt was under way. In fact the first signs of active rebellion had surfaced on October 19, when the rebels occupied Heilbron and trains were seized. Any thought of invading South-West Africa was put in abeyance and the assembled volunteers deployed against the rebels. Supporters urged Botha to deal with the rebels severely. Botha was always very aware of his Afrikaner background, and sensitive to the future of South Africa. "It is easy for you to talk," he said, "the responsibility is not yours. I am looking fifty years ahead. I do not wish to leave a wealth of bitterness behind, to keep my people divided forever."[265]

The threat of an impending rebellion had its impact upon Pretoria. The Governor-General, Buxton, was advised to move to Cape Town and on October 22 a night curfew was imposed.

Botha was able to mobilise a force of six thousand horsemen with several guns. Fortunately for him, the commandos of Maritz, Beyers and De Wet were not coordinated, and he was able to deal with them separately. De Wet's men were surprised at night, resting in a farmhouse at a place called Mushroom Valley near Winburg in the Orange Free State and dispersed with twenty-two casualties. De Wet escaped into the Kalahari Desert with a handful of his men, but was soon captured by Brits. Maritz was entrenched on the Cape border with a mixed contingent of rebels and Germans. Beyers fled towards German territory wading into the Vaal River to escape his pursuers. The river was high and flowing strongly; his pursuers fired from the banks. Hurt, Beyers slipped from his horse, disappeared into the torrent and was drowned.

The remaining rebel leader, Kemp, decided to join up with Maritz.

Of the two thousand men in his commando only 610 went with him, the rest trickling back to their homes and giving up the struggle. Kemp reached the Orange River on November 18. Botha himself took charge of the pursuers on November 21, and with 7,500 men swept down on Kemp, hoping to drive him into the arms of Ben Bouwer at Upington. Kemp saw the danger and rode north-east and then veered north-west into the desert where Bouwer's men surrounded them. Under cover of darkness most of them escaped and made their way towards Nakob on the border. The terrain was brutish – sand hills, stony and with harsh thornbushes which tore at the men's clothing. They reached Nakob on November 28 and there found Maritz waiting. Once the men had recovered from their ordeal, the two commandos joined forces and on December 1 jointly declared the independence of South Africa under a provisional government. Unfortunately they did not know the fate of their colleagues, and once they learned that De Wet had been captured and Beyers was dead, they realised there was no point in continuing the struggle.

Recognising their plight, the Germans were unwilling to supply food, clothing and arms. Peace feelers by Kemp and Maritz towards Botha were rejected, so in desperation Kemp and Maritz decided to go on the attack. On January 24, 1915 they descended upon Upington, but the town was a stronghold and they were easily held off. Kemp, seriously ill with blackwater fever, surrendered on February 2. Maritz refused to yield and headed for South-West Africa.

It is thought that some thirteen thousand men took part in the rebellion. 6,000 were captured or surrendered, and 4,000 yielded under an amnesty. The remainder simply melted away, and went home. 30,000 government troops were involved in opposing the rebels, of whom at least 20,000 were Afrikaners. This was a unique confrontation of brother against brother. 374 government troops were either killed or wounded; 540 rebels.

Botha saw the confrontation as not a revolt against the British Empire, but as an act of treachery against the Act of Union. The uprising caused him many a heartache. These were men he had fought with in the Boer war; men who shared his ideals and dreams for the Afrikaner nation. It says much for his leadership that he was able to deal with the rebels in a humane and generous way. Only one leader, Jopie Fourie, who had blown up railway lines and terrorised townships north of Pretoria, was executed for his part in the rebellion. General De Wet was sentenced to six years' imprisonment and a fine of £2,000. Kemp served 7 years and was fined £1,000. Botha was always mindful of the fact that the Afrikaners had to live together, and looked to the future. Merriman, who had been critical of Botha at the beginning of the rebellion, admitted his error:

> "I must own that I misjudged Botha. I was wrong, he has sacrificed what would have been an easy road to popularity, and he has done his duty in a way that compels one's admiration."[266]

Botha's suppression of the rebellion was very popular with the English-speaking citizens, but many of the Afrikaners never forgave him for what they saw as the betrayal of his people. They drew up a petition for clemency towards the rebel leaders. He responded with generosity, but the one person he could not forgive was General De Wet. In the Transvaal animosity towards Botha and Smuts was almost hysterical, and Hertzog seized the opportunity to seek the support of both Transvalers and Free Staters.

Smuts was later to write:

> "Few knew what Botha had gone through in the rebellion. He lost friendships of a lifetime, friendships he valued perhaps more than anything in life. But Botha's line remained absolutely consistent. No one else in South Africa could have stuck it out. You wanted a man for that, very broad-minded, large-hearted. People may say he went too far in that direction, but it is a policy that helped South Africa over its worst stile. It was quite on the cards that after the Boer war the bad old policy would revive. Botha managed to wean the people of that."[267]

chapter 19.
SOUTH-WEST AFRICA.

BOTHA.

With domestic affairs more or less under control, Botha turned again to South-West Africa. To subdue it would be a formidable task, for the territory was as large as the Transvaal and Orange Free State combined. Mainly desert, the terrain was in favour of defenders. Only two ports – Luderitz and Swakopmund – offered access from the sea, a 70-mile strip of desert protecting the hinterland from coastal invasion. The Germans had built 1,400 miles of railway routes with defence in mind; troops could be moved rapidly north and south to meet any threat. Branch lines connected with the two ports, and the main line ran from Angola in the north to Kalkfontein near the southern border.

Botha had been planning his assault for some time. Only he could command the force of 40,000 men, for only he could unite the English- and Afrikaans-speaking South Africans. In September 1914 Luderitzbucht was occupied, and plans to take Swakopmund were well advanced. Walvis Bay was recaptured. Botha sailed from Simonstown in the Cape on January 23, 1915. His force was a combination of British and South African regiments. The British soldiers were very impressed with him. He inspired confidence in the English officers, who found his personal charm and magnetism irresistible. This was just as well, for many of the South Africans were not happy about being pressed into service, and longed to return to their farms.

He found Swakopmund deserted. He planned to advance inland along the railway line, thereby moving swiftly. At the same time Smuts would advance from Kuruman in the east across the Kalahari Desert, Deventer would come from the Orange River in the south and the British commander, Mackenzie, from Luderitzbucht in the south-west. The Germans retreated inland, tearing up the railway tracks as they went and poisoning the wells. Many land mines were laid along the roads. Inability to use the railway, and the need to clear the way forward in such a fierce climate on inhospitable land, made Botha's progress slow.

Nevertheless the nature of warfare was changing. The advent of the motor car meant that commandos could be moved great distances rapidly. The plan was to travel light and fast, hoping to catch the Germans napping. Botha showed little regard for his personal safety by travelling with the advance force as they pushed the Germans back. Unwilling to take their enemy head on, the Germans retreated north without a fight, resorting to some desultory shelling and booby-traps.

The capital, Windhoek, was captured on May 12. This prompted the Germans to offer an armistice. They would remain in the north while Botha kept the territory he had conquered. When peace was agreed between England and Germany the future of South-West Africa could be decided between them. Botha was adamant: only unconditional surrender was acceptable.

The South Africans needed to rest their horses and recuperate, but Botha was concerned that the Germans would mount a guerrilla campaign that would prolong the war. By June 14 he was ready to move, and marched rapidly north, the Germans falling back before him. Ten miles north of Otavi they made their last stand.

Botha could see that a frontal attack on their position would incur heavy casualties, so he sent two columns in wide sweeping movements left and right of Otavi. The speed of this sweep caught the Germans by surprise. Although well entrenched with 3,400 men and a good supply of field and machine guns, they recognised that retreat to the north was now cut off. Their estimation of Botha's force was well in excess of the number he actually had, possibly because of the way he had divided his columns and the rapidity of their advance.

On July 9 the Germans laid down their arms and surrendered.

Although unconditional surrender was insisted upon, the German officers were well treated. All the Germans were interned, and reservists allowed to return to their farms on parole. They were given back their rifles for protective purposes. The territory was placed under military administration. Whittall, a British officer who participated in the campaign, wrote:

> "It is now British South-West Africa, and it must remain a Province of the Union. So ended a campaign that, though it scarcely produced a fight that could be dignified by the name of battle, especially in comparison with the colossal battles of Europe, was one of the most arduous of modern times in its demands on the determination and stamina of the armies engaged. The campaign was brought to a successful issue by a rare combination of consummate generalship and magnificent qualities of soldiership."[268]

Of the 40,000 South African and British troops engaged, Botha lost only 269 killed and 263 wounded.

Botha was given a rousing reception when he landed at Cape Town on July 30. In Pretoria a crowd of 12,000 awaited him. But when he addressed the crowd he could see only strangers and a few old friends. The Afrikaners were absent.

In fact, the gulf between the Afrikaans and English-speaking South Africans had never been wider. The pro-German sentiment made manifest by the extremists on the Afrikaans side repulsed the English-speakers, and their strong support of the British confirmed the fears of the Afrikaners that they were not true South Africans but imperialists who wished for continuing rule by the British.

chapter 20.
END GAME.

BOTHA.

THE GENERAL election of 1915 was to bring the differences between English and Afrikaans-speakers to a head. It was to be one of the bitterest elections ever held in South Africa. Merriman believed the feelings between the races to be irreconcilable. The National Party under Hertzog, supported by the elder statesman, President Steyn of the Orange Free State, was not only gathering strength but had significant organisations in the Transvaal as well as the Cape.

Rumours began to circulate concerning Botha and Smuts. It was said that De la Rey had been murdered – perhaps even Beyers. The Germans published pamphlets in Holland accusing Botha of being a traitor to his people. It was claimed that during the Boer War he had made decisions that benefitted the enemy, that he was even then a closet imperialist. Botha worked hard at campaigning, criss-crossing the country, addressing numerous public meetings, arguing consistently that the only way to take the Union forward was by racial conciliation, by which he meant Afrikaner and English-speaker.

It is noticeable that the black and coloured races were still not a factor in the argument: their rights and future were ignored. The Orange Free State was virtually unanimous in supporting Hertzog, while rural Cape and Transvaal opposed Botha as well. The English-speakers considered him by far the best man to lead their nation, but the way the Afrikaners were turning against him depressed Botha considerably.

At the general election Botha's South African Party emerged with the most number of seats: 54, down by 16. The Unionist Party, led by Sir Thomas Smartt, were steady at 40 seats but the dramatic gain was made by Hertzog's National Party, up from 8 seats to 26. Botha's supporters saw this as a victory of sorts in the face of great adversity, but Botha was sufficiently depressed to consider resigning. The results meant he would need the support of the Unionists to govern, and the Unionists were the "British Jingos" whom the Afrikaners hated even more than they did Botha. Their policies embraced compulsory military service overseas when conscription had not yet been introduced in Britain, and criticised Botha for not siding strongly enough with the British in the war!

Botha consulted the Governor-General, Lord Buxton, a good friend to him. Buxton pointed out that Botha's party was the only one strong enough to form a government, and urged him to stay on. Botha had known Buxton before the Union was formed. He had consulted him frequently on trade matters when Buxton was President of the Board of Trade in Britain, and Annie had stayed with his family while in England. The two men had developed a deep trust in each other, and talked frequently after Buxton was appointed Governor-General. Botha decided not to resign. He said:

> "Though I should like to get out, I made up my mind from the beginning of the war that I could not do so in the middle of the stream, it would be a cowardly thing to do."[269]

Aware of the threat posed by the Germans in East Africa, Botha raised troops to resist them in Tanganyika. These squads were known as the Burgher Brigades. Smuts had been asked by the British to take command in East Africa, and he worked closely with Botha. The call for volunteers and support for the British in East Africa exacerbated the ill-feeling towards Botha and Smuts from the Afrikaners.

In December 1915, De Wet was released from prison. Although he had promised Botha that he would not take part in politics or public meetings, he proved a rallying point for Afrikaner support. De Wet unwisely told the people to prepare for great things, which they took to mean the ascendancy of Afrikanerdom and the restoration of their republics. He protested that he simply foresaw the end of the Great War. Botha reminded him of his promise, and from then on he kept quiet.

Smuts remained out of the country for over three years. After his stint in East Africa he went to Europe, and became heavily involved in the peace negotiations between the allies and Germany. Botha thus lost his closest colleague and wisest adviser at a crucial time. Botha was very weary, both in body and spirit. He was frustrated that his attempt to reconcile English-speaking South Africans with Afrikaners was falling apart, and he feared for the future. By the middle of 1917 his health was failing: he could not sleep and he suffered from general exhaustion. His wife urged him to resign, but Botha was determined to hang on until the war was over. At the urging of his colleagues he took two months rest.

A speech by President Woodrow Wilson of the USA about the rights of small nations to self-determination was widely noticed in South Africa and encouraged Hertzog's group to believe the outside world was on their side. Increasingly Botha felt isolated and besieged. Attempts to form a coalition with the Unionists in order to strengthen the government came to nothing. Support grew for the National Party. Annie Botha was concerned for his health: swollen and painful legs prevented him from exercising, and his heart began to trouble him.

When the war in Europe ended Botha was invited to attend the Peace Conference at Versailles. He was not really fit enough to travel, but was determined to be present. He was excused most of the social engagements, and was shielded from any burden of work by Smuts, who took on South African business himself. Botha and Smuts were together for six months, which was a joy for Botha after such a long absence. He enjoyed hugely watching Smuts' keen mind at work.

During the peace talks the question of South-West Africa arose. South Africa's stock in Britain, thanks to Smuts and Botha, was very high. On May 7, 1919, South-West Africa was assigned to the protection of South Africa under terms that amounted to annexation.

Both Smuts and Botha were horrified at the harshness of the terms of surrender in Europe dictated to the Germans. Of all the people around the table, they were probably the only two apart from Marshal Foch to have experienced action in the field: the rest were politicians and diplomats. Botha predicted that Europe would not know peace for long if these terms were enforced. He had grave doubts about signing the peace terms. In the Hall of Mirrors at Versailles Botha rose to state his case, and recalled Vereenging:

> "You cannot, you must not destroy a nation. It was a hard peace for us to accept, but, as I know it now, when time has shown us the truth, it was not unjust – it was a generous peace that the British people made with us; and that is why we stand with them today side by side in the cause that has brought us all together. Remember, there was no spirit or act of vengeance in that peace; we were helped to rise again."[270]

Ironically, the man sitting next to him at the conference table was Alfred Milner. Milner – the man who had, in many people's eyes, provoked the Boer War. Milner, the stubborn Governor-General opposed to a generous peace, insistent upon Britain continuing to control South Africa.

Smuts declared to Botha that he would not sign the document, and started preparing to leave Versailles. Aware of the consequences, Botha implored him to stay. They went to see Lloyd George, who said: "Very well, sign first, and then protest afterwards, if protest you must."[271] The day after the Treaty was signed Smuts launched a highly critical, damning review of the document.

Botha, with a keen appreciation of reality, was more concerned to emphasize South Africa's position. His participation at Versailles confirmed South Africa's new status in the world, both within the Empire and outside. It enabled South Africa to become a member of the newly-formed League of Nations. With all its defects, Botha was keen to point out that peace was now established, and they should move forward. Interestingly, he chose this moment to reconfirm his allegiance to the British Empire. In his view the Great War was a war between Germany and France which Great Britain had chosen to join. He said:

> "I go back to South Africa more firmly convinced than ever that the mission of the British Empire now, and in the time to come, lies along the path of freedom and high ideals. Britain is the cornerstone upon which our civilization must rest. It largely depends upon her action and her spirit whether the new-born League of Nations

lies in the ideal brotherhood, in making the world a better place to live in."[272]

Encouraged by Wilson's championing of the small states, Hertzog and a number of his followers arrived in Paris to argue for a form of Republican Government in South Africa. Hertzog called on the Allied leaders to redeem their promises, but Lloyd George responded that only Botha as Premier had the right to speak for South Africa. Moreover, he stressed he

> "....would point to the status which South Africa now occupies in the world. It is surely no mean one. ....the South African people control their own national destiny in the fullest sense. In regard to the common Imperial concerns, they participate in the deliberations, which determine Imperial policy, on a basis of complete equality."[273]

Hertzog took this to mean that South Africa had the right to self-determination, which was enough for the moment.

The reception Botha and Smuts received on their return was rapturous. The declaration of peace had been greeted with joy in South Africa, and the two leaders were seen as national heroes, parading a resurgent South Africa on the world stage. Wherever they went formal receptions greeted them, and cheering crowds – English speaking and moderate Afrikaners – lined the streets.

Botha, unfortunately, was tired and ill, and the constant round took its toll. He was also profoundly depressed. His father had died when he was a year older than his (Louis') present age, and his elder brother had died at the same age. At fifty-seven, Botha felt forbodings of mortality, and so it turned out. In August he returned to his beloved farm, Rusthof, to see if everything was in order. He was never to leave it. Confined to bed initially with a cold, later suspected to be Spanish influenza, on August 27, 1919 he died. The official reason for his death was a heart attack.

Professor A.W.G. Raath asserts in his book that "Today it is general knowledge that General Louis Botha committed suicide by cutting his wrists." In substantiation of this claim it is said that his body was not embalmed, but placed in a lead coffin because he had committed a deed for which no statesman would receive a State funeral. A pastor, the Reverend Van der Holst, told a friend:

"Last night I returned from Pretoria. General Botha's corpse was lying in State in the church. It had become so rotten that the church had to be disinfected and the coffin lined with lead. Now I ask: Why was he not embalmed? Is it because the news might leak out about what really happened (to the General, that he did not die a natural death)? That he committed a deed for which no Statesman would receive a State funeral. Could a person believe that General Botha had committed suicide (because of the wrongs he had done his people?)."

Van der Holst was a friend of the seer, van Rensburg, and a supporter of Hertzog. The nature of what he said is subjective, and could have been the source for the rumours that arose.

The curator of the Bloemfontein Museum, who says it cannot be substantiated, refutes this explanation of Botha's death. Botha's private secretary, Dr F.V.Engelenburg, writes of visiting Botha on the day he died:

> "Late in the afternoon of Tuesday, August 26, 1919, Botha took to his bed, without there being any suspicion, on the part of either himself, his family, or his doctor, of worse to come…Twelve hours later…I was one of the first to whisper a few words of condolence to the widow. [Botha] never woke from his slumber; he breathed his last shortly before midnight. In the dead face I recognized the well-known, friendly expression, besides the will-power still delineated in his countenance."[274]

Whilst this does not categorically refute suicide, there is not even a hint that Botha was contemplating it, or was ready to die.

Botha was given a state funeral, with all the honours. He was buried in the old cemetery in Pretoria along with many of the Boer leaders of the past. There was only one possible successor to Botha as Prime Minister. A reluctant Jan Smuts was appointed in his place, to take a divided South Africa forward into the 1920's. At the funeral Smuts made one of the greatest speeches of his life, which will serve as a fitting epitaph:

> "His great work was the Union of South Africa; his untiring efforts through all difficulties were directed to the unity of the people of South Africa, to the promotion of a strong feeling of national brotherhood

among all sections of our community, to the healing of old wounds and the laying to rest of old enmities. Only quite recently he saw in Europe a whole continent torn and broken by the wild passions of the peoples, by race hatred raging on a colossal scale; and he returned from the Peace Conference more than ever convinced that for South Africa, just as for the people of Europe, salvation and healing were only to be found in a new spirit of humanity, of a more human sympathy, of forgiving and forgetting the old differences and wrongs."[275]

EPILOGUE.

What are we to make of the two men whose lives are outlined in this book?

On the one hand, Louis Botha was a humble farm boy who had little formal education but became skilled in fieldcraft, hunting and survival, with an affinity with people. Identified early in his life as a leader of men, he was a young man who demonstrated a genius for military tactics and manoeuvres. He was someone who listened; someone with good looks and a presence that drew people to him.

Botha rose rapidly to command the Boer army. Against overwhelming odds he showed an ability to resist the enemy and prolong the war. The Boer army was formed on democratic grounds. There was no high command structure similar to the British Army, and an independence of mind among the disparate commandos that made it difficult to persuade them to conform to an overall strategy. Each major decision Botha wished to make needed argument and persuasion with his peers before implementation.

It was his charismatic personality that enabled him to achieve so much.

At the end of the war Botha was faced with difficult decisions. The men he had grown up with, had fought with, distrusted the British and resisted any deal that sustained a British presence in South Africa. Botha saw very early in the process that without some sort of rapprochement the future of South Africa would be fraught with difficulty. The bitter legacy of the war, the underlying ambition of the Boers for independence and "purity" of race was impossible to reconcile with the way forward.

Had Britain allowed the Transvaal and Orange Free State their independence the future of the country would have taken a very different course. It was to Botha's credit that he saw this, and put aside his own nationalistic feelings for the greater good. In the process he lost the friendship of most of his military colleagues.

With Smuts, Botha forged the Union of South Africa. In doing this, he achieved the main aim of the white residents of South Africa: independence.

Since 1910 South Africa has been free to develop without the interference of Britain. The stability that came with the constitutional changes encouraged foreign investment and led to the foundation of a prosperous, modern economy based on the gold and diamond fields.

Although initially the South African government was dominated by Afrikaners, between 1910 and 1948 it was English-speaking South Africans, living in the urban communities, who largely took the lead in politics. In 1948 the National Party, Afrikaans-based, won the general election and took the country in a different direction. Many of the old dreams of the Boers who resisted the peace treaty with the British resurfaced. Apartheid – the separation of the races, coloured from white – was formalised, although in practice it had existed since the Union's inception. Both English-speaking and Afrikaans citizens feared that the indigenous races, which far outnumbered white residents, would come to rule South Africa if they were allowed the franchise. Denial of this was enshrined in the original Act of Union.

South Africa became a republic in 1961, further distancing it from the British Empire and taking it back to many Afrikaners' ideals. The problems this created came in time to effect the changes that led to the presence situation, with the African National Congress, the African people's party, in government.

Botha can justly be called the father of his nation.

In stark contrast Redvers Buller was born to English landed gentry, a privileged position in society and as good an education as Britain could offer. With significant parental financial assistance, he was able to become a professional soldier to his fingertips, rising quickly to prominence through his personal bravery and ability to lead men. Up to the commencement of the Boer his career was brilliant: he was considered one of Britain's finest soldiers. As a consequence his choice as commander in South Africa was almost automatic.

In many ways Buller was handed a poisoned chalice. British preparations for the war were slow and rather desultory. On landing in Cape Town Buller was faced with difficult choices. The British were not yet prepared to face the Boers on equal terms, and were fighting on separate fronts more than 1,000 miles apart. The sieges mounted at Kimberley, Mafeking and Ladysmith made the need for urgent action paramount. By deciding to assume command in Natal and leave the bulk of his army in the Cape, he knew he risked diffusing the leadership. He assessed, probably with some accuracy, that the relief of Ladysmith was his priority.

Although a fine soldier in the field as his record showed and a leader who inspired his men, he was inexperienced in overall command. Facing a difficult situation at Ladysmith, without adequate intelligence information against a well-entrenched enemy in difficult conditions, he faltered. Attack after attack failed; his hesitancy to press home any advantage acquired for him the nickname "Sir Reverse Buller." At the same time the advance in the Cape made slow, uneven progress. Finally Lord Roberts replaced him, and his reputation was sullied.

Unlike Botha, Buller was a private man, unused to being contradicted. He made political enemies, and this came to harm his career later. He detested the Press, and was short with reporters. He could be brusque and rude. Curiously though, his men adored him. They would follow him anywhere. Their confidence in him was complete.

Perhaps this explained Buller. His concern for the ordinary soldier's welfare was exceptional. It was said that he would not ask them to do anything, or go anywhere, that he would not experience himself. The care he took over their physical conditions – billets, medical facilities, food – was unusual for a general at that time. His reluctance to throw troops into conflict regardless of losses perhaps explains why he was so loath to take major risks in his attempts to relieve Ladsmith.

Once Ladysmith was relieved, Buller showed how much he had learnt in the field. His successes in clearing northern Natal and in winning battles in the eastern Transvaal demonstrated how adapting to South African conditions paid dividends.

When he returned to Britain he was faced with a strange dichotomy. The average citizen idolised him. He was a great military hero, feted wherever he went, drawing huge crowds. Yet the political and military establishment spurned him. He was dismissed from his post at Aldershot and submitted to stern criticism. He was blamed for many of the mistakes made during the Boer War. At least part of this was due to feuds within the British Army between Roberts' "Indian Ring" and Wolseley's "African Ring." Buller did not possess the tact or political skills to refute these accusations convincingly.

Thus the hero of the relief of Ladysmith, the ordinary soldiers' idol, died a sad and disillusioned man. In this he was not unlike his foe, Louis Botha.

In studying what Buller found himself up against in the Boer War, it is worth quoting Arthur Conan Doyle, who was in South Africa during the War:

> "Take a community of Dutchmen of the type who defended themselves for fifty years against all the power of Spain at a time when Spain was the greatest power in the world. Intermix with them a strain of those inflexible French Huguenots who gave up home and fortune and left their country for ever…The product must obviously be one of the most rugged, virile, unconquerable races ever seen upon earth. Take this formidable people and train them for several generations in constant warfare against savage men and ferocious beasts, in circumstances under which no weakling could survive, place them so that they acquire exceptional skill with weapons and in horsemanship, give them a country which is eminently suited to the tactics of the huntsman, the marksman and the rider. Then, finally, put a finer temper upon their military qualities by a dour fatalistic Old Testament religion and an ardent and consuming patriotism. Combine all these qualities and all these impulses in one individual, and you have the modern Boer – the most formidable antagonist who ever crossed the path of imperial Britain. Our military history has largely consisted in our conflicts with France, but Napoleon and all his veterans have never treated us so roughly as these hard-bitten farmers with their ancient theology and their inconveniently modern rifles."[276]

Neither of the subjects of this book was perfect: both had serious flaws that their enemies exploited. Despite these, both men achieved much in their lives. Botha was responsible for the formation of modern South Africa. Buller introduced important, fundamental reforms to the British Army that still exist today.

The two protagonists faced each other on the battlefield in South Africa, sworn enemies, intent on prevailing in a life and death struggle. Yet Buller had fought alongside Boers in the Zulu War. He liked and respected many of them. Botha came to be reconciled with the British. He spent much time in Britain, and was a major figure in the Commonwealth.

Like Buller, Botha was extremely popular with the British people, but unlike Buller he was highly respected by the establishment and received many honours.

The Boer War was, perhaps, the last "gentlemen's war." Despite the carnage, there was a respect between the two sides which has not prevailed in later conflicts.

Botha's action, in managing to bring British and Boer together in the running of South Africa was as epic as it was surprising.

APPENDIX.

Exchange of messages between Buller and White after the Battle of Colenso.

Buller to White, 16th December:

> "I tried Colenso yesterday, but failed; the enemy is too strong for any force, except with siege operations, and these will take one full month to prepare. Can you last so long? If not, how many days can you give me in which to take up defensive positions? After which I suggest your firing away as much ammunition as you can, and making best terms you can. I can remain here if you have alternative suggestions, but, unaided, I cannot break in. I find my infantry cannot fight more than ten miles from camp, and then only if water can be got, and it is scarce her."

This message was amended later the same day as follows:

> Add to the end of the message: "Whatever happens, recollect to burn your cipher and decipher and code books, and any deciphered messages."

White to Buller, 16th December:

> "Your [message] of today received and understood. My suggestion is that you take up strongest available position that will enable you to keep touch of the enemy and harass him constantly with artillery fire, and in other ways as much as possible. I can make food last for much longer than a month, and will not think of making terms until I am forced to. You may have hit enemy harder than you think. All our native spies report that your artillery fire made considerable impression on enemy. Have your losses been very heavy? If you lose touch of enemy, it will immediately increase his chances of crushing me, and have worst effect elsewhere. While you are in touch with him, and in communication with me, he has both our forces to reckon with. Make every effort to get reinforcements as early as possible, including India, and enlist every man in both Colonies who will serve and ride. Things may look brighter. The loss of 12,000 men here would be a heavy blow to England. We must not think of it. I fear I could not cut my way to you. Enteric fever is increasing alarmingly here. There are now 180 cases, all within the last month. Answer fully: I am keeping everything secret for the present till I know your plans."

BIBLIOGRAPHY.

Amery, Leo: *Chamberlain.*

Atkins, J.B.: *The Relief of Ladysmith;* 1900.

Barbary, James: *The Boer War;* Victor Gallancz, London, 1969.

Beckett, Ian F.W.: *The South African War and the Late Victorian Army.*

Bettesworth, Sheila: *Edmund Garrett in Cape Town;* 2011.

Buxton, Sydney Charles: *General Botha;* Murray, London, 1924.

Cain P.J. and Hopkins A.G.: *British Imperiallism 1688-2000;* Pearson, Harlow, 1993.

Castle, Ian: *Zulu War – Volunteers, Irregulars and Auxiliaries;* Osprey, Oxford, 2003.

Churchill, Winston S.: *London to Ladysmith Via Pretoria;* General Books, Memphis, Tennessee, 2010.

Coetzer, Owen: *The Anglo-Boer War, The Road to Infamy;* Arms & Armour, London, 1996.

Colville, Ian: *The Life of Jamieson;* Cassell, London, 1922.

David, Saul: *Zulu;* Penguin, London, 2005.

Davis, R.Harding: *With Both Armies in South Africa;* New York 1900.

De Souza, F.H.: *A Question of Treason*

De Wet, General C.R.: *Three Years War;* Charles Scribner, New York, 1902.

Doyle, Arthur Conan: *The Great Boer War;* Emereo, 1902.

Durbach, Renee: *Kipling's South Africa;* Chameleon Press, Plumstead, SA, 1988.

Engelenberg, Dr F.V.: *General Louis Botha;* George G. Harrap, London, 1929.

Evans, Martin: *Encyclopaedia of the Boer War;* Santa Barbara, 2000.

Farwell, Byron: *The Great Anglo-Boer War;* Harper and Row, London, 1976.

Fremont-Barnes, Gregory: *The Boer War;* Osprey, Oxford, 2003.

Garson, N.G.: *Louis Botha or John X. Merriman;* Athlone Press, London, 1969.

Headlam, Cecil: *The Milner Papers;* Cassell, London, 1933.

Jerrold, Walter: *Sir Redvers H. Buller;* Edwin Dalton, London, 1908.

Laband, John: *The Rise and Fall of the Zulu Nation*; Arms & Armour Press, London, 1997.

Le May, G.H.L.: *British Supremacy in South Africa;* Clarendon Press, Oxford, 1965.

Levi, N: *Jan Smuts;* Longmans, London, 1917.

Lyttleton, General Sir Neville: *Eighty Years;* Hodder & Stoughton, London.

Meintjies, Johannes: *General Louis Botha;* Cassell, London, 1970.

Melville, Charles Henderson: *Life of Buller;* Edward Arnold & Co, London, 1923.

Meredith, M.: *Diamonds, Gold and War;* Public Affairs, 2007.

Morris, Donald R.: *The Washing of the Spears;* Lowe & Brydone, London, 1966.

Padfield, Peter: *Aim Straight;* Hodder and Stoughton, London, 1966.

Pakenham, Thomas: *The Boer War;* Weidenfeld & Nicholson, London, 1979.

Powell, Geoffrey: *Buller: A Scapegoat?* Leo Cooper, London, 1994.

Reitz, Denis: *Commando;* Faber and Faber, London, 1929.

Smuts, J.C.: *Jan Christian Smuts;* Cassell, Cape Town, 1952.

Spender, Harold: *General Botha;* Constable & Company Limited, London, 1916.

Symons, Julian: *Buller's Campaign;* House of Stratus, Cornwall, 2001.

Thomas, Roy Digby: *The Rise and Fall of Bartle Frere;* Authorhouse, Milton Keynes, 2009.

Trew, Peter: *The Boer War Generals;* Sutton Publishing, Stroud, 1999.

Williams, Basil: *Botha Smuts and South Africa;* Hodder & Stoughton, London, 1946.

JOURNALS AND PERIODICALS.

1. With The Flag to Pretoria.
2. North American Review.
3. South African Military Journal.
4. Natal Witness.
5. The Courier.
6. The Standard.
7. Otago Witness.

ORIGINAL SOURCES.

1. National Archives, Kew.
2. British Library, London.
3. Devon Record Office.
4. Crediton Parish Church Records, Devon.
5. Talana Museum, Dundee, Natal.
6. Ladysmith Siege Museum, Ladysmith, Natal.
7. Bloemfontein Boer Museum, Orange Free State.
8. Memorandum to Royal Commission on War.
9. Transvaal Archives.
10. South African National Archives.
11. Buller's Address to the 80 Club, March 2, 1901.

ENDNOTES.

1. Meredith, M. :Diamonds, Gold and War P3/4
2. Thomas, R.D.: The Rise and Fall of Bartle Frere P195-199
3. Farwell, Byron: The Great Anglo-Boer War P12
4. Farwell P12
5. Farwell P13
6. Farwell P17
7. Farwell P18
8. Farwell P21
9. With the Flag to Pretoria Part 1, P13.
10. Bettesworth, Sheila: Edmund Garett in Cape Town P85
11. Bettesworth P134
12. Ferguson, Niall: Empire P273
13. Amery, Leo: Chamberlain.
14. Pakenham, Thomas: The Boer War P79
15. Fremont-Barnes, Gregory: The Boer War P7
16. CO417/279/17501
17. CO879/59/245-9
18. Meintjies, Johannes: General Louis Botha P29
19. Meintjies P19
20. Engelenburg, Dr F.V.: General Louis Botha P23
21. Engelenburg P24
22. Reitz, Deneys: Commando P15
23. Melville, Charles Henderson: Life of Buller P8
24. Engelenburg P16
25. Meintjies P6
26. Louis Botha's Daughter Looks Back; Sunday Times, June 11, 1972.
27. Melville P16
28. Meintjies P6
29. Powell, Geoffrey: Buller: A Scapegoat? P5
30. Melville P24
31. Melville P26
32. Engelenburg P33
33. Meintjies P12
34. Butler, quoted in Powell P30

35. Add.MS 50086; Letter from Buller to Hutton 25/2/1885 (217); British Library
36. Melville P88
37. Melville P88
38. Powell P32
39. Haggard, H. Rider: Days of My Life, 1926
40. Melville P93
41. Powell P34
42. Melville P108
43. David, Saul: Zulu P266
44. Melville P125
45. Crediton Parish Church Records
46. David P270
47. Vijn, Cetchwayo's Dutchman P38
48. Laband, John: The Rise and Fall of the Zulu Nation P263
49. Melville P127
50. Jerrold, Walter: Sir Redvers H.Buller The Story of His Life and Campaigns P148/9
51. Melville P131
52. Crediton Parish Church Records
53. Melville P135
54. Add. MS 50086: Letter to Hutton 19/4/1892 (31); British Library
55. Melville P145
56. Melville P147
57. Melville P151
58. Melville P147
59. Melville P152
60. Melville P153
61. Melville P158
62. Melville P166
63. Melville P168
64. Melville P169
65. Melville P179
66. Devon Record Office
67. Devon Record Office
68. Melville P188
69. Melville P193
70. Melville P253
71. North American Review, January 1900
72. Add. MS 50086: letter to Carnarvon 16/6/1887 (94); British Library
73. Add MS 50086: etter to Carnarvon 19/6/1887 (98): British Library
74. Bettesworth P84
75. Meintjies P27/8
76. Devon Record Office
77. Volume II Memorandum to Royal Commission on War; Melville Vol. II P1
78. Devon Record Office
79. Devon Record Office
80. Devon Record Office
81. Lyttleton, General Sir Neville: Eighty Years P200/1
82. Powell P118/9
83. Melville vol. II P9
84. Buller to Lansdowne, 2nd Sept. 1899; L
85. Natal Witness
86. Farwell P50
87. Meintjies P37
88. Natal Witness
89. Pakenham P139
90. Coetzer, Owen: The Anglo-Boer War P30
91. Farwell P40

92. Farwell P35
93. Farwell P89
94. Coetzer P50
95. With the Flag to Pretoria P490/1
96. Melville Vol. II P56
97. Coetzer P66
98. Churchill, Winston S.:London to Ladysmith Via Pretoria P14
99. Churchill P14
100. Ibid
101. Natal Witness 3rd November, 1899
102. Pakenham P170
103. Churchill P39

104. Churchill P40
105. With the Flag to Pretoria P242
106. Churchill P59
107. Melville P79
108. Melville Vol. II P80
109. Davis R.H.: With Both Armies in South Africa
110. John Atkins in Pakenham P209
111. Melville Vol. II P87
112. Pakenham P215
113. Melville Vol. II P93
114. Pakenham P215
115. Meintjies P47
116. Melville P100
117. Pakenham P221
118. Transvaal Archives; Leyds Archives 713c
119. Meintjies P49
120. Pakenham P231
121. Pakenham P239

122. Melville P120/1
123. Melville P122
124. Beckett
125. Pakenham P241
126. Melville P131
127. Davis
128. Devon Record Office
129. With the Flag to Pretoria P254
130. Ibid P252
131. Ibid P259
132. Ibid P264
133. Ibid P290
134. Ibid P291
135. Ibid P298
136. SA Military Journal
137. Reitz P80/1
138. 138 Pakenham P301
139. Melville Vol. II P159/60
140. Churchill P98: Melville P163/4
141. Ibid
142. Melville P170
143. RCWSA RB Q14963; Buller to Roberts 4/2/00
144. Farwell P190
145. Natal Witness
146. Symons, Julian: Buller's Campaign P263
147. Melville Vol. II P183
148. Melville Vol. II P184
149. Ibid
150. Coetzer P227
151. Churchill P113
152. Coetzer P229
153. Churchill P116
154. Davis
155. Major Wheldon; Pakenham P263

156. Churchill P132
157. Melville Vol. II P201
158. Pakenham P370
159. Pakenham P367
160. Pakenham P368
161. Pakenham P368
162. Pakenham P370
163. Powell P179
164. Roberts to the Queen, March 15, 1900. H&OI
165. Meintjies P60.
166. The Star, April 12, 1900
167. De Souza, F.H.: A Question of Treason P100
168. Ibid
169. Ibid
170. Engelenberg P51
171. Powell P180
172. National Archives
173. Ibid
174. Melville Vol. II P221/2
175. National Archives
176. Ibid
177. Powell P182
178. National Archives
179. Powell P185
180. The Courier, June 15, 1900
181. Pakenham P432
182. Meintjies P66
183. Pakenham P435
184. Proclamation no. 5 of 1900
185. Powell P186
186. Ibid
187. Powell P188
188. Reitz P120
189. Powell P189
190. Maurice, Boer War Vol. 3 P218
191. The Standard, October 22, 1900
192. The Courier September 5, 1900
193. Devon Record Office: Weekly Despatch, September 10, 1900
194. Reitz P125
195. The Milner Papers 1899-1905
196. Devon Record Office
197. Engelenberg P58
198. Meintjies P75
199. Meintjies P70
200. Meintjies P95
201. National Archives
202. National Archives
203. Botha's Papers; National Archives
204. Engelenberg P76
205. Meintjies P76
206. Le May, G.H.L.: British Supremacy in South Africa P98
207. Engelenberg P66
208. Wikisource
209. Meintjies P81
210. Amery Leo: Chamberlain Vol. IV P28
211. Engelenberg P79
212. Engelenberg P85
213. Ibid
214. Engelenberg P91/2
215. De Wet, General C.R.: Three Years War P428/9
216. Meintjies P103
217. Powell P126
218. Otago Witness; July 16, 1902
219. Beckett, Ian F.W.: The South

African War and the Late Victorian Army
220. National Archives
221. Ibid
222. Devon Record Office
223. Powell P196/7
224. Pakenham P230
225. Jerrold P264-266
226. Brodrick to Roberts, October 11, 1901: 7101-23-122-2-146
227. Ibid
228. National Archives; Buller 138/16
229. Powell P198
230. Powell P110
231. National Archives
232. Devon Record Office Bundle 6245-1
233. Ibid
234. Ibid
235. Devon Record Office
236. Meintjies P109
237. Ibid
238. Meintjies P116
239. Le May P164
240. Le May P174
241. Smuts J.C.: Jan Christian Smuts
242. The Milner Papers, edited by Cecil Headlam, Cassell 1933
243. Address to the 80 Club, Oxford, March 2 1901
244. Le May P192
245. Meintjies P144
246. Meintjies P148
247. Meintjies P149
248. Meintjies P153
249. Colville Ian; The Life of Jamieson
250. Smuts P
251. Buxton P232
252. Meintjies P193/4
253. Meintjies P195
254. Meintjies P197
255. Smuts P131
256. Meintjies P205
257. Meintjies P207
258. Buxton P173
259. Buxton: General Botha P173/4
260. Meintjies P218
261. Meintjies P222
262. Meintjies P223
263. Buxton P52
264. Meintjies P234
265. Meintjies P239
266. Meintjies P252
267. Levi, N.: Jan Smuts P246
268. Meintjies P271
269. Meintjies P278
270. Meintjies P296
271. Meintjies P298
272. Meintjies P299
273. Meintjies P297
274. Engelenberg P329
275. Meintjies P303/4
276. Conan Doyle: The Great Boer War, P2

INDEX.

A

Amery, Leo xxix, 83, 107, 165, 172, 173, 174, 229
Asquith, H.H. 190

B

Baden Powell, General R.S.S. 178
Balfour, Arthur J. 177, 178, 187
Baring, Evelyn 41
Benson, Colonel G.E. 160, 161
Beresford, Sir Charles 40
Beyers, General Christiaan 184, 198, 199, 202, 203, 204, 205, 206, 213
Bezuidenhout, Piet xxii
Bismarck 200
Botha, Annie (nee Emett) 158, 180, 215
Botha, Christiaan 141
Botha, Salomina 2
Botha Senior 3, 5
Bouwer, Major Ben 205
Brits, Coen 204
Broadwood, Brigadier-General Robert g. 136

Brodrick, St John 172
Buller, General Sir George 4
Buller, James Wentworth 4, 19
Burgher, Schalk 89, 111, 112, 116, 155
Butler, Lieutenant-General Sir William 53
Buxton, Lord 214

C

Cadogan, Lord 43, 44
Campbell-Bannerman, Sir Henry xxxi, 185
Carnarvon, Lord 43
Cetshwayo 7, 28, 29, 30
Chamberlain, Joseph xxviii, 165, 172, 181, 182
Chelmsford, Lord (General Thesiger) xxi, 19, 23, 31, 32
Churchill, Winston 77, 114, 123, 172
Clery, General Cornelius Francis 147
Coke, General John Talbot 110, 111
Colenso 74, 79, 80, 84, 85, 86, 88, 89, 90, 91, 92, 95, 96, 97, 98, 100, 101, 102, 106, 108, 114, 116, 117, 121, 122, 124, 125, 126, 127, 172, 173, 174, 175, 227

Colley, Sir George xxiii
Conynghame, Sir Arthur 19
Conyngham Greene, Sir W. xxxi
Cronje, General Pieter Arnoldud (Piet) xxii, 61, 136

D

De la Rey, General Jacobus Herculeas 67, 133, 134, 135, 145, 159, 167, 168, 169, 180, 186, 200, 201, 202, 203, 204, 213
Deventer 210
De Wet, Christiaan 57
Dinizulu 7, 8, 16
Disraeli, Benjamin xx
Duke of Cambridge 27, 33, 41
Dundonald, Earl of; Douglas Mackinnon Baillie Hamilton Cochrane 103, 104, 105, 123, 140

E

Edward VII, King 19, 169, 180
Elandslaagte 65, 67, 72, 77
Emett, Annie 13

F

Fingoes 20
Fitzpatrick, Percy 191
Fourie, Christian 94
French, Major-General John 65
Frere, Bartle xx, xxi, xxvii, xxix, 22, 86, 190, 231
Frost, Commandant 20

G

Gatacre, Sir William 76
Gcalekas 20
Gladstone, William xxi
Gordon, General Charles 39
Gough, Lieutenant-Colonel Hubert 128
Graham, Fred xxx

H

Haggard, H. Rider 22
Haig, General Douglas 75
Hamilton, General Sir Ian ix, xxiv, 58, 65, 66, 130, 144, 153, 154
Hartington, Lord 41
Hart, Major-General Arthur Fitzroy 93
Hawley, Robert Beaufoy 11, 12
Hertzog, James Barry Munnik 163, 183, 184, 187, 189, 191, 193, 194, 195, 196, 200, 201, 202, 203, 204, 207, 213, 214, 215, 217, 218
Hicks Beach, Sir Michael 53
Hicks, General 39
Hildyard, General H.J. 76, 80, 83, 95, 124, 142
Hill, Colonel A.W. 111
Hlangwane 90, 91, 92, 95, 121, 122, 123, 124, 125
Howard, Charlotte Juliana Jane 4
Hunter, General Archibald 86

I

Isandhlwana xxi, 30

J

Jameson, Leander Starr xxvi, 187
Joubert, General Piet 133

K

Kaiser Wilhelm II 199
Kambula 24, 26, 27, 28, 30, 34, 56
Kemp, Field Cornet Jan 113
Kemp, General Christoffel Greyling 205, 206, 207
Khartoum 39, 41, 42, 75
Kimberley xix, 72, 74, 75, 76, 77, 87, 97, 125, 223
Kitchener, Lod Herbert Horatio 136, 137, 147, 157, 159, 161, 163, 164, 165, 166, 167, 168, 169, 180, 196

Kruger, Paul xxi, xxii, xxv, xxvi, xxvii, xxviii, xxix, xxx, xxxi, 34, 47, 48, 49, 50, 51, 56, 57, 61, 78, 89, 91, 92, 94, 113, 126, 133, 134, 135, 143, 148, 151, 154, 155, 158, 182

L

Lansdowne, Marquis of (Henry Charles Keith Petty-Fitzmaurice) 52, 53, 54, 55, 56, 58, 83, 96, 99, 140, 156, 172, 173
Lloyd George, David 216, 217
Long, Colonel Charles J. 80, 93
Lyttleton, Colonel Neville 56, 76, 83, 97, 103, 105, 117, 121, 154, 230

M

Mackenzie, Colonel C.J. 210
Mafeking xvii, 72, 74, 75, 223
Majuba xvii, xxiii, xxiv, xxx, xxxi, 33, 48, 66, 131, 136, 141, 190
Mapelo 1, 6
Maritz, Colonel Salomon Gerhardus 204, 205, 206
McDougall, William 14
Merriman, John X. 187, 190, 191, 207, 213, 230
Methuen, Lord Paul sanford 76, 87, 88, 89, 99
Meyer, Lukas 7, 8, 16, 62, 63, 66, 67, 69, 77, 89, 94, 124, 126, 134, 180
Milner, Sir Alfred xxvii, xxviii, xxix, xxx, xxxi, 50, 51, 56, 57, 58, 72, 73, 75, 76, 83, 155, 165, 167, 168, 169, 179, 181, 182, 183, 184, 185, 186, 188, 196, 216, 230
Mnayamana 29, 30
Mohammed Ahmed (Mahdi) 39

N

Nellmapius, Hugo 50

P

Penn Symons, Major General Sir William 53, 58, 59, 63, 64, 67
Pretorius, M.W. xxii, 134

Q

Queen Victoria 32, 87, 132, 156, 176, 177

R

Rawlinson, Sir Henry 58, 129, 130
Reitz, Deneys 3, 66, 112, 133, 150, 155, 231
Reitz, Francis 133
Rhodes, Cecil xxvi, xxvii, 33, 49, 75, 87, 194
Roberts, General Frederick Sleigh 52, 54, 115, 173
Roberts, Lieutenant Frederick 52
Russell, Lieutenant Colonel 25, 26

S

Salisbury, Marquis of xxviii, 147, 172, 176, 177
Scott, Captain Percy 67, 68, 86
Sekukuni 23
Selbourne, Lord William 186, 188, 190
Shepstone, Theophilus 5
Smartt, Sir Thomas 214
Smuts, Jan xxix, 48, 49, 50, 51, 61, 134, 143, 144, 159, 168, 169, 182, 183, 184, 185, 186, 189, 191, 194, 196, 197, 201, 203, 204, 207, 210, 213, 214, 215, 216, 217, 218, 222, 230, 231
Smyth, Lieutenant-General Sir Leicester 33
Spion Kop xvii, 104, 105, 107, 108, 109, 113, 114, 116, 174, 177
Stephenson, General T.E. 41
Stewart, General 42
Steyn, Marthinus Theunis xxviii, 50, 55, 57, 136, 143, 144, 154, 155,

163, 167, 169, 187, 189, 195, 196, 213

T

Talana 64, 65, 66, 67, 140, 235

U

Ulundi 23, 31, 34
Usibebu 7, 8, 16

V

Vaal Krantz 102, 105, 116, 117, 118, 121, 174

W

Wallace, Edgar 170
Warren, Lieutenant-Colonel Sir Charles ix, 100, 103, 104, 105, 107, 108, 110, 111, 112, 113, 114, 115, 121, 122, 177
Watson, Lieutenant W.W.R. 144
White, Lieutenant-General Sir George ix, xxiv, xxv, 24, 58, 59, 65, 67, 68, 69, 73, 74, 75, 78, 83, 86, 88, 89, 95, 96, 97, 98, 99, 112, 115, 117, 118, 122, 125, 128, 129, 130, 131, 172, 173, 174, 175, 227, 228
Wilson, Major Henry 121
Wilson, Sir Charles 42
Wolseley, General Garnett xxi, 14, 15, 16, 17, 20, 32, 37, 38, 41, 42, 45, 52, 53, 54, 56, 74, 99, 115, 132, 139, 156, 171, 172, 178, 224
Wood, Colonel Evelyn 20
Woodgate, General E.R.P. 108, 110

Y

Yule, General James H. 67